at Pearl Harbor?

Documents Pertaining to the Japanese Attack of December 7, 1941, and Its Background.

Edited with an Introduction by
HANS LOUIS TREFOUSSE

 COLLEGE AND UNIVERSITY PRESS
New Haven, Connecticut

© *Copyright 1958, Edited by Hans Louis Trefousse*

Library of Congress Catalog Card Number: 58-14292

REPRINTED WITH PERMISSION OF TWAYNE PUBLISHERS, INC.
BY COLLEGE AND UNIVERSITY PRESS, PAPERBACK DIVISION

MANUFACTURED IN THE UNITED STATES OF AMERICA BY
UNITED PRINTING SERVICES, INC.
NEW HAVEN, CONN.

**What Happened at
Pearl Harbor?**

What Happened

Contents

INTRODUCTION   13

PART ONE: THE EVENTS AT PEARL HARBOR

Admiral Husband E. Kimmel's Reports   25
Testimony of Admiral Husband E. Kimmel (Concerning his actions at Pearl Harbor)   32
Testimony of General Walter C. Short (Concerning his actions at Pearl Harbor)   59
Testimony of Sergeants George E. Elliott and Joseph L. Lockard (Who first spotted Japanese planes and were told to disregard them)   79
Testimony of Lt. Colonel (then Lt.) Kermit Tyler (Who told Elliott and Lockard to disregard the information)   95
Testimony of Captain William W. Outerbridge (Who fired the first shot in the Pacific after sighting an unidentified submarine)   103
Testimony of Lieutenant Commander Harold Kaminski and Captain John B. Earle (Who received Outerbridge's information)   110

PART TWO: THE EVENTS IN WASHINGTON

Statement by Henry L. Stimson (Concerning the background of the Pearl Harbor attack)   121
Testimony of General George C. Marshall (Concerning measures taken to alert Pearl Harbor and the evaluation of "magic" intercepts)   147
Testimony of General Sherman Miles (Concerning the G-2's evaluation of "magic" intercepts)   173
Testimony of General George C. Marshall (Resumed)   175

Testimony of Captain Laurence F. Safford (Concerning the 14 part and "winds execute" messages)   183

Testimony of Captain Alwin D. Kramer (Concerning the 14 part and "winds execute" messages)   193

Testimony of Commander Lester Robert Schulz   219

The Fourteen Part and Related Messages   225

PART THREE: THE EVENTS IN TOKYO

Agenda for the Imperial Conferences of July 2 and September 6, 1941 (Concerning the broad outlines of Japanese policy)   241

Excerpts from the Memoirs of Prince Fumimaro Konoye and the Diary of Marquis Koichi Kido (Concerning the fall of the Third Konoye Cabinet)   246

Excerpts from the Diary of Marquis Koichi Kido and the Interrogation of General Hideki Tojo (Concerning the final Japanese decision for war with the United States and Great Britain)   250

Excerpts from the Interrogation of Admiral Osami Nagano and Navy Minister Shigetaro Shimada (Concerning the preparations for the Pearl Harbor attack)   254

Excerpts from the Diary of Marquis Koichi Kido (Concerning Japanese reactions to the Pearl Harbor attack)   259

PART FOUR: THE EVENTS IN BERLIN

Excerpts from the Tripartite Pact (Which confirmed the alliance between Germany, Italy, and Japan)   263

Excerpts from the Falkenstein Memorandum (Which indicated Hitler's ultimate intentions concerning the United States)   265

Excerpts from Intercepts of Messages from and to the Japanese Embassy in Berlin (Concerning the breakdown of conversations with the United States)   266

Testimony of Joachim von Ribbentrop (Concerning his relations with the Japanese prior to the Pearl Harbor attack)   269

Excerpts from the Diary of Count Galeazzo Ciano (Concerning the immediate background of the Pearl Harbor attack) 271

Testimony of Paul Otto Schmidt (Concerning the German reaction to the Pearl Harbor attack) 273

PART FIVE:
THE AMERICAN-JAPANESE CONVERSATIONS

Memorandum by the Secretary of State, August 17, 1941 (Concerning a conversation between President Roosevelt and the Japanese Ambassador) 277

Memorandum of Conversation, August 28, 1941 (Between the Secretary of State and the Japanese Ambassador concerning a projected meeting between President Roosevelt and Premier Konoye) 281

Memorandum by the Secretary of State, September 3, 1941 (Concerning a conversation between President Roosevelt and the Japanese Ambassador) 284

Memorandum by the Adviser on Political Relations (Hornbeck), September 5, 1941 (Concerning the projected meeting between President Roosevelt and Premier Konoye) 286

The Ambassador in Japan (Grew) to President Roosevelt, September 22, 1941 (Concerning the internal situation in Japan) 290

The Secretary of State to President Roosevelt and President Roosevelt to the Secretary of State, September 28, 1941 (Concerning the negotiations with Japan) 291

The Ambassador in Japan (Grew) to the Secretary of State, October 1, 1941 (Concerning the proposed meeting between President Roosevelt and Prince Konoye) 292

Memorandum by the Ambassador in Japan (Grew), October 25, 1941 (Concerning the implications of the resignation of Premier Konoye) 293

The Ambassador in Japan (Grew) to the Secretary of State, November 3, 1941 (Concerning the precarious situation in Japan and the danger of sudden war) 295

Memorandum by the Ambassador in Japan (Grew), November 10, 1941 (Concerning a conversation with the Japanese Foreign Minister)   298

The Ambassador in Japan (Grew) to the Secretary of State, November 17, 1941 (Reemphasizing previous warnings)   302

Draft Proposal Handed by the Japanese Ambassador (Nomura) to the Secretary of State on November 20, 1941 (The final Japanese offer)   303

Memorandum by Mr. Joseph W. Ballantine to the Secretary of State, November 22, 1941 (Concerning the final Japanese offer)   304

Memorandum of a Conversation, November 26, 1941 (Between the Secretary of State and the Japanese envoys concerning what turned out to be the final American offer)   306

Document Handed by the Secretary of State to the Japanese Ambassador (Nomura) on November 26, 1941 (Secretary Hull's final offer to the Japanese)   309

The Secretary of State to the Ambassador in Japan (Grew), November 28, 1941 (Concerning the proposal of November 26, 1941)   314

The Ambassador in Japan (Grew) to the Secretary of State, December 1 and 5, 1941 (Concerning the seriousness of the situation in Japan)   316

INDEX   319

Selected Bibliography

I. SOURCES USED IN THIS VOLUME

    International Military Tribunal. *Trial of the Major War Criminals Before the International Military Tribunal.* Nuremberg, 1947-1949, 42 vols.

    International Military Tribunal for the Far East. Record of Proceedings . . . (Mimeographed).

    United States, Congress. *Pearl Harbor Attack, Hearings Before the Joint Committee on the Investigation of the Pearl Harbor Attack,* 79th Congress, 2nd Session, Public Document #79716. Washington, 1946. 39 vols.

    United States, Department of State. *Foreign Relations of the United States: Diplomatic Papers, 1941, Volume IV, The Far East.* Washington, 1956.

    United States, Department of State. *Papers Relating to the Foreign Relations of the United States, Japan*: 1931-1941. Washington, 1943. 2 vols. 78th Congress, 1st Session, House Document #339.

    United States, Office of United States Chief Counsel For Prosecution of Axis Criminality. *Nazi Conspiracy and Aggression.* Washington, 1946-1948. 11 vols.

II. REMINISCENCES AND PARTICIPANTS' ACCOUNTS

    Churchill, Winston S. *The Second World War.* Boston, 1948-1953. 6 vols.

    Grew, Joseph C. *Ten Years in Japan.* New York, 1944.

    Hull, Cordell. *The Memoirs of Cordell Hull.* New York, 1948.

    Kimmel, Husband E. *Admiral Kimmel's Story.* Chicago, 1955.

    Stimson, Henry L., and Bundy McGeorge. *On Active Service in Peace and War.* New York, 1948.

    Togo, Shigenori. *The Cause of Japan.* New York, 1956.

III. OTHER WORKS

Beard, Charles A. *President Roosevelt and the Coming of the War.* New Haven, 1946.

Chamberlin, William Henry. *America's Second Crusade.* Chicago, 1950.

Davis, Forest, and Lindley, Ernest K. *How War Came.* New York, 1942.

Feis, Herbert. *The Road to Pearl Harbor.* Princeton, 1950.

Flynn, John T. *The Roosevelt Myth.* New York, 1948.

Gunther, John. *Roosevelt in Retrospect.* New York, 1950.

Langer, William L., and Gleason, S. Elliott. *The Undeclared War, 1940-1941.* New York, 1953.

Lord, Walter. *Day of Infamy.* New York, 1957.

Millis, Walter. *This Is Pearl!* New York, 1947.

Morgenstern, George. *Pearl Harbor, The Story of the Secret War.* New York, 1947.

Rauch, Basil. *Roosevelt: From Munich to Pearl Harbor.* New York, 1950.

Sanborn, Frederick C. *Design for War.* New York, 1951.

Sherwood, Robert E. *Roosevelt and Hopkins.* New York, 1948.

Tansill, Charles C. *Back Door to War.* Chicago, 1952.

Theobald, Robert A. *The Final Secret of Pearl Harbor.* New York, 1954.

Trefousse, Hans L. *Germany and American Neutrality, 1939-1941.* New York, 1951.

Personnel Of The Joint Committee On The Investigation Of The Pearl Harbor Attack

ALBEN W. BARKLEY, Senator from Kentucky, *Chairman*
JERE COOPER, Representative from Tennessee, *Vice Chairman*

WALTER F. GEORGE, Senator from Georgia
SCOTT W. LUCAS, Senator from Illinois
OWEN BREWSTER, Senator from Maine
HOMER FERGUSON, Senator from Michigan
J. BAYARD CLARK, Representative from North Carolina
JOHN W. MURPHY, Representative from Pennsylvania
BERTRAND W. GEARHART, Representative from California
FRANK B. KEEFE, Representative from Wisconsin

Counsel

(Through January 14, 1946)

WILLIAM D. MITCHELL, *General Counsel*
GERHARD A. GESELL, *Chief Assistant Counsel*
JULE M. HANNAFORD, *Assistant Counsel*
JOHN E. MASTEN, *Assistant Counsel*

(After January 14, 1946)

SETH W. RICHARDSON, *General Counsel*
SAMUEL H. KAUFMAN, *Associate General Counsel*
JOHN E. MASTEN, *Assistant Counsel*
EDWARD P. MORGAN, *Assistant Counsel*
LOGAN J. LANE, *Assistant Counsel*

Introduction

What happened at Pearl Harbor? As long as Americans take an interest in their history, this question will be asked, and, judging by a similar question about Fort Sumter, the answers will depend on the point of view of the writer. Certain it is that the tangled web of events leading up to the destruction of the United States Pacific Fleet at its anchorage on December 7, 1941, is among the most fascinating sequences of historical drama ever enacted. All the great powers of the world at war but one . . . that last one on the brink of war, in possession of the secret codes of its enemies, forewarned but wholly surprised, and finally forced to enter the greatest conflict of all times with a sense of shame, anger, and feeling of deception by someone, somewhere, sometime . . . . It is a story without parallel. That Americans have wondered ever since whether they were duped by the enemy, let down by their leaders, or taken in by a sinister conspiracy, is hardly surprising. Depending on their political and ideological preconceptions, they have sought varying answers to these questions.

During the first week of December, 1941, the United States was in the midst of a serious diplomatic crisis which had been developing for many years. Ever since Japan invaded Manchuria in 1931, there had been no real peace in the Far East, and ever since Hitler assumed power in Germany in 1933, there had been no real basis for peace in Europe. As the most industrialized of the great powers, America had been unable to escape from the effects of the shifting balance of power in Europe and Asia; as the world's largest democracy, the United States had been threatened by the rise of Fascism and Nazism. When Germany and Japan signed the Anti-

Comintern Pact in 1936, they served notice that the two dissatisfied powers in opposite corners of the world must henceforth be considered as part of a common threat, and when Hitler withdrew his military mission from Chiang Kai-shek after the outbreak of open war between China and Japan in 1937, the previous notice of German-Japanese collaboration was confirmed. Nor could American observers console themselves any longer with the notion that the two troublemakers in Europe and Asia were simply fighting the Bolsheviks—Chiang Kai-shek's hostility to Communism was well known.

War broke out in Europe in 1939. There was little question that Americans sympathized with the British and French, and even those who had considered Communism a greater menace than Nazism could say little while Hitler and Stalin were linked by a non-aggression pact. Nevertheless, nine out of ten Americans had no desire to see their country once more drawn into conflicts started by others and hoped that the European democracies would be able to take care of themselves without open American intervention. As for China, then fighting desperately against the Japanese invaders, most Americans gave the matter but little thought; they hoped that the Chinese would win, but were not particularly interested in the Far East.

As the two wars in Europe and Asia went on, and as the Germans and Japanese scored success after success, America's position shifted. It became obvious that without American help, Hitler could never be defeated, and, when Germany and Japan signed a military alliance clearly directed against the United States, the inherent connection between the war in Europe and the war in Asia was made clear for all to see. President Roosevelt was fully aware of the dangerous implications of a German and Japanese victory to America's position as a great power, but because of the strength of isolationist feeling, he had to move slowly. Relying on his great popularity and Americans' natural sympathy for peoples of similar ideology and culture, he gradually but effectively brought the majority of Congress and the country to a realization that America must help the Allies by methods short of war.

INTRODUCTION

As a result, by the fall of 1941, the United States stood deeply committed to an Allied victory. The President had traded fifty overage destroyers to Great Britain; Congress had passed the Lend-Lease Act to enable the Allies to obtain ammunition and the tools of war; American troops had temporarily occupied Greenland and Iceland, and American ships had engaged in a number of outright skirmishes with the German navy on the high seas. However, the United States was not yet a belligerent; the isolationists were still strong, and although the President had been reelected in 1940 for an unprecedented third term, he was by no means certain of unqualified support in Congress or the country.

The Japanese were aware of these developments. They knew that in order to complete their dream of hegemony over East Asia they must make the most of the difficulties of the European powers because of the war and the embarrassments of the United States because of domestic dissension. Yet as long as the American navy continued to challenge their own fleet in the Pacific, they did not dare undertake any further large-scale overseas adventures which might meet with American disapproval. Therefore they either had to obtain American consent to their plans for a Tokyo-dominated "East Asian Co-Prosperity Sphere," or compel American compliance by means of war. To be sure, they had a third alternative, peaceful economic expansion, but the military elements in the Japanese Empire had decided against such a policy long before, when, in 1937, they committed their Government to war in China. In spite of the fact that negotiations with the United States had begun early in the spring of 1941, the Japanese continued their policy of expansion and invaded southern Indo-China in July of 1941. America responded by freezing Japanese funds and embargoing Japanese-bound tools of war, including oil, so that Japan was faced with the necessity of coming to a decision. She could not continue her military operations without the embargoed supplies; she might seize them in the Dutch East Indies and neighboring territories, but such a step would entail the danger of American interference. Consequently, the

Japanese decided to try once more to come to an understanding with the United States. Should this effort fail, the militarists made it quite clear to the civilian government of Prince Fumimaro Konoye that the consequences would be drastic.

American observers were by no means ignorant of developments in Japan. By July, 1941, United States intelligence units had succeeded in breaking the secret Japanese code employed by the Imperial diplomatic service. The messages sent to the various Japanese embassies—telegrams containing reports of top secret decisions and conversations—were now obtainable in Washington almost as quickly as they were sent from Tokyo. "Magic" was the code name given to this fortuitous aid to American planning, a triumph of intelligence efforts. Henceforth, Japan could keep few secrets from the State Department in Washington. Unfortunately, however, the Japanese did not rely entirely upon their codes. In very exceptional cases, they made no mention of their plans or movements to any of their embassies, so that, in these instances, there were no codes to decipher. The plan for an attack on Pearl Harbor was such a case.

By the fall of 1941, relations between the United States and Japan had taken a dramatic turn. Prince Fumimaro Konoye, the Japanese Premier, had suggested a personal meeting with President Roosevelt somewhere in the Pacific. However, because no advance agreement could be reached on outstanding problems, especially the Japanese demand for a free hand in China, the President turned down the request. Konoye fell, and the militarist, General Hideki Tojo, became Prime Minister. Tojo was determined to preside over Japanese expansion. To achieve that objective, he was willing to negotiate once more with the United States, but should the attitude of the State Department fail to change in his favor, he was prepared to go to war, not with Russia, as his German allies were urging, but with the United States. And in order to make sure of unobstructed lines of communication in the Pacific, he gave his sanction to plans to wipe out the American fleet at Pearl Harbor. He entrusted his diplomatic decisions to the code messages sent to his representatives abroad; his military decisions, however, he kept secret.

In line with Tojo's wishes, negotiations in Washington were reaching a climax. A special envoy, Saburo Kurusu, had arrived to assist Ambassador Kichisaburo Nomura; Japan presented a final *"modus vivendi"* plan for an overall adjustment, but on November 26, 1941, Secretary of State Cordell Hull turned it down. He would not and could not agree to Japanese domination of China, and although he offered a plan of his own, for all practical purposes, negotiations had come to an end. What action Japan would take next remained to be seen.

The events of the two weeks following Secretary Hull's rejection of the Japanese *modus vivendi* have received close attention ever since. Because of the "magic" intercepts, it was known in Washington that the Japanese were planning some radical move. One of the messages had indicated that the words "East wind rain," inserted in regular Japanese language news broadcasts, would mean imminent rupture of relations with the United States, and diplomatic messages indicated that after November 29, things were going to happen automatically. Neither the Japanese Embassy in Washington nor the State Department knew exactly what was going to happen, nor where it was going to happen, but warnings of danger were received.

The Chief of Staff of the United States Army, General George C. Marshall, did not remain idle in the face of the Japanese threat. After conferring with President Roosevelt and members of the Cabinet, he sent messages to American commanders in the Philippines, Panama, and Hawaii, informing them that war was imminent and that measures were to be taken accordingly. The commanders received the warning, but because of instructions not to alarm the civilian population, General Walter C. Short, Commanding General of the Hawaiian Department, decided to institute only a sabotage alert. Although he informed the Chief of Staff of his action, somehow or other, this misreading of the situation escaped General Marshall's attention, and the Chief of Staff did nothing to clear up Short's misunderstanding.

Even without formal warning, newspaper reports of the seriousness of the diplomatic crisis between the United States and Japan tended to alert Americans to the danger. Of course neither the authorities in Washington nor the commanders in Hawaii had any premonition of peril to Pearl Harbor; the Japanese had made ominous references to British Malaya, especially the Isthmus of Kra, and Japanese troop concentrations were reported in southern Indo-China. If the Japanese were actually going to attack any American installations, they might conceivably choose the Philippines, but it was not even absolutely certain that they were going to attack any American installations at all. That they were going to strike was known —new intercepts indicated that they considered the negotiations to be at an end and that they were instructing their diplomats to destroy their codes—but when, where, and how they were going to strike was not known. Therefore the reply to Hull's offer of November 26 was expected with great interest: It might yield the answer to these questions.

The reply seemed to be forthcoming on Saturday, December 6, 1941. President Roosevelt had just made ready a last message to the Emperor of Japan, when, through "magic," he was informed that the answer to Hull's note was expected. The Japanese authorities indicated that they were about to broadcast a fourteen-part message and instructed the Ambassador to delay the presentation of the note until such time as he would be specifically ordered to communicate the contents to the Secretary of State. Thirteen parts of the code message were deciphered before midnight. The President remarked to Harry Hopkins that it looked like war, but when Mr. Hopkins said it was a pity that we could not strike the first blow, Mr. Roosevelt replied that as a democracy, we could do no such thing. Then, presumably, he went to bed to await the most significant part of the communication, part fourteen, which had not yet arrived.

The Japanese did not wait long to forward the last part

of the message. The ominous final reply to Hull, clearly evincing Japan's bellicose attitude, reached the decoding rooms in Washington at about 4 o'clock in the morning of December 7. By 10 o'clock, the message was in the hands of the President, but General Marshall could not be found immediately because he had gone for a horseback ride early that morning. At about 10:30, an additional message arrived, instructing the Japanese diplomats to present the 14 part note at 1 p.m. that day. Here was at least the crucial time—the exact place was never revealed—and after all the important officials concerned in the matter had been assembled, General Marshall prepared a warning message to be sent immediately to Hawaii, Panama, and Manila. Because of security considerations, he did not use a scrambler telephone; nor could he know that because of atmospheric conditions, the army's radio-telegraph would be unable to establish contact with Pearl Harbor and that the message would be transmitted by commercial cable. When it arrived, it was too late; the messenger boy who was bicycling to headquarters with it was caught by Japanese bombers and had to seek cover. One important warning had thus been wasted. Whether another, the "East wind rain" broadcast, had ever been heard, long remained a matter of controversy.

In the meantime, a Japanese fleet which had left Tankan Bay in the Kuriles on November 26, was approaching Pearl Harbor. It was proceeding under strict radio silence; few people in Japan knew of its course, and it is more than likely that the Japanese ambassadors in Washington did not have the vaguest idea of its existence. Without mishap, it arrived within striking distance of the great American naval base at Pearl Harbor, where the entire American Pacific fleet with the exception of the aircraft carriers lay at anchor. The Japanese had prepared carefully for the attack. They expected to wipe out the fleet elements at Pearl Harbor and to retire; yet they did not know that the United States had made such progress in radar that it would be possible to monitor the approach of any hostile force on the radar screen. Ordinarily, this lack of knowledge would have proved their undoing, but luck was with them. To be sure, an alert young American radar operator who was testing the equipment in order to get some more experience in his specialty, was on the job on Sunday morning, December 7, 1941, and spotted the approaching Japanese planes. But when he told his lieutenant about them, he was told to forget it, in view of the fact that no planes were expected from the northwest. Another important warning had been disregarded.

To compound the weird events of Pearl Harbor day, naval units had also established the presence of unidentified forces in Hawaiian waters early that Sunday morning. An American destroyer sighted an unidentified submarine and fired upon it. However, by the time reports of the action had been verified, it was too late—a third warning thrown to the winds.

The Japanese succeeded only too well with their mission. They virtually wiped out the Pacific fleet, destroyed many planes on the ground, and inflicted over 3,000 casualties. America found herself at war as the result of the worst naval disaster in American history. Germany joined her Far Eastern partner a few days later, and at long last the war the isolationists had tried so desperately to prevent was upon them.

Many of the errors and blunders committed in connection with the Pearl Harbor disaster might, under normal circumstances, have been ascribed to human weakness. In effect, however, it was the Japanese who committed the gravest blunder. By attacking the American fleet, they unified the United States overnight. Isolationists now had no choice; they were patriots and rushed to the defense of their country. Roosevelt's dilemma —the question of how to aid the Allies whose survival was essential for the survival of America—had been solved for him. Japan's ill-considered attack so simplified the President's problems that his enemies began to suspect that not blunders, but devilish planning had been responsible for Pearl Harbor. And the more they reflected upon the problem, the more they tended to convince themselves. Why, they asked, were the capital ships anchored at Pearl Harbor at a time of crisis? Why were the carriers at sea at the same time? Was it because Roosevelt was trying to set a trap for the Japanese, using the

American fleet as bait? And why, if "magic" was used properly, were the commanding officers at Hawaii not better informed? Did General Marshall refuse to use the scrambler telephone because he did not wish the commanders in the field to receive warning in time? And why was he cantering through the Virginia countryside at the very time when the final part of the Japanese fourteen-part message was expected? Willing to believe the worst of the men they had come to hate, they arrived at the most sinister conclusions. A conspiratorial theory about the origins of the Pacific War has grown up, just as similar theories concerning other wars have developed. Reminiscences and memoirs have poured from the presses; tons of testimony have been taken and recorded, and still the debate rages. In the following pages, the most pertinent documents concerning the fateful and dramatic events leading up to Pearl Harbor have been reproduced. Four different locations—Pearl Harbor, Washington, Tokyo, and Berlin—have been selected as foci for an understanding of the circumstances surrounding the attack. A separate section dealing with the Hull-Nomura conversations has been included, and an effort has been made to let the witnesses speak for themselves. Perhaps the atmosphere thus re-created will contribute to the understanding of that tragic day.

PART ONE

The Events at Pearl Harbor

The Events at Pearl Harbor

When the Japanese attacked Pearl Harbor on December 7, 1941, they succeeded in damaging all American battleships in the Pacific but one and inflicted over 3,000 casualties. The following three documents, Admiral Husband E. Kimmel's battle reports, are designed to give the setting of the attack.

Pearl Harbor Attack, XXXVII, 1207, 1213-1214, 1215-1216, (Hewitt Inquiry Exhibit No. 72, 73).

Dispatch From Commander In Chief, Pacific Fleet, To The Chief Of Naval Operations, 8 December 1941

Pearl Harbor Attack, XXXVII, 1207.

Cincpac And Cincpoa

		Classified outgoing
		Grp. Ct.:
Date:	8 December 1941	Classification: Secret
From:	Cincpac	C.W.O.: HRF
To:	Opnav	System: 18

First evidence of hostilities was presence of submarine in Pearl Harbor defense area at about 0715 local X There were only a few minutes warning of approach of aircraft which arrived at 0747 X Their first attacks against our aircraft on ground at Pearl Harbor Eva Kaneohe Hickam and Wheeler were so effective that practically none were immediately available except 10 VPB which were in air X Enemy carriers were not sighted but indications of at least 1 north and 1 south Oahu as there appeared to be 3 separate attacks ending about 0930 X Dive bombing and torpedoing most effective and in spite of magnificent

25

and courageous work by gun crews not more than dozen enemy shot down including those by Army pursuits X Add to report of casualties Arizona blew up and most of her officers and men including Rear Admiral Kidd were lost X Floating drydock sunk X Personnel casualties estimated 2800 about one half dead X Attempted bombing of dock facilities in Honolulu killed about 200 civilians X No other damage from mines X Pearl channel usable X In addition to ship based and planes in carriers about 30 VPB 15 Army pursuits and 13 Army bombers available X Lexington and 4 heavy cruisers from position east of Midway attempting to intercept southern carrier X Enterprise with other available light forces guarding against repetition of raid X Wake reports heavy damage from bombing by 30 planes X Guam reported being attacked by aircraft

Certified to be a true copy.

       Lt (JG) A S Gordon
      A S GORDON LT (JG) USNR

Report Of Casualties Sustained By U. S. Navy At Pearl Harbor, December 7, 1941

Pearl Harbor Attack, XXXVII, 1213-1214.

      UNITED STATES PACIFIC FLEET
      U.S.S. PENNSYLVANIA, Flagship
     Pearl Harbor, T. H., December 12, 1941

L11-1 (1)/ (50) (02019)
Secret
To: Commander-in-Chief, United States Pacific Fleet.
From: The Chief of Naval Operations
Subject: Damage to Ships of the Pacific Fleet resulting from
    Enemy Attacks at Pearl Harbor, 7 December 1941.

. . . .

1. The following report relative to damage sustained by ships

of the Pacific Fleet resulting from enemy attacks on 7 December 1941 is submitted. . . .:

(a) *BATTLESHIPS.*

ARIZONA sunk at berth as result of aircraft torpedoes and heavy bombs which exploded forward magazines. Ship is considered to be a total wreck.

CALIFORNIA sunk at berth as a result of hits by two or more aircraft torpedoes; also received one large bomb hit amidships which caused serious fire. Recommendations regarding salvage and repairs will be forwarded later.

NEVADA damaged by heavy bombs, possibly mine in the channel and aircraft torpedoes. Beached across from hospital point to prevent sinking after an attempt to sortie. Batteries intact and manned though no power is on the ship. Recommendations regarding salvage and repairs will be made later.

OKLAHOMA capsized at berth as a result of receiving three or more hits by aircraft torpedoes. Recommendations regarding salvage will be made later.

PENNSYLVANIA slightly damaged by bomb hit, starboard side of boat deck while in drydock number 1, Navy Yard, Pearl Harbor. Repairs have been completed and ship is ready for service.

MARYLAND damaged by bomb hit on forecastle and near miss. Ship was moved to the Navy Yard on 11 December and expected to be fully ready for service 13 December.

TENNESSEE received one heavy bomb through turret top which did not explode, but put 2 rammers out of commission. Also one bomb hit aft which cracked one 14" gun. Heat from the *ARIZONA* fire melted and ignited paint in after portion of the second deck which was badly burned out. Ship is now heavily wedged to mooring by reason of the *WEST VIRGINIA* leaning against her. Steps are being taken to dynamite the mooring to permit the removal of the *TENNESSEE.* Repairs are proceeding and it is estimated that by 14 December ship will be ready for service less one 14" gun.

WEST VIRGINIA sunk at berth as result of four aircraft torpedoes and one bomb hit. There is considerable damage from fire. Recommendations regarding salvage and repairs will be made later.

(b) *CRUISERS*

HELENA damaged by bomb hit at frame 30, starboard side, opening up side under armor belt for distance of about 50 feet. Number one and two fire rooms and forward engine room flooded. Ship is now in drydock #2 Navy Yard, Pearl Harbor to effect repairs to make seaworthy. It is estimated that new shell and framing will be completed within two weeks and ship will be able to operate with two shafts and with all gun batteries in commission. It is recommended that ship proceed to Mare Island for completion of repairs to hull and machinery.

HONOLULU damaged by near miss at approximately frame 40 port side. Hole approximately 20 feet by 6 feet underwater. Ship being docked in drydock #1 today and it is estimated that work will be completed to make her fully effective by 16 December.

RALEIGH damaged by one aircraft torpedo which flooded forward half of machinery plant. Also hit by small bomb forward which penetrated three decks and went out ship's side and did not explode. It is proposed to dock the *RALEIGH* following completion of the *HONOLULU* to effect underwater repairs to make seaworthy. Recommendations as to whether all repairs to make the ship fully serviceable should be undertaken at Navy Yard, Pearl Harbor or a mainland navy yard, will be forwarded later.

(c) *DESTROYERS.*

CASSIN and *DOWNES* damaged by bomb in number one drydock, Pearl Harbor ahead of *PENNSYLVANIA*. Bomb hit *DOWNES* exploding her torpedo warheads and causing serious oil fire. *CASSIN* was damaged by fire and knocked off drydock blocking and fell over on *DOWNES*. *DOWNES* appears to be total loss except for salvageable parts and materials. Recommendations regarding salvage and repairs to *CASSIN* will be forwarded later.

SHAW hit by bomb while docked on floating drydock. Forward part of ship and floating drydock badly damaged by fire resulting from oil and powder. After part of ship not seriously damaged. Recommendations regarding repairs will be forwarded later.

(d) *AUXILIARY VESSELS.*

OGLALA sunk by aircraft torpedo and near miss by bomb at ten-ton dock at Navy Yard, Pearl Harbor. Recommendations regarding salvage and repairs will be forwarded at a later date.

UTAH damaged and capsized as a result of hits by aircraft torpedoes. Recommendations regarding salvage and repairs will be forwarded later.

CURTISS damaged by enemy plane out of control which flew into crane mast and bomb which exploded damaging hanger is entirely seaworthy. Repairs are proceeding and ship will be ready for operations less one amidships crane by 15 December.

VESTAL damaged by a bomb hit aft while at berth at Pearl Harbor, is undertaking repairs with own repair force. It is estimated that the ship will be fully ready as a repair ship by 17 December. Docking may not be required.

2. It is believed that the sinking of the *OKLAHOMA, NEVADA, CALIFORNIA* and *WEST VIRGINIA* is in large part due to the ships having been in condition *XRAY*. Had time been available to set condition *ZED* before receiving damage, progressive flooding might have been avoided.

H. E. Kimmel.

Copy to:
Buships
Buord

Excerpts From Admiral Kimmel's Report Of Action Of 7 December 1941

Pearl Harbor Attack, XXXVII, 1215-1216.

UNITED STATES PACIFIC FLEET
U.S.S. PENNSYLVANIA, Flagship
Pearl Harbor, T. H., Dec. 21, 1941

A16-3/ (02088)
To: Rear Admiral H. E. Kimmel, U. S. Navy.
From: The Secretary of the Navy.
Via: The Chief of Naval Operations.
Subject: Report of Action of 7 December 1941.

. . . .

1. The first indication of the attack on Pearl Harbor on the morning of 7 December 1941 was a telephone report received by the Staff Duty Officer from the Fourteenth Naval District Duty Officer at about 0720 (LCT). It reported an attack by the WARD on a hostile submarine off the entrance of Pearl Harbor. Twenty minutes thereafter another telephone report from Operations Officer Patrol Wing TWO, was received that a patrol plane had sunk a hostile submarine south of the entrance buoy. This was followed by an additional telephone report from the Fourteenth Naval District stating the WARD was towing a sampan into Honolulu. At about 0752 a telephone report was received from the Navy Yard Signal Tower as follows: *"Enemy Air Raid—Not Drill."* Almost simultaneously Japanese planes were observed over the Fleet. Dive bombers were bombing the adjacent air fields, accompanied by torpedo plane attacks on the ships in the harbor. From then on there was almost continuous enemy air activity of some kind over the harbor, but there seemed to be separate periods of intense activity as if different new waves were arriving prior to departure of last one. The first of these periods lasted from about 0755 to around 0820. Another period was from about 0900 to 0930 and consisted mainly of dive bombers, a third wave, by high altitude bombers, interspersed with dive bombing and strafing came over about

0930. Meanwhile enemy submarines were reported in Pearl Harbor. One submarine was rammed and sunk by the *MONAGHAN*. All enemy planes withdrew about 1000.

2. It appears that the raid on OAHU was excellently planned and executed in that every air field on the island was bombed and strafed in an attempt to demobilize all planes.

Admiral Husband E. Kimmel, Commander-in-Chief, United States Pacific Fleet, has become one of the key figures in the controversies about Pearl Harbor. The following document shows his side of the story, as presented to the Joint Congressional Committee investigating the Pearl Harbor attack on January 15, 1946.

Pearl Harbor Attack, VI, 2497-2552, footnotes omitted.

TESTIMONY OF REAR ADM. HUSBAND E. KIMMEL, UNITED STATES NAVY (RETIRED)

Pearl Harbor Attack, VI, 2497-2552.

The CHAIRMAN. You may be seated.
The Chair understands that you have a written statement which you desire to read to the committee.
Admiral KIMMEL. That is correct, sir.
The CHAIRMAN. You may proceed, sir.
Admiral KIMMEL. Thank you.

. . . .

This is the first opportunity I have had to speak to the representatives of the American people. I propose to give an account of my stewardship as commander in chief of the Pacific Fleet. . . .

I took command of the Pacific Fleet on February 1, 1941. I had served for more than 40 years in the Navy. I entered the Naval Academy in 1900 and graduated in the class of 1904. I went around the world with the fleet in 1908 as a junior officer. During World War I, I served on Admiral Rodman's staff. He was in command of the United States battleships operating with the British Grand Fleet. I commanded a destroyer division in the Asiatic Fleet, and did additional duty in the Philippines and China from 1923 to 1925.

After a tour of duty at the Naval War College and in the Office of the Chief of Naval Operations I commanded a destroyer squadron in the Battle Fleet from 1928 to 1930.

THE EVENTS AT PEARL HARBOR 33

I was Director of Ship Movements in the Office of the Chief of Naval Operations from 1930 to 1933.

I commanded the battleship *New York* in 1933 and 1934, and during the next year served as chief of staff to Admiral Craven, commander, battleships of the fleet.

I was budget officer of the Navy Department from 1935 to 1938. As a rear admiral, I commanded a heavy cruiser division of the Scouting Force of the fleet in 1938.

I was type commander of the cruisers in the Battle Force in 1939. I held this position until I was appointed Commander in Chief of the Pacific Fleet.

. . . .

The fleet was not ready for war in 1940. I set out to make it ready. This required an intensive training program. In carrying out this program, we were handicapped by the detachment, from time to time, of officers and men in large numbers to meet the demands of the expanding procurement and training agencies on shore, and the supply of trained personnel to man new ships.

. . . .

It became apparent soon after I took command that the existing organization of the United States Fleet was not a proper one to meet the tasks which would be required in a Pacific war. Early in 1941, therefore, the vessels of the Pacific Fleet were reorganized into three task forces, including one fast carrier task force, one amphibious task force and one battleship task force. In their operations at sea, these task forces were operated under wartime conditions. Fueling at sea, a requirement for long range operations, was stressed.

The operating schedule was so arranged that there was always at least one of these task forces, and usually two, at sea. Frequently during fleet maneuvers the entire fleet was at sea. Periods in port were of course necessary for all ships. At no time during 1941 were all of the ships of the fleet in Pearl Harbor.

It was recognized that the Pacific Fleet was inferior to the Japanese Fleet in every category of fighting ship. No one in authority expected that the Pacific Fleet could meet the Japanese head on.

. . . .

In his letter to the Secretary of War on January 23, 1941, the Secretary of the Navy listed an air torpedo plane attack as one of the possible forms of hostile action against Pearl Harbor. Subsequently, the Chief of Naval Operations forwarded to the Fleet and the Commandant, 14th Naval District, detailed technical advice which practically eliminated from consideration an air torpedo plane attack as a serious danger to ships moored in the shallow waters of Pearl Harbor.

. . . .

My relations with General Short, which were once the subject of considerable confusion in the public mind, have now been clarified by exhaustive investigations . . . . It has been established that our official and social relations were friendly, that we frequently conferred on official matters of common interest and invariably did so when either of us received messages which had any bearing on the development of the United States-Japanese situation, or on our several plans in preparing for war.

. . . .

In summary, the Pacific Fleet in 1941 established and maintained the highest degree of security measures at sea and in port consistent with our assigned mission of intensive preparation for war. . . .

We needed only one thing which our own resources could not make available to us. That vital need was the information available in Washington from the intercepted dispatches which told when and where Japan would probably strike. I did not get this information.

. . . .

In this part of my statement, I shall describe the information available to me prior to the attack and the actions which I took upon the basis of that information.

. . . .

On November 24, 1941, the Chief of Naval Operations sent me a dispatch stating that the chances of a favorable outcome

THE EVENTS AT PEARL HARBOR

of negotiations with Japan were very doubtful and that, in his opinion, an aggressive movement in any direction, including an attack on the Philippines or Guam was a possibility. . . . During the time these dispatches were sent, the Navy Department knew just what my program in Hawaii was. My fleet-operating schedules were filed with the Navy Department, where the location and movement of substantially every ship in the fleet was known at all times. No dispatch or letter contained any order or suggestion for departure from my operating schedules.

. . . .

It is one thing to warn commanders at a particular base of the probable outbreak of war in theaters thousands of miles away, knowing and expecting that they will continue their assigned tasks and missions after the receipt of such warning, and that the very nature of the warning emphasized to them the necessity for continuing such tasks and missions.

It is quite another thing to warn commanders at a particular base of an attack to be expected in their own locality.

. . . .

On November 27, the Chief of Naval Operations sent to me and to the Commander in Chief of the Asiatic Fleet, the following dispatch:

> This dispatch is to be considered a war warning. Negotiations with Japan looking toward stabilization of conditions in the Pacific have ceased and an aggressive move by Japan is expected within the next few days. The number and equipment of Japanese troops and the organization of naval task forces indicates an amphibious expedition against either the Philippines Thai or Kra Peninsula or possibly Borneo. Execute an appropriate defensive deployment preparatory to carrying out the tasks assigned in WPL 46. Inform District and Army authorities. A similar warning is being sent by War Department. SPENAVO inform British. Continental Districts Guam Samoa directed take appropriate measures against sabotage.

. . . .

The so-called "war warning" dispatch of November 27 did

not warn the Pacific Fleet of an attack in the Hawaiian area. It did not state expressly or by implication that an attack in the Hawaiian area was imminent or probable. It did not repeal or modify the advice previously given me by the Navy Department that no move against Pearl Harbor was imminent or planned by Japan. The phrase "war warning" cannot be made a catch-all for all the contingencies hindsight may suggest. It is a characterization of the specific information which the dispatch contained.

In brief, on November 27, the Navy Department suggested that I send from the immediate vicinity of Pearl Harbor the carriers of the fleet which constituted the fleet's main striking defense against an air attack.

On November 27, the War and Navy Departments suggested that we send from the island of Oahu, 50 percent of the Army's resources in pursuit planes.

These proposals came to us on the very same day of the so-called "war warning."

In these circumstances no reasonable man in my position would consider that the "war warning" was intended to suggest the likelihood of an attack in the Hawaiian area.

From November 27 to the time of the attack, all the information which I had from the Navy Department or from any other source, confirmed, and was consistent, with the Japanese movement in southeast Asia described in the dispatch of November 27.

. . . .

In short, all indications of the movements of Japanese military and naval forces which came to my attention confirmed the information in the dispatch of 27 November—that the Japanese were on the move against Thailand or the Kra Peninsula in southeast Asia.

. . . .

I shall now describe the nature and extent of distant reconnaissance from the Hawaiian area on and after November 27, 1941.

. . . .

When the *Enterprise* completed its delivery of planes to Wake,

I withdrew a squadron of patrol planes from Wake. This squadron then proceeded to Midway, searching the ocean areas en route. It then moved from Midway to Pearl Harbor, conducting a reconnaissance sweep en route.

In the week before December 7, these reconnaissance sweeps of the patrol plane squadrons moving from Midway to Wake; from Pearl Harbor to Johnston and from Johnston to Midway; from Wake to Midway and Midway to Pearl Harbor, covered a total distance of nearly 5,000 miles. As they proceeded, each squadron would cover a 400 mile strand of ocean along its path. They brought under the coverage of air search about 2,000,000 square miles of ocean area.

In addition to these reconnaissance sweeps, submarines of the fleet on and after November 27 were on war patrols from Midway and Wake Islands continuously.

At Oahu before the attack, there were 49 patrol planes which were in flying condition. Eight other planes were out of commission and undergoing repair. In addition, on December 5, a squadron of patrol planes returned to Pearl Harbor after an arduous tour of duty at Midway and Wake. This squadron consisted of obsolete PBY-3 planes, approaching 18 months' service and overdue for overhaul. It was not available for distant searches.

. . . .

To insure an island base against a surprise attack from fast carrier-based planes, it is necessary to patrol the evening before to a distance of 800 miles on a 360° arc. This requires 84 planes on one flight of 16 hours. Of course, the same planes and the same crews cannot make that 16-hour flight every day. For searches of this character over a protracted period, a pool of 250 planes would be required. These are fundamental principles. You will find them in the testimony of expert aviation officers before the naval court; and in the very comprehensive letter Fleet Admiral Nimitz wrote to the commander in chief, United States Fleet, on January 7, 1942, on the subject Airplane Situation in Hawaiian Area.

It is clear that I did not have a sufficient number of planes to conduct each day a 360° distant search from the island of Oahu. That fact is beyond controversy.

. . . .

I shall now discuss the dispositions of the capital ships of the Pacific Fleet on and after November 27. On November 28 Admiral Halsey left for Wake with a carrier task force and on December 5 Admiral Newton left for Midway with another carrier task force. These missions were in pursuance of an explicit suggestion from the Navy Department. When Admiral Halsey left for Wake on November 28 the three battleships of his task force accompanied him out of Pearl Harbor so as to avoid creating the impression that there was anything unusual about the movement of his task force. However, immediately on clearing the channel Admiral Halsey diverted his battleships and instructed them to carry out exercises in the Hawaiian area. He then headed west with the remainder of his task force.

It would have been unwise for Admiral Halsey to have taken along the battleships. The maximum speed of the battleships was 17 knots. The fleet units which he took to Wake could make 30 knots. To take his battleships with him would have meant the loss of 13 knots of potential speed. He was bound for dangerous waters where curtailed speed might spell disaster. He needed all the mobility his force could attain. Three battleships did not furnish sufficient supporting strength to warrant the risks of reduction in speed and mobility which their presence in the expedition to Wake would entail. Moreover, it was necessary to complete the Wake operation as quickly as possible so that the ships engaged might be ready for further eventualities.

. . . .

The absence of the carriers from the Hawaiian area temporarily limited the mobility of the battleships which were left behind.

While the carriers were absent on the assigned missions to Midway and Wake, the battleships force was kept in Pearl Harbor. To send them to sea without air cover for any prolonged period would have been a dangerous course. The only effective defense at sea from air attack, whether it be a bombing attack or a torpedo-plane attack, is an effective air cover. Surface ships, such as destroyers and cruisers, are much less effective against an air attack. That is so today. It was the more so prior to 7 December because of the existing inadequacies of anti-aircraft guns.

The carriers furnished air coverage for the battleships at sea. The few planes that battleships and cruisers carry for use by catapult are not fighters. Their function is only scouting and reconnaissance. They are ineffective as a defense against enemy air attack. The battleships at sea without carriers had no protection from air bombing attack. In Pearl Harbor they had the protection of such antiaircraft defenses as the Army had. At sea, in deep waters, there were no physical barriers to the effectiveness of torpedo-plane attack. In Pearl Harbor, where the depth of water was less than 40 feet, a torpedo-plane attack was considered a negligible danger. The battleships of the fleet at sea, without carriers, sighted by a force of such character as to have a chance of successful air attack on the Hawaiian Islands appeared to be more subject to damage than in port.

Vice Admiral Pye, commander of the Battle Force, and I discussed these considerations in a conference after the receipt of the so-called war-warning dispatch.

At the time of our discussion—at that time and later—we did not have before us the intercepted Japanese messages indicating that the ships in port in Pearl Harbor were marked for attack. We had no information that an air attack upon Pearl Harbor was imminent or probable. The fact that the Navy Department proposed at this time that our carriers be sent to the outlying islands indicated to us that the Navy Department felt that no attack on Pearl Harbor could be expected in the immediate future.

. . . .

Upon receipt of the so-called war warning dispatch of November 27, 1941, I issued orders to the fleet to exercise extreme vigilance against submarines in operating areas and to depth bomb all contacts expected to be hostile in the fleet operating areas. My dispatch of November 28 to the fleet containing this order was forwarded to the Navy Department on that day. On December 2, I wrote to the Chief of Naval Operations directing his personal attention to this order. The Navy Department, in the 10 days prior to the attack, did not approve or disapprove my action.

For some time there had been reports of submarines in the operating areas around Hawaii. . . . The files of the Commander in Chief, Pacific Fleet, contain records of at least three suspicious contacts during the 5 weeks preceding Pearl Harbor.

On November 3, 1941, a patrol plane observed an oil slick area in latitude 20-10, longtiude 157-41. The patrol plane searched a 15-mile area. A sound search was made by the U.S.S. *Borden,* and an investigation was made by the U.S.S. *Dale,* all of them producing negative results. On November 28, 1941, the U.S.S. *Helena* reported that a radar operator without knowledge of my orders directing an alert against submarines was positive that a submarine was in a restricted area. A search by a task group with three destroyers of the suspected area produced no contacts. During the night of December 2, 1941, the U.S.S. *Gamble* reported a clear metallic echo in latitude 20-30, longitude 158-23. An investigation directed by Destroyer Division Four produced no conclusive evidence of the presence of a submarine. On the morning of the attack, the U.S.S. *Ward* reported to the Commandant of the Fourteenth Naval District that it had attacked, fired upon and dropped depth charges upon a submarine operating in the defensive sea area. The Commandant of the Fourteenth Naval District directed a verification of this report with a view to determining whether the contact with the submarine was a sound contact or whether the submarine had actually been seen by the *Ward.* He also directed that the ready-duty destroyer assist the *Ward* in the defensive sea area. Apparently, some short time after reporting the submarine contact, the *Ward* also reported that it had intercepted a sampan which it was escorting into Honolulu. This message appeared to increase the necessity for a verification of the earlier report of the submarine contact.

Between 7:30 and 7:40 I received information from the Staff

Duty Officer of the *Ward's* report, the dispatch of the ready-duty destroyer to assist the *Ward*, and the efforts then under way to obtain a verification of the *Ward's* report. I was awaiting such verification at the time of the attack. In my judgment, the effort to obtain confirmation of the reported submarine attack off Pearl Harbor was a proper preliminary to more drastic action in view of the number of such contacts which had not been verified in the past.

PART III.

INFORMATION WITHHELD FROM THE FLEET
AND ITS SIGNIFICANCE

. . . .

In the month of July 1941 the Chief of Naval Operations sent me at least seven dispatches which quoted intercepted Japanese diplomatic messages from Tokyo to Washington, Tokyo to Berlin, Berlin to Tokyo, Tokyo to Vichy, Canton to Tokyo. These dispatches identified by number the Japanese messages they quoted and gave their verbatim text.

I was never informed of any decision to the effect that intelligence from intercepted Japanese messages was not to be sent to me. In fact, dispatches sent to me by the Navy Department in the week before the attack contained intelligence from intercepted messages. On December 1, a dispatch from the Chief of Naval Operations, sent to me for information, quoted a report of November 29 from the Japanese Ambassador in Bangkok to Tokyo which described a Japanese plan to entice the British to invade Thai, thereby permitting Japan to enter that country in the role of its defender. On December 3, a dispatch to me from the Chief of Naval Operations set forth an order from Japan to diplomatic agents and expressly referred to this order as "Circular 2444 from Tokyo." Another dispatch from the Chief of Naval Operations on December 3 referred to certain "categoric and urgent instructions which were sent yesterday to Japanese diplomatic and consular posts."

The Navy Department thus engaged in a course of conduct calculated to give me the impression that intelligence from important intercepted Japanese messages was being furnished to me. Under these circumstances a failure to send me important information of this character was not merely a withholding of intelligence. It partook of the nature of an affirmative misrepresentation. I had asked for all vital information. I had been assured that I would have it. I appeared to be receiving it. My current estimate of the situation was formed on this basis. Yet, in fact, the most vital information from the intercepted Japanese messages was not sent to me. This failure not only deprived me of essential facts. It misled me.

I was not supplied with any information of the intercepted messages showing that the Japanese Government had divided Pearl Harbor into five subareas. Each area was given an alphabetical symbol. Area A was the term prescribed to describe the waters between Ford Island and the arsenal. Area B was the term prescribed to describe the waters south and west of Ford Island. Area C was the term prescribed to describe East Loch; area D, Middle Loch; Area E, West Loch and communicating water routes. The dispatch stated:

> With regard to warships and aircraft carriers, we would like to have you report on those at anchor, (these are not so important), tied up at wharves, buoys, and in docks. (Designate types and classes briefly. If possible we would like to have you make mention of the fact when there are two or more vessels alongside the same wharf.)

This dispatch was decoded and translated on October 9, 1941. This information was never supplied to me.

.   .   .   .

In the volume of intercepted Japanese dispatches eliciting and securing information about American military installations and naval movements, the dispatches concerning Pearl Harbor, on and after September 24, 1941, stand out, apart from the others. No other harbor or base in American territory, possessions was divided into subareas by Japan. In no other area was the Japanese Government seeking information as to whether two or more vessels were alongside the same wharf. Prior to the dispatch of September 24, the information which the Japanese sought and obtained about Pearl Harbor, followed the general pattern of their interest in American Fleet movements in other localities. One might suspect this type of conventional espionage. With the dispatch of September 24, 1941, and those which followed, there was a significant and ominous change in the character of the information which the Japanese Government sought and obtained. The espionage then directed was of an unusual character and outside the realm of reasonable suspicion. It was no longer merely directed to ascertaining the general whereabouts of ships of the fleet. It was directed to the presence of particular ships in particular areas; to such minute detail as what ships were double-docked at the same wharf. In the period immediately preceding the attack, the Jap Consul General in Hawaii was directed by Tokyo to report even when there were no movements of ships in and out of Pearl Harbor. These Japanese instructions and reports pointed to an attack by Japan upon the ships in Pearl Harbor. The information sought and obtained, with such painstaking detail, had no other conceivable usefulness from a military viewpoint. Its utlilty was in planning and executing an attack upon the ships in port. Its effective value was lost completely when the ships left their reported berthings in Pearl Harbor.

No one had a more direct and immediate interest in the security of the fleet in Pearl Harbor than its commander in chief. No one had a greater right than I to know that Japan had carved up Pearl Harbor into subareas and was seeking and receiving reports as to the precise berthings in that harbor of the ships of the fleet. I had been sent Mr. Grew's report earlier in the year with positive advice from the Navy Department that no credence was to be placed in the rumored Japanese plans for an attack on Pearl Harbor. I was told then, that no Japanese move against Pearl Harbor appeared "imminent or planned for in the foreseeable future." Certainly I was entitled to know when information in the Navy Department completely altered the information and advice previously given to me. Surely, I was entitled to know of the intercepted dispatches between Tokyo and Honolulu on and after September 24, 1941, which indicated that a Japanese move against Pearl Harbor was planned in Tokyo.

Knowledge of these intercepted Japanese dispatches would have radically changed the estimate of the situation made by me and my staff. It would have suggested a reorientation of our planned operations at the outset of hostilities. The war plans of the Navy Department, and of the Pacific Fleet, as well as our directives and information from Washington prior to the attack indicated that the Pacific Fleet could be most effectively employed against Japan through diversionary raids on the Marshalls, when the Japanese struck at the Malay Barrier. Knowledge of a probable Japanese attack on Pearl Harbor afforded an opportunity to ambush the Japanese striking force as it ventured to Hawaii. It would have suggested the wisdom of concentrating our resources to that end, rather than conserving them for the Marshall expedition.

The intercepted dispatches about the berthing of ships in Pearl Harbor also clarified the significance of other intercepted Japanese dispatches, decoded and translated by the Navy Department prior to the attack. I refer particularly to the intercepted dispatches which established a deadline date for agreement between Japan and the United States. When this date passed without agreement, these dispatches revealed that a Japanese plan automatically took effect.

The deadline date was first established in a dispatch No. 736 from Tokyo to Washington on November 5, 1941. . . .

This dispatch was decoded and translated by the Navy on the date of its origin, November 5, 1941. This information was never supplied to me.

The deadline was reiterated in a dispatch from Tokyo to Washington on November 11, 1941. . . . This information was never supplied to me.

The deadline was again emphasized in a dispatch from Tokyo to Washington November 15, 1941. This dispatch stated:

> Judging from the progress of the conversations, there seem to be indications that the United States is still not fully

aware of the exceedingly criticalness of the situation here. The fact remains that the date set forth in my message No. 736 (November 25) is absolutely immovable under present conditions. It is a definite deadline and therefore it is essential that a settlement be reached by about that time. The session of Parliament opens on the 15th (work will start on (the following day?)) according to schedule. The government must have a clear picture of things to come in presenting its case at the session. You can see, therefore, that the situation is nearing a climax, and that time is indeed becoming short * * *"

This dispatch was decoded and translated by the Navy Department on November 12, 1941. This information was never supplied to me.

The deadline was again emphasized in a dispatch from Tokyo to Washington on November 15, 1941. . . . This information was never supplied to me.

The deadline was again reiterated on November 16 with great emphasis upon its importance. A dispatch from Tokyo to Washington on that date was as follows:

For your Honor's own information:

1. I have read your #1090 and you may be sure that you have all my gratitude for the efforts you have put forth, but the fate of our Empire hangs by the slender thread of a few days, so please fight harder than you ever did before.

2. * * * In your opinion we ought to wait and see what turn the war takes and remain patient. However, I am awfully sorry to say that the situation renders this out of the question. I set the deadline from the solution of these negotiations in my #736 and there will be no change. Please try to understand that. You see how short the time is; therefore, do not allow the United States to sidetrack us and delay the negotiations any further. Press them for a solution on the basis of our proposals and do your best to bring about an immediate solution.

This dispatch was decoded and translated on November 17, 1941. This information was never supplied to me.

The deadline was finally extended on November 22 for a period of 4 days. On that date a dispatch from Tokyo to Washington instructed Nomura and Kurusu:

> It is awfully hard for us to consider changing the date we set in my #736. You should know this, however, I know you are working hard. Stick to our fixed policy and do your very best. Spare no efforts and try to bring about the solution we desire. There are reasons beyond your ability to guess why we wanted to settle Japanese-American relations by the 25th, but if within the next three or four days you can finish your conversations with the Americans; if the signing can be completed by the 29th (let me write it out for you—twenty-ninth); if the pertinent notes can be exchanged; if we can get an understanding with Great Britain and the Netherlands; and in short, if everything can be finished, we have decided to wait until that date. This time we mean it, that the deadline absolutely cannot be changed. After that things are automatically going to happen. Please take this into your careful consideration and work harder than you ever have before. This, for the present, is for the information of you two Ambassadors alone.

This dispatch was decoded and translated on the date of its origin, November 22, 1941. This information was never supplied to me.

Again on November 24, 1941, Tokyo specifically instructed its Ambassadors in Washington that the November 29 dead line was set in Tokyo time. This dispatch was decoded and translated on November 24, the date of its origin. This information was never supplied to me.

In at least six separate dispatches, on November 5, 11, 15, 16, 22, and 24, Japan specifically established and extended the dead line of November 25, later advanced to November 29. The dispatches made it plain that after the deadline date the Japanese plan was automatically going into operation. The plan was of such importance that as the deadline approached, the Government of Japan declared: "The fate of our Empire hangs by the slender thread of a few days."

When the dead line date of November 29 was reached with no agreement between the United States and Japan, there was no further extension. The intercepted dispatches indicated that the crisis deepened in its intensity after that day passed. On the 1st of December, Tokyo advised its ambassadors in Washington:

> The date set in my messages #812 has come and gone and the situation continued to be increasingly critical.

This message was translated by the Navy on the 1st of December. This information was never supplied to me.

An intercepted Japanese dispatch from Tokyo to Washington of November 28, 1941, made it clear that the American proposal of November 26 was completely unsatisfactory to Japan and that an actual rupture of negotiations would occur upon the receipt of the Japanese reply. A dispatch on November 28, decoded and translated on the same day, stated:

> Well, you two ambassadors have exerted superhuman efforts but, in spite of this, the United States has gone ahead and presented this humiliating proposal. This was quite unexpected and extremely regrettable. The Imperial Government can by no means use it as a basis for negotiations. Therefore, with a report of the view of the Imperial Government on this American proposal which I will send you in two or three days, the negotiations will be de facto ruptured. This is inevitable. * * *

After receipt by Tokyo of the American note of November 26, the intercepted Japanese dispatches show that Japan attached great importance to the continuance of negotiations to conceal from the United States whatever plan automatically took effect on November 29. Thus the dispatch from Tokyo to Washington on November 28, cautions the Japanese Ambassadors in Washington:

> * * * I do not wish you to give the impression that the negotiations are broken off. Merely say to them that you are awaiting instructions and that, although the opinions of your government are not yet clear to you, to your own

way of thinking the Imperial Government has always made just claims and has borne great sacrifices for the sake of peace in the Pacific * * *

This information was never supplied to me.

Again the dispatch from Tokyo to Washington of December 1, 1941, advising the Japanese Ambassador that the dead line date had come and gone and the situation continues to be critical, contains this further information:

* * * to prevent the United States from becoming unduly suspicious we have been advising the press and others that though there are some wide differences between Japan and the United States, the negotiations are continuing. (The above is for only your information.)

This information was never supplied to me.

Again in the trans-Pacific telephone conversation intercepted on November 27, and translated by the Navy Department on November 28, Yamamoto in Tokyo explicitly instructed Kurusu: "Regarding negotiations, don't break them off."

In another trans-Pacific telephone conversation between Kurusu and Yamamoto, intercepted and translated by the Navy on November 30, Kurusu noted the change in the Japanese attitude with respect to the duration of the American-Japanese negotiations. Before the deadline date Kurusu and Nomura had been urged by Tokyo to press for a conclusion of negotiations. Now they were instructed to stretch them out. Kurusu asked, "Are the Japanese-American negotiations to continue?" Yamamoto replied, "Yes." Kurusu then stated: "You were very urgent about them before, weren't you; but now you want them to stretch out. We will need your help. Both the Premier and the Foreign Minister will need to change the tone of their speeches! Do you understand? Please use more discretion."

The information from these telephone conversations was never supplied to me.

Again on November 29, an intercepted Japanese dispatch from Tokyo contains cautious representations to be addressed to the United States. The following instructions accompanied them:

THE EVENTS AT PEARL HARBOR

* * * In carrying out this instruction, please be careful that this does not lead to anything like a breaking off of negotiations. * * *

This dispatch was decoded and translated by the Navy on November 30 and never sent to me.

The intercepted Japanese diplomatic dispatches show that on and after November 29, a Japanese plan of action automatically went into effect; that the plan was of such importance that it involved the fate of the empire; and that Japan urgently wanted the United States to believe that negotiations were continuing after the deadline to prevent suspicion as to the nature of the plan.

What was this plan? Why such elaborate instructions to stretch out negotiations as a pretext to hide the operation of this plan? Anyone reading the Japanese intercepted messages would face this question.

Certainly the concealed Japanese plans which automatically went into effect on November 29 would hardly be the Japanese movement in Indo-China. "* * * No effort was made to mask the movements or presence of the naval forces moving southward, because physical observations of that movement were unavoidable and the radio activity of these forces would provide a desirable semblance of normalcy." (testimony of Admiral Inglis, p. 453) The troop movements to southern Indo-China were the subject of formal diplomatic exchanges between the two governments of Japan and the United States.

On December 2, 1941, Mr. Welles handed to Mr. Nomura and Mr. Kurusu a communication which the President of the United States wished to make to them. This communication was as follows:

I have received reports during the past days of continuing Japanese troop movements in southern Indo-China—Please be good enough to request the Japanese ambassador and Ambassador Kurusu to inquire at once of the Japanese government what the actual reasons may be for the steps already taken and what I am to consider is the policy of the Japanese government as demonstrated by this recent and rapid concentration of troops in Indo-China. . .

Thus, it was apparent to the Japanese Government from this formal representation of the United States that our Government was aware of the movement in Indo-China. The United States expressed its concern about potential Japanese action against the Philippines, the East Indies, Malaya, or Thailand. There was, therefore, very little reason for Japan to keep up a pretext of negotiations for the purpose of disguising these objectives.

Consequently, as time went on after November 29, and as Japan insisted to her envoys upon the continuance of negotiations as a pretext to divert the suspicion of the United States, it must have been apparent to a careful student of the intercepted dispatches that Japan on a dead-line date of November 29 had put into effect an operation, which was to consume a substantial time interval before its results were apparent to this Government, and which appeared susceptible of effective concealment in its initial phases.

The messages as to the berthings of ships in Pearl Harbor would have given the reader of these intercepted dispatches an insight as to one of the probable directions of the plan which went into effect automatically on November 29, and which Japan was so anxious to conceal. All these dispatches taken together would have pointed to Pearl Harbor as a probable objective of this plan. Yet, because I was not furnished with these intercepted dispatches, nor given in summary form any indication of the dead-line date, the automatic execution of a plan by Japan on that date, and the continuance of negotiations thereafter as a pretext to hide that plan, I was deprived of the opportunity to make this deduction, which the dispatches as a whole would warrant, if not compel.

After November 27, there was a rising intensity in the crisis in Japanese-United States relations apparent in the intercepted dispatches. I was told on November 27 that negotiations had ceased and 2 days later that they appeared to be terminated with the barest possibilities of their resumption. Then I was left to read public accounts of further conversations between the State Department and the Japanese emissaries in Washington which indicated that negotiations had been resumed.

The Navy Department knew immediately of the reaction of

Nomura and Kurusu to the American note of November 26—"Our failure and humiliation are complete."

The Navy Department knew immediately of the reactions of the Japanese Government to the American note of November 26.* Japan termed it—

> a humiliating proposal. This was quite unexpected and extremely regrettable. The Imperial Government can by no means use it as a basis for negotiations. Therefore with a report of the views of the Imperial Government on this American proposal which I will send you in two or three days, the negotiations will be de facto ruptured. This is inevitable.

The Navy Department knew that Nomura and Kurusu suggested to Japan on November 26 one way of saving the situation—a wire by the President to the Emperor.

The Navy Department knew that the Japanese Government advised Nomura and Kurusu on November 28 that the suggested wire from the President to the Emperor offered no hope: "What you suggest is entirely unsuitable."

The Navy Department knew that on November 30, Japan gave Germany a detailed version of the negotiations with the United States. Japan stated that "a continuation of negotiations would inevitably be detrimental to our cause," and characterized certain features of the American proposal of November 26 as "insulting"—"clearly a trick." Japan concluded that the United States had decided to regard her as an enemy.

The Navy Department knew that Japan had instructed her ambassadors in Berlin on November 30 to inform Hitler:

> The conversation begun between Tokyo and Washington last April * * * now stand ruptured—broken. Say very secretly to them (Hitler and Ribbentrop) that there is extreme danger that war may suddenly break out between the Anglo-Saxon nations and Japan through some clash of arms and add that the time of the breaking out of this war may come quicker than anyone dreams.**

---

* See p. 309.
** See p. 268.

All this vital information came from intercepted dispatches, decoded and translated in Washington, either on the day they were sent or a day or two later. None of this information was supplied to me.

On November 19, 1941, the Japanese Government set up a system for informing its representatives throughout the world of the time when Japan was to sever diplomatic relations or go to war with the United States, Great Britain, or Russia. This decision was to be made known through a false weather broadcast from Japan. The words "east wind rain" in the broadcast meant that Japan had decided to sever relations or go to war with the United States. The words "west wind clear" would denote such action against England. The words "north wind cloudy" would denote such action against Russia.

The interception of the false weather broadcast was considered by the Navy Department to be of supreme importance. Every facility of the Navy was invoked to learn as speedily as possible when the false weather broadcast from Japan was heard and which of the significant code words were used. Extraordinary measures were established in the Navy Department to transmit the words used in this broadcast to key officers in Washington as soon as they were known.

The Naval Court of Inquiry heard substantial evidence from various witnesses on the question of whether or not Japan gave the signal prescribed by the winds code. The Naval Court of Inquiry found the facts on this matter to be as follows:

> On 4 December an intercepted Japanese broadcast employing this code was received in the Navy Department. Although this notification was subject to two interpretations, either a breaking off of diplomatic relations between Japan and the United States or war, this information was not transmitted to the Commander in Chief, Pacific Fleet, or to other Commanders afloat.
>
> It was known in the Navy Department that the Commanders-in-Chief, Pacific and Asiatic Fleets, were monitoring Japanese broadcasts for this code, and apparently there was a mistaken impression in the Navy Department that the execute message had also been intercepted at Pearl Harbor,

when in truth this message was never intercepted at Pearl Harbor. No attempt was made by the Navy Department to ascertain whether this information had been obtained by the Commander-in-Chief, Pacific, and by other Commanders afloat. Admiral Stark stated that he knew nothing about it, although Admiral Turner stated that he himself was familiar with it and presumed that Admiral Kimmel had it. This message cannot now be located in the Navy Department.

From various intercepted Japanese messages it was apparent that the high point in the crisis in Japanese-American affairs would be reached when the Japanese reply to the American note of November 26 was received. As the Naval Court of Inquiry put it:

> The reply to this note was anxiously awaited by the high officials of the War and Navy Departments because of the feeling that Japan would not accept the conditions presented, and that diplomatic relations would be severed or that war would be declared.

On the afternoon of December 6, 1941, there was intercepted, decoded, and translated in the Navy Department, a dispatch from Japan to her Ambassadors in Washington known as the "pilot message." This stated:

> 1. The Government has deliberated deeply on the American proposal of the 26th of November and as a result we have drawn up a memorandum for the United States contained in my separate message #902 (in English).
>
> 2. This separate message is a very long one. I will send it in fourteen parts and I imagine you will receive it tomorrow. However, I am not sure. The situation is extremely delicate, and when you receive it I want you to please keep it secret for the time being.
>
> 3. Concerning the time of presenting this memorandum to the United States, I will wire you in a separate message. However, I want you in the meantime to put it in nicely

drafted form and make every preparation to present it to the Americans just as soon as you receive instructions.

The first 13 parts of the Japanese reply were intercepted and received by the Navy Department at about 3 p.m., December 6, 1941, and were translated and made ready for distribution by 9 p.m., Washington time, on that date. These 13 parts contained strong language. The following expressions are fairly typical of the tenor of those 13 parts:*

> The American Government, obsessed with its own views and opinions, may be said to be scheming for the extension of the war (Part 9)—it is exercising in conjunction with Great Britain and other nations pressure by economic power. Recourse to such pressure as a means of dealing with international relations should be condemned as it is at times more inhumane than military pressure (Part 9)—It is a fact of history that the countries (of East Asia for the past hundred years or more have) been compelled to observe the status quo under the Anglo-American policy of imperialistic exploitation and to sacrifice (themselves) to the prosperity of the two nations. (Part 10).

Mr. Hull described the whole document on December 7:

> In all my 50 years of public service I have never seen a document that was more crowded with infamous falsehoods and distortions on a scale so huge that I never imagined until today that any government of this planet was capable of uttering them.

The 13 parts and the pilot message instructing the Japanese envoys that a specific hour was later to be fixed for its delivery could mean only one thing; that war with the United States was imminent. An hour had been fixed for the delivery of the Japanese ultimate and for the probable outbreak of hostilities. The hour fixed would be communicated to the Japanese emissaries in Washington in a separate message to be expected shortly.

---

* See p. 225.

THE EVENTS AT PEARL HARBOR

Not a word of these supremely critical developments of Saturday, December 6, was sent to me. This vital information which was available at 9 p.m., Washington time, was distributed to the most important officers of the Government in Washington by midnight, Washington time. The President of the United States had it. The Secretary of the Navy had it. The Chief of Military Intelligence had it. The Director of Naval Intelligence had it. Apparently, the Secretary of War and the Secretary of State were apprised of these momentous events on that same evening. Nine p.m. in Washington was 3:30 in the afternoon in Hawaii. At midnight in Washington it was early evening, 6:30 p.m., in Hawaii.

The dispatch fixing the hour for the delivery of the Japanese ultimatum to the United States as 1 p.m., Washington time, was intercepted and decoded by the Navy Department by 7 on the morning of December 7—7 a.m., Washington time, 1:30 a.m., Hawaiian time—nearly six and a half hours before the attack. The translation of this short message from the Japanese was a 2-minute job. Not later than 10:30 a.m. the Chief of Naval Operations was informed of it. This information was not supplied to me prior to the attack.

I cannot tell what the evidence at this investigation will ultimately show as to the precise hours on the morning of December 7, when various responsible officers of the Navy Department knew that 1 p.m., Washington time, was the hour fixed for the delivery of the Japanese ultimatum to this Government. This much I know. There was ample time, at least an interval of approximately 2½ hours, in which a message could have been dispatched to me.

Regardless of what arguments there may be as to the evaluation of the dispatches that had been sent to me, I surely was entitled to know of the hour fixed by Japan for the probable outbreak of war against the United States. I cannot understand now—I have never understood—I may never understand—why I was deprived of the information available in the Navy Department in Washington on Saturday night and Sunday morning.

On November 28, 1941, the Navy Department could have informed me of the following vital facts:

(1) Japan had set November 29 as an immovable dead-line date for agreement with the United States.

(2) The United States gave to Japan certain proposals for a solution of Japanese-American relations on November 26. I might remark parenthetically that an authoritative statement from my Government as to the general nature of these proposals would have been most enlightening.

(3) Japan considered the United States proposals of November 26 as unacceptable and planned to rupture negotiations with the United States when the reply to them was delivered to this Government.

(4) Japan was keeping up a pretext of negotiations after November 26 to conceal a definite plan which went into effect on November 29. This was the type of information which I had stated in May I needed so urgently in making the difficult decisions with which I was confronted.

The question will arise in your minds, as it has in mine: Would the receipt of this information have made a difference in the events of December 7? No man can now state as a fact that he would have taken a certain course of action 4 years ago had he known facts which were then unknown to him. All he can give is his present conviction on the subject, divorcing himself from hindsight as far as humanly possible, and re-creating the atmosphere of the past and the factors which then influenced him. I give you my views, formed in this manner.

Had I learned these vital facts and the "ships in the harbor" messages on November 28, it is my present conviction that I would have rejected the Navy Department's suggestion to send carriers to Wake and Midway. I would have ordered the third carrier, the *Saratoga,* back from the west coast. I would have gone to sea with the fleet and endeavored to keep it in an intercepting position at sea. This would have permitted the disposal of the striking power of the fleet to meet an attack in the Hawaiian area. The requirement of keeping the fleet fueled, however, would have made necessary the presence in Pearl Harbor from time to time of detachments of various units of the main body of the fleet.

On December 4, ample time remained for the Navy Department to forward me the information which I have outlined, and in addition the following significant facts, which the Navy Department learned between November 27 and that date:

(1) Japan had informed Hitler that war with the Anglo-Saxon powers would break out sooner than anyone dreams;

(2) Japan had broadcast her winds code signal using the words "east wind rain," meaning war or a rupture of diplomatic relations with the United States.

Assuming that for the first time on December 5 I had all the important information then available in the Navy Department, it is my conviction that I would have gone to sea with the fleet, including the carrier *Lexington* and arranged a rendezvous at sea with Halsey's carrier force, and been in a good position to intercept the Japanese attack.

On December 6, 15 hours before the attack, ample time still remained for the Navy Department to give me all the significant facts which I have outlined and which were not available to me in Hawaii. In addition, the Navy Department could then have advised me that 13 parts of the Japanese reply to the American proposals had been received, that the tone and temper of this message indicated a break in diplomatic relations or war with the United States, and that a Japanese reply was to be formally presented to this Government at a special hour soon to be fixed. Had I received this information on the afternoon of December 6 it is my present conviction that I would have ordered all fleet units in Pearl Harbor to sea, arranged a rendezvous with Halsey's task force returning from Wake, and been ready to intercept the Japanese force by the time fixed for the outbreak of war.

Even on the morning of December 7, 4 or 5 hours before the attack, had the Navy Department for the first time seen fit to send me all this significant information, and the additional fact that 1 p.m., Washington time, had been fixed for the delivery of the Japanese ultimatum to the United States, my light forces could have moved out of Pearl Harbor, all ships in the harbor would have been at general quarters, and all resources of the fleet in instant readiness to repel an attack.

It is my conviction that action by the Navy Department at any one of these significant dates in furnishing me the information from intercepted messages would have altered the events of December 7, 1941.

The Pacific Fleet deserved a fighting chance. It was entitled to receive from the Navy Department the best information available. Such information had been urgently requested. I had been assured that it would be furnished me. We faced our problem in the Pacific confident that such assurance would be faithfully carried out.

. . . .

Lieutenant General Walter C. Short, the Commanding General of the Hawaiian Department, like his naval opposite, has become another key figure in the controversy concerning the Pearl Harbor attack. The following document consists of excerpts from his own account of events as presented to the Joint Congressional Committee investigating the Pearl Harbor attack on January 22, 1946.

Pearl Harbor Attack, VII, 2921-2964, paragraph numbers and footnotes omitted.

Testimony Of Maj. Gen. Walter C. Short, United States Army, Retired

(Having been first duly sworn by the Chairman.)

The Chairman. General, the Chair understands that you have a statement here which you desire to read, or to have read, due to the fact that you have been somewhat indisposed.

If you would like to have someone else read it, it would be entirely agreeable to the committee, or if you wish to read it yourself, why, you may proceed.

General Short. Mr. Chairman, I have been in the hospital with pneumonia, and have not entirely recovered my strength, but I shall make every effort to go through my testimony before this committee without interruption.

I prefer to read it myself.

The Chairman. You may proceed.

General Short. Mr. Chairman, I want to thank you and the members of the committee for giving me, after 4 long years, the opportunity to tell my story of Pearl Harbor to the American public. I appeared before the Roberts commission but was not permitted to hear the other witnesses nor given the privilege of cross-examination. I was not given the opportunity to read the evidence taken before the Roberts commission until August

1944. I appeared before the Army Pearl Harbor board, but again was not permitted to hear the other witnesses nor given the privilege of cross-examination; however, I was furnished a copy of the hearings except for the part considered top secret. The Army board labeled certain evidence top secret and I was never permitted to see that until this committee was about to meet. Both boards took testimony of the record which has not been made available to me.

Before taking up my statement in detail, there are a few points that I would like to mention for emphasis. These will be elaborated upon later.

1. On Pearl Harbor day I was carrying out orders from the War Department as I understood them.

2. At no time since June 17, 1940, had the War Department indicated the probability of an attack on Hawaii. In none of the estimates prepared by G-2 War Department was Hawaii mentioned as a point of attack, but the Philippines was mentioned repeatedly.

3. There was in the War Department an abundance of information which was vital to me but was not furnished to me. This information was absolutely essential to a correct estimate of the situation and correct decision. My estimate of the situation and my decision were made without the benefit of this vital information. Had this information been furnished to me, I am sure that I would have arrived at the conclusion that Hawaii would be attacked and would have gone on an all-out alert.

4. When I made the decision, based on the information available to me, to go on alert to prevent sabotage (No. 1), I reported measures taken as follows:

    Reurad 472 27th Report Department alerted to prevent sabotage. Liaison with the Navy.

The War Department had 9 days in which to tell me that my action was not what they wanted. I accepted their silence as a full agreement with the action taken. I am convinced that all who read the report thought that my action was correct or I would have received instructions to modify my orders.

. . . .

Appointment to Hawaii

The Chief of Staff selected me as the commanding general of the Hawaiian Department. I was first notified in December 1940. I held conferences in Washington, D. C., with General Marshall the first week in January 1941. I also conferred with General Gerow in the War Plans Division. I talked with some officer about the equipment of the Hawaiian Department. I talked with Colonel (now General) Spaatz about the Air Corps problem.

Assumption of Command

At the time I assumed command on February 7, 1941, the Hawaiian Department was amply prepared for defense against the submarine danger and against sabotage and espionage, but was not adequately prepared for defense against an air raid, either by bomber or by torpedo planes or both. On February 7, 1941, the Chief of Staff sent me a letter, detailing his policies regarding the Army mission in Hawaii and stressing his interest in strengthening our air power and antiaircraft defense. In that letter he deplored the fact that all defenses would be inadequately equipped because of the over-all shortage of aircraft and antiaircraft equipment.

Effort To Strengthen Defenses

10 months' efforts

During the 10 months immediately following my assumption of command, in full cooperation with the Navy, I made strenuous efforts to improve the defense system of the Hawaiian Islands.

. . . .

Pre-War Alerts

Marshall-Herron alert

Prior to the time that I assumed command in Hawaii, General Marshall had definitely indicated his intention to direct personally any genuine prewar alert. As commanding general and as a matter of training I was, of course, fully authorized to conduct drills, maneuvers, and practice alerts. Numerous maneuvers, general and special practice alerts were, in fact held. However, as a part of my orientation, on the day before I assumed command, General Herron, my predecessor, acquainted me with the relation which had existed between himself and General Marshall during the all-out alert which began June 17, 1940. In that alert, General Marshall had directed the alert and had closely supervised its continuance, as disclosed in committee exhibit No. 52, Communications Between War Department and General Herron Concerning 1940 Alert. The following message began the alert:

June 17, 1940. No. 428. Immediately alert complete defensive organization to deal with *possible* trans-Pacific raid, to greatest extent possible without creating public hysteria or provoking undue curiosity of newspapers or alien agents. Suggest maneuver basis. Maintain alert until further orders. Instructions for secret communication direct with Chief of Staff will be furnished you shortly. Acknowledge.

ADAMS

Supervision by Chief of Staff

The record is clear that at the time of the 1940 alert the Chief of Staff had sufficient time and sense of personal responsibility toward the Hawaiian Department to order and to supervise the Hawaiian alert. In addition, he had information which caused him to state that—

* * * In any event it would have been foolhardy not to take special precautions.

Expected action of Chief of Staff

It was my expectation that if the Chief of Staff once again had information causing him to expect a "trans-Pacific raid" against Oahu, he would follow the course he had previously set as an example. I felt that a Chief of Staff who had personally supervised the long-continued 1940 alert would certainly have the time and interest not only to read and to understand my succinct report, "Reurad four seven two 27th Report Department alerted to prevent sabotage. Liaison with the Navy," but to send further word in the event that he disagreed in any way with the measures I had taken in obedience to his November 27 directive. At the time that the previous alert had been modified, on July 16, 1940, the Chief of Staff had thought that the sabotage menace continued, even though the air raid danger had subsided. He had said that he wanted the Air Corps training resumed in such manner that the "aerial patrol measures" could be reestablished on short notice.

. . . .

Information Furnished Hawaiian Department

. . . .

Do-Don't Message

On November 27 I received the following radiogram from the Chief of Staff which, on account of its conflicting instructions, the Army Pearl Harbor Board called the "Do or Don't message":

> No. 472. Negotiations with the Japanese appear to be terminated to all practical purposes with only the barest possibilities that the Japanese Government might come back and offer to continue. Japanese future action unpredictable but hostile action possible at any moment. If hostilities cannot, repeat cannot, be avoided the United States desires that Japan commit the first overt act. This policy should not, repeat not, be construed as restricting you to a course of action that might jeopardize your defense. Prior to hostile

64   WHAT HAPPENED AT PEARL HARBOR?

> Japanese action you are directed to undertake such reconnaissance and other measures as you deem necessary but these measures should be carried out so as not, repeat not, to alarm the civil population or disclose intent. Report measures taken. Should hostilities occur, you will carry out the tasks assigned in Rainbow Five so far as they pertain to Japan. Limit the dissemination of this highly secret information to minimum essential officers.

The impression conveyed to me by this message was that the avoidance of war was paramount and the greatest fear of the War Department was that some international incident might occur in Hawaii and be regarded by Japan as an overt act. That this opinion was in accordance with the views of **General Marshall** is shown by the following quotation from his testimony:

> So far as public opinion was concerned, I think the Japanese were capitalizing on the belief that it would be very difficult to bring our people into a willingness to enter the war. That, incidentally, was somewhat confirmed by the governmental policy on our part of making certain that the overt act should not be attributed to the United States, because of the state of the public mind at the time. Of course, no one anticipated that that overt act would be the crippling of the Pacific Fleet.

No mention was made of a probable attack on Hawaii since the alert message of June 17, 1940. An examination of the various Military Intelligence Estimates prepared by G-2 WD, shows that in no estimate did G-2 ever indicate the probability of an attack on Hawaii. There was nothing in the message directing me to be prepared to meet an air raid or an all-out attack. "Hostile action at any moment" meant to me that as far as Hawaii was concerned the War Department was predicting sabotage. Sabotage is a form of hostile action.

Sabotage Emphasis

The only additional information received from the War Department after the receipt of message No. 472 (November 27) was contained in three messages on sabotage and subversive measures. The first from G-2 War Department to G-2 Hawaiian Department received November 27 read as follows:

> Japanese negotiations have come to practical stalemate. Hostilities may ensue. Subversive activities may be expected. Inform Commanding General and Chief of Staff only.

. . . .

Report by General Short

I replied as follows to the radiogram from the Chief of Staff November 27:

CHIEF OF STAFF,
> War Department, Washington, D. C.
>
> Reurad four seven two 27th Report Department alerted to prevent sabotage. Liaison with the Navy.
>
> SHORT

. . . .

November 28 Sabotage message and report

On November 28 the following message, relating entirely to sabotage and subversive measures, was received from the War Department:

HAWN DEPT FT SHAFTER, TH

> 428 28th Critical situation demands that all precautions be taken immediately against subversive activities within field of investigative responsibility of War Department. . . . Also desired that you initiate . . . all additional measures necessary to provide for protection of your establishments, property, and equipment against sabotage, protection of your personnel against subversive propaganda and protection of all activities against espionage. This does not, repeat not, mean that any illegal measures are authorized. Protective measures should be confined to those essential to security, avoiding unnecessary publicity and alarm. To insure speed

of transmission identical telegrams are being sent to all air stations but this does not, repeat not, affect your responsibility under existing instructions. ADAMS.

When this message was received from the War Department I felt that it had been prepared after consideration had been given to my message reporting measures taken pursuant to War Department message No. 472. I sent the following message in reply and was careful to refer directly to the War Department number, "482":

THE ADJUTANT GENERAL,
War Department, Washington, D. C.

Re your secret radio 282 28th, full precautions are being taken against subversive activities within the field of investigate responsibility of War Department. . . . SHORT.

General Arnold's radiogram

On November 28 General Arnold, Chief of the Air Corps, sent to the Commanding General, Hawaiian Air Forces, a message relating entirely to sabotage and subversive activities, similar in tone to War Department message No. 482, signed "ADAMS." General Martin, replying to this message on December 4, gave a detailed report of measures taken by him against sabotage and subversive activities and added:

This entire department is now operating and will continue to operate under an alert for prevention of sabotage.

We received no reply disagreeing in any way with the action reported.

November 28 to December 7, 1941

From November 28, 1941, until the war began, I received only one more message from the War Department, that of November 29, 1941, regarding preparations to move two Army pursuit squadrons on short notice, and informing me that the Army would take over the defense of advance Pacific bases, except for furnishing antiaircraft equipment. This message stated that Christmas and Canton Islands would be garrisoned from Hawaii, and replacements would be sent from the United States. This was the last information from the War Department until the final message from the Chief of Staff of December 7, which arrived 7 hours after the attack.

I do not believe that message has been placed in evidence.

. . . .

The message sent by the Chief of Staff of December 7, which arrived 7 hours after the attack, was as follows:

H<small>AWN</small> D<small>EPT</small> F<small>T</small> S<small>HAFTER</small>, TH

>529 7th Japanese are presenting at 1:00 P.M. Eastern Standard Time today what amounts to an ultimatum also they are under orders to destroy their code machine immediately. Just what significance the hour set may have we do not know but be on alert accordingly. Inform naval authorities of this communication.
>
>> M<small>ARSHALL</small>

Delay of December 7 Message

The message was filed at 12:18 p.m., December 7, eastern time (6:48 a.m., December 7, Honolulu time). It was received by the R. C. A. in Honolulu at 7:33 a.m., December 7, and delivered to the Signal Office, Fort Shafter, at 11:45 a.m. (Delivery was undoubtedly delayed by the Japanese attack.) The deciphered message was delivered to the adjutant general, Hawaiian Department, at 2:58 p.m., December 7.

Delay in deciphering due to not being marked "Priority" in Washington. Thus, this vital message was received 7 hours after the attack.

If this message had been sent by scrambler telephone there would have been time to warm up the planes and put them in the air, thus, at least, avoiding a large loss of planes in the initial attack at 8 a.m. This would not necessarily have lessened the naval losses. The fact that the War Department sent this message by radio in code instead of telephoning it in clear and putting it through in the minimum amount of time indicates that the War Department, even as late as 6:48 a.m., December 7th, Honolulu time, did not consider an attack on Honolulu as likely enough to warrant drastic action to prepare the islands for the sneak attack.

. . . .

Staff procedure re communications

It is standard staff procedure and doctrine that all important or emergency messages should be sent by all available means of communication, which in this case would have included the scrambler telephones which had been frequently used between the War Department and Fort Shafter. Colonel Phillips and General Marshall did confer by scrambler phone later in the day on December 7, 1941. If security would have been violated by sending the information by phone, then the War Department should have issued the necessary alert orders which they would have known that I would have issued at once if I had the information which they possessed. . . .

Action Taken—November 27 To December 7, 1941

Alert Plans

The standing operation procedure, headquarters, Hawaiian Department, 5 November 1941, provided for the following alerts:

. . . .

Alert No. 1.—a. This alert is a defense against acts of sabotage and uprisings within the islands, with no threat from without. * * *

. . . .

Alert No. 2.—a. This alert is applicable to a more serious condition than Alert No. 1. Security against attacks from hostile subsurface, surface, and aircraft, in addition to defense against acts of sabotage and uprisings, is provided.

Alert No. 3.—a. This alert requires the occupation of all field positions by all units, prepared for maximum defense of Oahu and the Army installations on outlying islands. * * *

Conferences November 27

When I received the November 27, 1941, message signed "Marshall," I immediately talked it over with my Chief of staff, Colonel Phillips, and then made my decision to order alert No. 1. This decision was then communicated to G-2 and to the echelon commanders. On that same afternoon, I conferred on the matter with General Martin and with General Burgin. The general contents of the radiogram were also made known to the two division commanders through staff officers. In view of the restrictive orders against wide dissemination of the information, I withheld it from the other Army personnel. At the same time that I ordered alert No. 1 into effect, I directed that the interceptor command, including the aircraft warning service and information center, should operate from 4 a.m. until 7 a.m. daily. In addition, the six mobile stations operated daily, except Sunday, from 7 a.m. to 11 a.m. for routine training and daily, except Saturday and Sunday, from 12 until 4 p.m. for training and maintenance work.

. . . .

Information Not Sent By War Department

Policy to withhold information

As this joint committee's investigation has already revealed, there was a vast amount of highly significant information available in the War Department which no responsible military man could exclude from consideration in forming an estimate of the situation. The War Department was aware of the fact that I did not have this information and had already decided that I should not get this information. It was therefore their duty not only to make the estimate of the situation but to make the decision as to what military action it required, and to give me orders to go on an all-out alert instead of permitting my sabotage alert to stand. This was in line with their centralized peace time control system. It is my firm conviction that they did not estimate the situation, that they expected only sabotage and subversive activities in Hawaii, and that on reading my report, "Department alerted to prevent sabotage. Liaison with Navy," they dismissed the matter from their minds because I had done exactly what they desired.

. . . .

Hindsight evaluation

I do not want to attempt to summarize or even to list all the information here which the War Department had but which I did not have. I want to refrain from hindsight evaluation of this information. But I also want to call the committee's attention to some very obvious items which had they been given to me, would have necessarily changed the picture which I then had of the crisis between the United States and Japan.

Military commitments in Far East

I did not know that the United States Army officers at Singapore had made tentative military commitments, not approved by the President, that the United States would fight, along with the Netherlands and the British, to defend the Dutch East Indies and Singapore.

Japanese knowledge of United States policy

I did not know that the War Department knew that the Japanese suspected or had somehow learned of this joint military program. . . .

November 20 ultimatum

I had not been told, but Washington knew, that the Secretary of State regarded the November 20, 1941, Japanese proposal as an ultimatum and that from then on it was merely a question of trying to stall off the final break as long as possible, and, quoting Secretary Hull:

> in the hope that somewhere even then something might develop suddenly and out of the sky.

Deadlines

I did not know, but the War Department knew that the Japanese had set a deadline after which their armed forces would move. . . .

Code destruction

Another thing I did not know is the fact that the Japanese were under orders to destroy their codes and code machines. The War Department knew of this code destruction as early as 1 December 1941 and knew specifically of the orders to destroy the codes in the United States on 3 December 1941. I should certainly have been told of this intelligence. . . .

Ships in harbor report

While the War Department G-2 may not have felt bound to let me know about the routine operations of the Japanese in keeping track of our naval ships, they should certainly have let me know that the Japanese were getting reports of the exact location of the ships in Pearl Harbor, which might indicate more than just keeping track, because such details would be useful only for sabotage, or for air or submarine attack in Hawaii. As early as October 9, 1941, G-2 in Washington knew of this Japanese espionage. This message, analyzed critically, is really a bombing plan for Pearl Harbor.

Winds code

I was not informed, but the War Department knew, of the so-called "winds" code or of the fact that the so-called implementing message had been received, definitely confirming the fact that diplomatic relations would be severed between Japan and the United States.

Hull's "ultimatum" to Japan

I was not informed of Secretary Hull's note of November 26,* proposing a 10 point plan which the Japanese considered an ultimatum.

War considered inevitable

I did not know that sometime in the fall of 1941 the Chief of Staff had come to the conclusion that war with Japan was inevitable.

Jap reply — 13 parts

Critical information (the first 13 parts of the long Japanese memorandum) finally terminating relations with the United States was received in the War Department by 9 p.m. on December 6. The so-called "pilot" message from Tokyo to Washington December 6, 1941, No. 901, had been received in the War Department sometime during the afternoon of December 6.** This message stated definitely that the long Japanese memorandum would be sent as message No. 902 and would be presented to the Americans as soon as instructions were sent.

Part 14, Jap reply

The fourteenth part of the long memorandum and the short message of the Japanese directing the Ambassador to deliver the long memorandum at 1 p.m. on the 7th were in the hands of the War Department between 8:30 and 9 a.m. December 7. This message indicated a definite break of relations at 1 p.m., and pointed directly to an attack on Hawaii at dawn. Had this information been communicated to Hawaii by the fastest possible means, we would have had more than 4 hours to make preparations to meet the attack which was more than enough for completing Army preparations. The Navy might have had time to get all ships out of the harbor.

* See p. 309.
** See p. 225.

Delay of December 7 message

Not until 7 hours after the attack was I informed that the Japanese Ambassador had been directed to deliver the 14-part memorandum to the Secretary of State at 1 p.m., December 7. This message was received in the War Department from a naval courier between 8:30 a.m. and 9 a.m., December 7 (3 a.m. to 3:30 a.m. Honolulu time). This message definitely pointed to an attack on Pearl Harbor at 1 p.m., Washington time. If this message had been delivered to me by the most rapid possible means of communication I would have had 4 hours, more than enough time, to fully alert the Army forces against an air raid.

Delay translation December 6 Pearl Harbor message

A more prompt decoding and translation of one of the December 6 intercepts would have pointed out clearly to the War and Navy Departments that a surprise attack on Pearl Harbor was planned. After discussing the lack of barrage balloon defense, the consul at Honolulu reported as follows to Tokyo:

> * * * However, even though they have actually made preparations, because they must control the air over the water and land runways of the airports in the vicinity of *Pearl Harbor, Hickam, Ford* and *Ewe,* there are limits to the balloon defense of *Pearl Harbor*. I imagine that in all probability there is considerable opportunity left to take advantage for a *surprise attack against these places.*

I would like to set up my conclusions. There will be a certain amount of repetition, but I think it is desirable.

Conclusions

Obeyed instructions

On December 7, 1941, I was obeying my instructions from Washington as I understood them, and as the War Department had every reason to know that I understood them, and was acting in accordance with the information which was available to me at that time. Little information was available to me. The little that was given to me in the War Department message of November 27 did not give an accurate picture of the prospects of war. The War Department knew definitely by 9 p.m., December 6, that the hour had struck and that war was at hand. By 9 a.m., December 7, the War Department knew the hour of attack. None of this information was given to me.

War Department responsibility

If for any possible reason the War Department felt that it could not give me the information, then it was the responsibility of the War Department to direct me to go on an all-out alert particularly since it well knew that we were on an antisabotage alert. The Hawaiian Department was not provided with agencies for obtaining Japanese information outside of Hawaii, and was dependent on the War Department for such information.

War Department estimate

When the War Department was informed that the Hawaiian Department was alerted against sabotage, it not only did not indicate that the command should be alerted against a hostile surface, subsurface, ground or air attack, but replied emphasizing the necessity for protection against sabotage and subversive measures. This action on the part of the War Department definitely indicated to me that it approved of my alert against sabotage. The War Department had 9 more days in which to express its disapproval. The action of the War Department in sending unarmed B-17's from Hamilton Field, Calif., on the night of December 6, to Honolulu confirmed me in my belief that an air raid was not probable.

. . . .

Army-Navy cooperation

During this period I held frequent conferences with the commander in Chief of the United States Fleet and the commandant of the Fourteenth Naval District, and at no time was anything said to indicate that they feared the probability of an air attack by the Japanese. In fact, the sentiment was expressed by a naval staff officer that there was no probability of such an attack. With a large part of the United States Navy in Hawaiian waters and with their sources of information, I was convinced that the Navy would be able either to intercept any carrier attempting to approach Oahu or at least to obtain such information from task forces or by reconnaissance as to make them aware of the presence of carriers in the Hawaiian waters and of the probobility of an air attack.

Expectations from War Department

I felt that I had a right to expect the War Department to inform me by the most rapid means possible if a real crisis arose in Japanese relations. I did not expect that when the crisis arose the message would remain in the hands of General Miles and Colonel Bratton without action from 9 a.m. till 11:25 a.m., and that when action was finally taken the desire for secrecy would be considered more important than the element of time. Had the message in regard to the Japanese ultimatum and the burning of their code machines been given me by telephone as an urgent message in the clear without loss of time for encoding and decoding, delivery, etc., or if I had been directed by telephone to go on an all-out alert for a dawn trans-Pacific raid, without being told the reason, I would have had approximately 4 hours in which to make detailed preparations to meet an immediate attack.

Follow-up of orders

When any department of the Army has issued an order on any matter of importance, it has performed only one-half of its function. The follow-up to see that the order has been carried out as desired is at least as important as issuing the order. The War Department had 9 days in which to check up on the alert status in Hawaii and to make sure that the measures taken by me were what was desired, which it did not do. The check-up would have required no more than a reading of my report of measures taken.

Supervision by Chief of Staff

Repeatedly, from the time I took command in Hawaii in February 1941, the Chief of Staff had written me at length advising me on policies and details of operation. However, after October 28, 1941, with the War Department receiving information almost daily which indicated that war was imminent, he communicated to me none of those personal messages containing the inside information.

Erroneous estimate of situation

My decision to put the Hawaiian Department on an alert to prevent sabotage was based upon a belief that sabotage was our gravest danger and that air attack was not imminent. I realize that my decision was wrong. I had every reason to believe, however, that my estimate of the situation coincided with that of the War Department General Staff, which had the signal advantage of superior sources of intelligence as to enemy intentions.

Hindsight value of information withheld

I know it is hindsight, but if I had been furnished the information which the War Department had, I do not believe that I would have made a mistaken estimate of the situation. To make my meaning clear, I want to add that I do not believe that my estimate of the situation was due to any carelessness on my part or on the part of the senior Army and Navy officers with whom I consulted. Nor do I believe that my error was a substantial factor in causing the damage which our Pacific Fleet suffered during the attack.

Intelligence complacency

I have been more than astounded to learn the complacency of the War Department General Staff with relation to so-called magic intelligence. The War Department could have devised a method to paraphrase the information obtained and send it by courier to me, without, if they chose, disclosing to me that it resulted from an ability to decipher Japanese messages. I want to quote for the committee the following pertinent paragraph from the Operations Manual then current:

> From adequate and timely military intelligence the commander is able to draw logical conclusions concerning enemy lines of action. Military intelligence is thus *an essential* factor in the estimate of the situation and the conduct of operations.

General Marshall and Admiral Wilkinson have pointed out that the security of our cryptanalytic ability was risked for the slight, temporary exultation of shooting down Yamamoto's plane. Surely, then, supplying the data to me and to Admiral Kimmel would not have been inconceivably risky.

. . . .

Adequate sabotage defense

I had been furnished adequate means to prevent sabotage. I used those means with complete success, as the testimony has shown. No one can say to what extent sabotage would have occurred if the Army had not taken such measures to prevent it.

Inadequate means for air defense

I had not been furnished adequate means to defend against a surprise air raid. The War Department was aware of the inadequacy of our aircraft and antiaircraft defense establishment. . . .

Army failure — Heroism of troops

Due to the fact that the War Department did not make available to Hawaii the information in its possession, the Army forces in Hawaii were unable to prevent the terrific destruction caused by the Japanese attack. However, the fine action of the Hawaiian troops when struck by the surprise attack should not be overlooked. Every officer and man did his full duty with promptness, precision and efficiency. All organizations moved quickly to their battle positions and took up their prescribed duties. Acts of heroism were the rule, not the exception.

. . . .

Unjust War Department treatment

I do not feel that I have been treated fairly or with justice by the War Department. I was singled out as an example, as the scapegoat for the disaster. My relatively small part in the transaction was not explained to the American people until this joint congressional committee forced the revelation of the facts. I fully appreciate the desire of the War Department to preserve the secrecy of the source of the so-called magic, but I am sure that could have been done without any attempt to deceive the public by a false pretense that my judgment had been the sole factor causing the failure of the Army to fulfill its mission of defending the Navy at Pearl Harbor. I am sure that an honest confession by the War Department General Staff of their failure to anticipate the surprise raid would have been understood by the public, in the long run, and even at the time. Instead, they "passed the buck" to me, and I have kept my silence until the opportunity of this public forum was presented to me.

War Department's 4-year silence

The War Department had 4 years to admit that a follow-up should have been made on the November 27 message and on my report of the same date, but no such admission of responsibility was made public until General Gerow and General Marshall testified before this committee.

First opportunity to present story

I want to thank all the members of this committee for the thorough manner in which you have tried to bring out the facts and particularly for the opportunity to present my story to you and through you to the American public.

. . . .

The attacking Japanese planes did not approach Pearl Harbor entirely unobserved. Two American soldiers, Privates George E. Elliott and Joseph L. Lockard, intercepted the hostile flight by means of radar. When they reported the unknown planes to the information center, however, the officer on duty, Lieutenant Kermit Tyler, told them to forget it, as the following excerpts from testimony before the Joint Congressional Committee and the Army Pearl Harbor Board show.

Pearl Harbor Attack, X, 5027-5035; *ibid.,* XXVII (Proceedings of the Army Pearl Harbor Board), 526-533, 566-571.

TESTIMONY OF GEORGE E. ELLIOTT, JR., FORMERLY SERGEANT, ARMY OF THE UNITED STATES, FEBRUARY 20, 1946

(Having been first duly sworn by the Chairman.)

Mr. RICHARDSON. Sergeant Elliott, will you state your name for the record?

Mr. ELLIOTT. George E. Elliott, Jr.

Mr. RICHARDSON. How old are you?

Mr. ELLIOTT. Twenty-eight, sir.

Mr. RICHARDSON. You are not in the service at present?

Mr. ELLIOTT. No, sir; I am lucky enough to have been discharged 4 months ago.

Mr. RICHARDSON. You were on duty in Hawaii at the time of the Japanese attack on Pearl Harbor?

Mr. ELLIOTT. That is right, sir.

Mr. RICHARDSON. In what division of the Army?

Mr. ELLIOTT. I was in the Signal Corps, Aircraft Warning.

Mr. RICHARDSON. And that brought you in contact with the radar sets that the Army had on Oahu?

Mr. ELLIOTT. Yes, sir.

Mr. RICHARDSON. You were present at one of those mobile radar sets on the morning of the attack?

Mr. Elliott. Yes, sir.

Mr. Richardson. Can you indicate on this map, Sergeant, where the mobile station was located and where you were on the morning of the attack?

Mr. Elliott. Yes, sir.

Mr. Richardson. Indicate on this map where the station is located where you were on the morning of the attack.

Mr. Elliott. The station was located at the top of the mountain, I believe they call it Opana, at the northernmost point of the island of Oahu, as I indicate here [indicating].

Mr. Richardson. Now, coming to this map, Sergeant, this colored chart of what is supposed to be a radar chart of approaching Japanese planes prior to the attack, you were at this point? [indicating].

Mr. Elliott. That is correct.

Mr. Richardson. Will you indicate with the pointer where you saw any indication of approaching planes, where it would be on this map?

Mr. Elliott. At this point up here [indicating] 3° northeast at the azimuth that they came in on.

We picked them up at the mileage of 136 or 137 miles. That was the very first indication of the flight that we had picked up.

Mr. Richardson. Now, follow with our pointer, just generally how the planes came down toward your station.

Senator Brewster. Will you place the time so it can be identified?

Mr. Richardson. What was the time when you first found any information of planes?

Mr. Elliott. That was 7:02.

Mr. Richardson. All right; now follow with your pointer the course, as nearly as you can recall it, that the planes followed as you watched them on the radar.

Mr. Elliott. I believe that they came in on a very straight line. I do not recall of their [sic] being any differences, as indicated here. It was fairly straight.

Mr. Richardson. Now, when they approached your station, did they disappear finally from your radar?

Mr. ELLIOTT. Yes, sir; they disappeared at approximately 15 to 20 miles away from the island. We lost them due to distortion from a back wave from the mountains, and it was impossible to follow them further than we had.

Mr. RICHARDSON. Up to the time they disappeared, had there been any diversion of the planes? Were they still all in the main group which you had seen at 7:02?

Mr. ELLIOTT. Yes, sir; they were all in the same group, so far as I know.

Mr. RICHARDSON. That is the last you saw of them?

Mr. ELLIOTT. Yes, sir.

Mr. RICHARDSON. Who was with you, Sergeant, at the time these planes were sighted?

Mr. ELLIOTT. Another private, Joseph L. Lockard.

Mr. RICHARDSON. Who first saw these planes? You or Lockard?

Mr. ELLIOTT. We actually both saw them together.

Mr. RICHARDSON. What discussion was there between you with reference to the matter when you saw them?

Mr. ELLIOTT. At the time I was receiving instructions on the operations of the scope. Lockard looking over my shoulder noticed that there was a target, so he, knowing more about the operation of the scope, actually took over the control there. I went over to the plotting board, and we got an azimuth and mileage and figured out a reading as to the location where the flight was, where the target was.

Mr. RICHARDSON. How long did that take you, would you say?

Mr. ELLIOTT. Well, just a very short time.

Mr. RICHARDSON. A minute or two?

Mr. ELLIOTT. Less than a minute.

Mr. RICHARDSON. All right, go ahead.

Mr. ELLIOTT. At that time I suggested to Private Lockard that we send it in to the Information Center. Private Lockard figuring that our problem was over at 7 o'clock, disagreed as to sending the reading.

Mr. RICHARDSON. What do you mean by your problem was over at 7?

Mr. Elliott. The normal operating period at that time was from 4 in the morning until 7 in the morning.

Mr. Richardson. Was that true on weekdays as well as on Sundays?

Mr. Elliott. Yes, sir, I believe it was.

Mr. Richardson. For how long a period prior to the morning of the 7th had you been on the 4 to 7 status?

Mr. Elliott. Well, our particular station at that time had only been set up, it was only in operation about 2 weeks before December 7.

Mr. Richardson. Then, as a matter of fact, from 4 until 7 on the morning of the 7th you two were the only men at that station?

Mr. Elliott. Yes, sir. We were the only two at that station from noon of December 6 through 8 o'clock on the morning of December 7.

Mr. Richardson. And that was the station at Opana?

Mr. Elliott. Yes, sir.

Mr. Richardson. At the farthest north station?

Mr. Elliott. Yes, sir.

Mr. Richardson. The station most immediately adjacent to the whole northwest sector north of Oahu?

Mr. Elliott. Yes, sir.

Mr. Richardson. All right. Now, at 7:02 you two men discovered planes on your target?

Mr. Elliott. Yes, sir.

Mr. Richardson. You suggested that you contact the information center?

Mr. Elliott. Yes, sir.

Mr. Richardson. At first Lockard did not approve of that?

Mr. Elliott. Yes, sir. That was after we had figured out the reading from the azimuth and mileage. At that time I spoke to Private Lockard. I even recall saying to him since he did not want to send it in, even if we sent it in and the Army and Navy would work together, they may not know just whose planes they are, but if worked out through the information center and had it not on any scheduled problem, that it would be more effective as to actually going out there and intercepting like, say, the Army go out and intercept planes, or vice versa.

Finally, after mentioning a few of those things to Private Lockard, he finally told me to go ahead and send it in if I liked.

Mr. RICHARDSON. How long from the time you discovered the planes was it until you concluded to phone the information center? How many minutes?

Mr. ELLIOTT. I would say offhand 7 or 8.

Mr. RICHARDSON. During that time, you could still see the target on your charts, these planes coming from the north?

Mr. ELLIOTT. Yes, sir.

Mr. RICHARDSON. You called up the information center?

Mr. ELLIOTT. Yes, sir. We had two phones in the mobile unit: One was a direct line, a tactical line, as it was called. That was from the plotting board directly to the information center which was located at Fort Shafter.

Mr. RICHARDSON. Which phone did you use?

Mr. ELLIOTT. I picked up the tactical phone on the plotting board, and I found nobody on the other end at the information center. After that, I went to the administrative line and called the information center.

After getting the information center—

Mr. RICHARDSON. Who answered?

Mr. ELLIOTT. A corporal or Private McDonald answered the phone. He was a switchboard operator at the information center.

Mr. RICHARDSON. All right.

What conversation occurred?

Mr. ELLIOTT. At that time, I explained to Private McDonald what we had seen, and he told me that there was nobody around there, and he did not know what to do about it.

I asked him if he would get somebody that would know what to do and pass on the information, and have him take care of it.

Well, a few minutes later—

Mr. RICHARDSON. How many minutes? Just make a guess.

Mr. ELLIOTT. Two or three, I would say.

Mr. RICHARDSON. Two or three. All right.

Mr. ELLIOTT. Two or three minutes later, this lieutenant that is referred to, or was first referred to in the Roberts report, called back to the station, and Private Lockard picked up the phone and spoke to the lieutenant.

It was at this time that the lieutenant told us to forget about the flight.

Mr. RICHARDSON. Well, now, you, of course, did not hear what the lieutenant said over the telephone.

Mr. ELLIOTT. No, sir. I did not.

Mr. RICHARDSON. What did you hear Lockard say over the telephone, to whomever he was talking?

Mr. ELLIOTT. Well, he only acknowledged that we were to forget it, that we were to forget the flight.

Mr. RICHARDSON. Did Lockard say anything to the lieutenant about having discovered planes coming on the chart?

Mr. ELLIOTT. Yes, sir; I believe he did. He again repeated the distance that we had picked up these planes.

Mr. RICHARDSON. When Lockard had finished his telephone conversation, what did he tell you the lieutenant on the other end said?

Mr. ELLIOTT. He told me that the lieutenant said to forget it.

Mr. RICHARDSON. Did he say anything about the lieutenant mentioning what these planes might be, or from where the planes might be coming? Did he make any statement that the lieutenant had mentioned that subject to him over the telephone?

Mr. ELLIOTT. I do not recall whether or not he did.

Mr. RICHARDSON. I am referring to the question of whether the lieutenant mentioned the fact that a flight of B-17's from San Francisco was expected in that morning, and that these planes were probably those planes.

Was there any discussion on that subject by Lockard in reporting the telephone conversation to you?

Mr. ELLIOTT. That is what I do not quite remember. I cannot place it together, whether we received that information then, or whether it came out after the publicity of the Roberts Commission.

I cannot say for sure.

Mr. RICHARDSON. Now, what did you continue to do after

the end of the conversation over the telephone with the lieutenant at the information center? What did you and Lockard continue to do, if anything?

Mr. ELLIOTT. Private Lockard at that time wanted to shut down the unit and just go off the air, and the original intention was that I was to have gotten further training on the unit. I insisted again, and we continued to operate.

Mr. RICHARDSON. You could still see the plane target?

Mr. ELLIOTT. Yes, sir.

Mr. RICHARDSON. And you followed it in until it got within about 20 miles of your station?

Mr. ELLIOTT. That is right, sir.

Mr. RICHARDSON. Now, then, did you make any chart of the course of these planes?

Mr. ELLIOTT. Yes, sir; we had an overlaid chart; that is, a transparent paper that is put over the map itself, of the island, with true north on the overlay. That is, the grid lines on the overlay were true north on the map, and in the center is a radius, a mileage radius rule.

From your azimuth and your mileage you can plot exactly where your location is on the map. That is used so that you could have a record of all the flights that you had.

In other words, as you posted your target on this overlay, you could take it off of there and put it on a new sheet of transparent paper and continue on again.

Mr. RICHARDSON. Now, you did complete a chart following the course of those planes as they approached your station?

Mr. ELLIOTT. Yes, sir.

Mr. RICHARDSON. Did you make any readings?

Mr. ELLIOTT. Yes, sir; we had a running log, a record of reading sheets that covered the time, mileage, azimuth, and coordinate readings.

Mr. RICHARDSON. And you filled that out?

Mr. ELLIOTT. Yes, sir.

Mr. RICHARDSON. When did you leave the station that morning?

Mr. ELLIOTT. It was approximately 15 minutes of 8.

Mr. RICHARDSON. Where did you go?

Mr. Elliott. Our station at Opana was 9 miles away to our camp where we billeted and of course coming down the mountain to the highway took some time, and then the 9 miles was from the highway.

Mr. Richardson. How did you go?

Mr. Elliott. At approximately just shortly before 15 minutes of 8, a private—

Mr. Richardson. (interposing). How did you go, by shank's mare or in a car?

Mr. Elliott. That is just what I am going to explain.

Mr. Richardson. All right.

Mr. Elliott. Just a few minutes before a quarter of 8, Private Farnback came out in a truck to pick us up, and take our bedding and ourselves back to the camp.

Mr. Richardson. He took you back to camp?

Mr. Elliott. Yes, sir.

Mr. Richardson. What time did you get back to the camp, do you think?

Mr. Elliott. It was very close to 8 o'clock.

Mr. Richardson. Did you have with you either your chart or your readings?

Mr. Elliott. We only had the record of readings, the log.

Mr. Richardson. Did your record or reading log show the direction from which these planes were coming?

Mr. Elliott. It could have been replotted on the map with the information given to get the exact location of the flight.

Mr. Richardson. What did you do with that log?

Mr. Elliott. That log was turned over to a Lieutenant Upson, the commanding officer of the two platoons that were out in that particular camp.

Mr. Richardson. Was it turned over immediately upon your return to the camp?

Mr. Elliott. Yes, sir. We were very proud of the reading that we had gotten; that is the distance out, and we brought it along, not knowing what was taking place, but it was just the fact that the reading was a very good reading.

We brought it back to show off, so to speak.

Mr. RICHARDSON. Now, you gave it to your platoon commander?
Mr. ELLIOTT. Yes, sir.
Mr. RICHARDSON. Do you know what he did with it?
Mr. ELLIOTT. No, sir; I do not.
Mr. RICHARDSON. Who was your platoon commander?
Mr. ELLIOTT. A First Lieutenant—at that time Second Lieutenant John Upson.
Mr. RICHARDSON. And he was in the Aircraft Warning Division?
Mr. ELLIOTT. Yes, sir.
Mr. RICHARDSON. Who was his superior, if you know?
Mr. ELLIOTT. A Captain Tetley.
Mr. RICHARDSON. And where was he stationed?
Mr. ELLIOTT. He was stationed in Schofield Barracks, at the headquarters. That is where the main body of the company stayed. . . .
Mr. RICHARDSON. Where and to whom would your platoon commander have reported to his superior?
Mr. ELLIOTT. He would have reported directly to Captain Tetley.
Mr. RICHARDSON. At Schofield Barracks?
Mr. ELLIOTT. At Schofield Barracks; yes, sir.
Mr. RICHARDSON. Do you know who was over Tetley?
Mr. ELLIOTT. Off hand, I believe it was Colonel Powell, although I am not sure of the chain of command.
Mr. RICHARDSON. They were all in the aircraft warning section?
Mr. ELLIOTT. I am not sure about Colonel Powell. I believe he was head of the Signal Corps installations.
Mr. RICHARDSON. And the material which you had given to your platoon commander could have been read by any competent person to whom it came, and would indicate where you saw the planes, the direction from which they came, and when they disappeared from your view?
Mr. ELLIOTT. Yes, sir; very definitely, sir.
Mr. RICHARDSON. With the times of day involved?

Mr. ELLIOTT. Yes, sir; an identical chart could have been made, as is indicated up there on the map.

Mr. RICHARDSON. Did you remain in camp after you arrived there and during the attack?

Mr. ELLIOTT. No, sir; we stayed in camp only long enough to get up our main belongings that we would need, and we went right back to the unit 9 miles away.

Mr. RICHARDSON. You stayed at the unit the rest of the day?

Mr. ELLIOTT. Yes, sir; we stayed there day and night from then on; we did not go back to the camp.

Mr. RICHARDSON. There were two operating phones to that unit?

Mr. ELLIOTT. Yes, sir.

Mr. RICHARDSON. Did anyone call you up while you were there . . . concerning what you discovered and the details?

Mr. ELLIOTT. No, sir; they did not call me. They called back, but Private Lockard answered the phone.

Mr. RICHARDSON. Who called him, do you know?

Mr. ELLIOTT. Well, as I said before, it is explained as this lieutenant through the Roberts report. That is the only knowledge I have actually as to who called.

Mr. RICHARDSON. Someone called him?

Mr. ELLIOTT. Well, the information was relayed by Corporal McDonald at the switchboard to the lieutenant.

Mr. RICHARDSON. You do not get what I mean, I don't think, Sergeant.

Mr. ELLIOTT. You mean the lieutenant called—

Mr. RICHARDSON. After you came back from the camp on the morning of the attack, after you came in at 8 o'clock and turned over your reading, you then went back to the station, as I understand it.

Mr. ELLIOTT. Yes.

Mr. RICHARDSON. While you were at the station did anyone contact you to find out what you knew about the incoming planes?

Mr. ELLIOTT. That, sir, I could not answer.

When we went back to the unit, we did not go back to—at least I did not, and I do not recall just what Private Lockard did—we did not go back to the operation. The operation of the unit was being manned by other men in the platoon.

As I recall, we were busy setting up tents, since we were not going to travel back and forth to our old camp.

Mr. RICHARDSON. Well, but, Sergeant, did anybody come to you during that day and ask you to tell them what you saw in the radar at 7 o'clock that morning?

Mr. ELLIOTT. No, sir; only the men at our individual camp that were interested to know just what had gone on.

. . . .

Mr. RICHARDSON. When did you first know of the attack?

Mr. ELLIOTT. At the time that we arrived at our camp. However as we were going to the camp, we noticed from our truck all of the men from the camp driving very fast in the opposite direction in which we were going. They were going to the unit. They had their field packs, and helmets, and what not. We still had no indication as to what had happened until we arrived at the camp, when we were told that we had been attacked by the Japanese.

Mr. RICHARDSON. I have no further questions.

. . . .

TESTIMONY OF FIRST LT. JOSEPH L. LOCKARD,
SIGNAL CORPS, UNITED STATES ARMY,
Before the Army Pearl Harbor Board, August 17, 1944

(Consecutive numbering of questions and answers omitted)

(The witness was sworn by the Recorder and advised of his rights under Article of War 24.)

Colonel WEST. Will you state to the Board your name, rank, organization, and station?

Lieutenant LOCKARD. Joseph L. Lockard, First Lieutenant, Signal Corps, 01634176, 934th Signal Battalion, Esler Field, Louisiana.

. . . .

General Frank. What was your rank on the morning of December 7, 1941?

Lieutenant Lockard. I was a third-class specialist, sir.

General Frank. A private?

Lieutenant Lockard. Under the old specialist system I had a third-class specialist rating.

General Frank. To what organization did you belong at that time?

Lieutenant Lockard. S.C., A.W., H.—Signal Corps, Aircraft Warning, Hawaii, was all the designation we knew at that time.

General Frank. What were your duties on that morning? Did you have any regularly assigned duties?

Lieutenant Lockard. Yes, sir. Under the hours we were working at that time, Sundays and holidays called for operation from 4 until 7 o'clock; that is, a.m. I was assigned, and Private Elliott and myself were sent to operate the station for that particular Sunday, those particular hours.

General Frank. How long had you been on duty with that station?

Lieutenant Lockard. We moved that station from Schofield Barracks and set it up around Thanksgiving time. I cannot give you the exact date.

General Frank. Was it September or October?

Lieutenant Lockard. It was in November. It had formerly been set up in Schofield, and they were planning a more appropriate coverage with the equipment.

General Frank. Do you remember when those sets arrived from the mainland?

Lieutenant Lockard. I cannot be exactly definite about that. It was the latter part of July or the first part of August. That is the first I knew.

General Frank. That is the best your memory serves you?

Lieutenant Lockard. Yes, sir.

General Frank. How long had you been there?

Lieutenant Lockard. I landed there on the 10th of December 1940.

General Frank. How long had you been on this type of work?

Lieutenant Lockard. Since we had the equipment.

General Frank. How much training had you had?

Lieutenant Lockard. As far as any school was concerned, we did not have any.

General Frank. How did you get your instruction?

Lieutenant Lockard. Instruction was by actual work with the equipment.

. . . .

General Frank. When did you start on this work?

. . . .

Lieutenant Lockard. Around the first part of August.

General Frank. You had been in training and operating it since August?

Lieutenant Lockard. Yes, sir.

. . . .

General Frank. Did the location of the set at Opana Point result in any unusual radio phenomena?

Lieutenant Lockard. About the only thing that would be unusual about it was our reception. Most of the men were in accord that it probably was the best site they had.

. . . .

General Frank. You were at the set on the morning of December 7, were you?

Lieutenant Lockard. Yes, sir.

General Frank. When did you go there?

Lieutenant Lockard. We went up there the night before.

General Frank. Did the set start operating on the morning of December 7?

Lieutenant Lockard. Yes, sir. We started operation.

General Frank. What time?

Lieutenant Lockard. Around four o'clock.

General Frank. Who operated the set? Who was at the oscilloscope?

Lieutenant Lockard. I was.

General Frank. From what time until what time?

Lieutenant Lockard. The whole period.

General Frank. When did you start?

Lieutenant Lockard. At what time?

General Frank. Yes.

Lieutenant Lockard. Around four o'clock.

General Frank. What was picked up that morning and at what times, so far as your memory will serve you?

Lieutenant Lockard. It was a rather dull morning. There was not much activity.

General Frank. Up until what time? Did you pick up any planes before seven o'clock?

Lieutenant Lockard. If we did, sir, it was one or two or a small number.

General Frank. When did you pick up this flight that was coming in from the north?

Lieutenant Lockard. Around 7:02.

General Frank. What were the circumstances surrounding the situation as it then existed? Where you at the oscilloscope, or was Elliott?

Lieutenant Lockard. I was still at the oscilloscope, sir. We were going to close down, but we figured that we might as well play around, because the truck had not come in yet to take us back for chow. So I was just checking the adjustments and was going to let Elliott operate them a while. He had not been in the outfit very long; he was a new man with us. I was going to let him operate. To me it looked like two main pulses. That is why I thought there was something wrong with the equipment, and I was checking to see if there was anything wrong. Apparently there was not.

General Frank. Proceed and tell us what happened.

Lieutenant Lockard. Well, I showed it to Elliott. I fooled around some more trying to determine exactly whether it was something coming in or whether it was a defect in the equipment, and finally decided that it must be a flight of some sort. Since it was the only activity we had had that morning, I decided to plot it. Elliott plotted it.

General Frank. Who did the plotting?

Lieutenant Lockard. Elliott. We picked it up at 136 miles, and when it got to 132 we called the information center—it was just a few minutes after seven—and there was no one. I knew the switchboard operator there, and I asked if there was anyone around.

General FRANK. You called the information center, or did the other man?

Lieutenant LOCKARD. No, sir. I was watching the track, and he made the phone call, and the switchboard operator told us there was no one around; so we asked him to look around; and, contrary to regulations, he left the switchboard and looked, and he found someone; but first, we told him about what we had, and he told this individual.

General FRANK. Do you know who that was?

Lieutenant LOCKARD. No, sir; I had never seen him.

General FRANK. You do not know whom he told?

Lieutenant LOCKARD. I know his name. I think I know his name.

General FRANK. What was it?

Lieutenant LOCKARD. Miller. I believe he was a liaison officer.

General FRANK. Miller, or Tyler?

Lieutenant LOCKARD. The best that I can remember, sir, it was Miller.

General FRANK. All right.

Lieutenant LOCKARD. This individual—well, the switchboard operator came back and said that, "O. K.—it's all right," something to that effect. I can't tell you the conversation anymore, because I haven't too good a memory and we insisted—I asked—

General FRANK. You insisted what?

Lieutenant LOCKARD. I asked the switchboard operator if I couldn't speak to this person; which I did; and I gave him all the information that we had—the direction, the mileage, and the apparent size of whatever it was; and that was about the end of it, right there.

General FRANK. What did he tell you?

Lieutenant LOCKARD. Well—

General GRUNERT. You are not incriminating anybody. Tell us. What did he tell you? Did he say, "Forget it," or that it did not amount to anything, or what?

Lieutenant LOCKARD. Something to that effect. I mean, "O. K."

General Frank. Did he tell you to forget it, or what did he say?

Lieutenant Lockard. Well, he didn't—he wasn't very committal. He just said, "O. K.," or something to that effect— "You needn't"—

General Frank. When you picked it up and had followed it, so that it had come from 137 or thereabouts down to a shorter distance from the sight, what did the oscilloscope show? Did it show that it was a single plane, or that it was a large group of planes? What was your interpretation of it?

Lieutenant Lockard. Well, sir, it was the largest group I had ever seen on the oscilloscope. It looked, as I said, like a main pulse, and that is why I was confused, at first, as to whether it was a flight or not. I had never seen one. It maybe was the exceptional reception in that particular spot, but it still produced the largest echo on the 'scope that I had seen.

General Frank. Did you tell the man, then, at the information center, that it looked like an unusually large number of planes?

Lieutenant Lockard. Yes, sir.

General Frank. And that didn't seem to excite him in any way?

Lieutenant Lockard. No, sir.

General Frank. What followed from then on? Did you continue?

Lieutenant Lockard. Well, sir, we went as far as we thought was reasonably safe in our argument.

General Frank. What do you mean? In your argument with whom? With the man at the information center?

Lieutenant Lockard. Yes, sir.

General Frank. All right.

Lieutenant Lockard. Then we continued to follow the flight, and to plot it, till it got within about 22 miles—20 to 22 miles of the Island, at which time we lost it in this blacked-out area. Then we proceeded to close down the station and go back to Kawailoa for breakfast. The truck had arrived—or, had not arrived, yet, but there was nothing else working.

General Frank. There were no additional targets in the distance behind that, were there? Do you remember whether or not you attempted to find out if there were any more coming in?
Lieutenant Lockard. Oh, we looked around somewhat.

. . . .

Testimony Of Lt. Col. Kermit A. Tyler, Air Corps, Orlando, Fla., Army Air Force Board, Before the Army Pearl Harbor Board, August 17, 1944

(Consecutive numbering of questions and answers omitted).

(The witness was sworn by the Recorder and advised of his rights under Article of War 24).

General Grunert. Colonel, the Board is trying to get at the facts; that is, as to things leading up to what happened at Pearl Harbor . . . . General Frank will lead in propounding the questions, and then the other members of the Board will fill in wherever they see fit. General Frank.

General Frank. What was your assignment?

Colonel Tyler. My duty on that morning was "pursuit officer." That was the assignment that was written on the order assigning.

General Frank. I know, but on what duty were you? What was your permanent assignment at that time?

Colonel Tyler. I was second ranking officer in the 78th Pursuit Squadron. It was then "pursuit," now "fighter."

General Frank. How long had you been in Honolulu?

Colonel Tyler. On that duty, sir?

General Frank. No. When did you arrive in the Hawaiian Islands?

Colonel Tyler. On the 22nd of February 1941, sir.

General Frank. You had been there about six months?

Colonel Tyler. More than that, sir; almost ten months.

General Frank. They had a practice of sending officers down to the information center, to break them in in the various duties to which they would be assigned, when the information center became operative, is that correct?

Colonel TYLER. Sir, I believe that that was the intention, on the morning of the 7th, when I was assigned, there. I had been assigned there, one previous date, but there was only one other person there besides myself, and that was the telephone operator.

General FRANK. So you got little or no instruction on the previous date?

Colonel TYLER. That is right, sir. I had, however, been through information center, once before. They took a tour of officers.

General FRANK. Were you familiar with the detailed operation of the information center?

Colonel TYLER. Well, I understood how the thing worked; yes, sir. I think I understood it quite well.

General FRANK. Had you had any instructions on the duties of a pursuit officer in the information center?

Colonel TYLER. I had no instruction before I went on this first tour of duty. At that time I reported for duty, and, there being only a telephone operator and myself, I called the operations officer, Major Bergquist, now Colonel Bergquist, and asked him what my duties were, then, because, obviously, it seemed to me, I had no reason to be there, if there wasn't an operator there.

General GRUNERT. May I interrupt, here? Will you explain what a "pursuit officer in an information center" is? I know what a control officer is, but just what is a "pursuit officer in an information center"?

Colonel TYLER. At that time, the pursuit officer's duty was to assist the controller in actually controlling the planes in the air. The pursuit officer is the one who would give the actual instruction of the fighter planes after they were ordered off. A controller's job, however, was to order the planes off.

General FRANK. To be a little more specific, when an enemy plane was sighted, instructions were issued from the information center to provide what—an interception?

Colonel TYLER. The instruction that would come to me

THE EVENTS AT PEARL HARBOR

would be from the controller, to order a certain number of flights off, from such and such a squadron.

General Frank. To accomplish what?

Colonel Tyler. To take off and make interception.

General Frank. And from the time that they left the ground until the interception was made, who was giving them instructions?

Colonel Tyler. That was the pursuit officer's duty, sir, except at such time as the controller might.

General Grunert. That is what I wanted in the record.

General Frank. So on this morning, you were assigned there for instructional purposes, to learn about being a pursuit officer?

Colonel Tyler. Yes, sir.

General Frank. Who was there, this morning, to teach you anything about that?

Colonel Tyler. I was the senior—in fact, I was the only officer there, and all that I could learn would be what I would learn by observing. By that I mean, there were about five or six plotters placing the plots (arrows) on the board, and there was a—

General Frank. Was it a very well organized activity for the purpose of giving you instruction?

Colonel Tyler. I would say that the previous tour that I had through the information center was clear enough in giving me a set-up of the thing, but actually, there being no officers there to identify plots, nor no senior controller there, then, I wouldn't say that I was very well instructed that morning.

General Frank. All right. Was the aircraft warning service, including the information center, operating that morning?

Colonel Tyler. Yes, sir; it was.

General Frank. Were there any plots made on the board prior to 7 o'clock?

Colonel Tyler. I am quite sure there were, sir. There were a number of plots around the Island. As to whether they were just before 7, or started apearing about 7, I am not certain as to that.

General Frank. Do you remember the occasion on which a flight from the north was picked up by the Opana station?

Colonel TYLER. Yes, sir.

General FRANK. You remember that?

Colonel TYLER. Yes, sir.

General FRANK. Will you give us the circumstances surrounding that? Can you give us a narrative concerning it?

Colonel TYLER. Just as a matter of interest, I saw this lad who was keeping the historical record. There is a record made of every plot that comes into the station, and I had not yet observed that activity, so I went over to see what he was doing, and it happened to be just about 7 o'clock, or roughly thereabout; and he had these plots out probably 130 miles, which I looked at, and there were other plots on the board at that time. It was just about 7, or a little bit after, I think, and then, right at 7 o'clock, all the people who were in the information center, except the telephone operator, folded up their equipment and left. There were just the operator and myself again; and about 7:15, the radar operator from Opana called the telephone operator to say that he had a larger plot than he had ever seen before, on his 'scope, and the telephone operator relayed the call to me; so I took the call, and, inasmuch as I had no means of identifying friendly plots from enemy, nor was I led to believe that there would be any occasion to do so, I told him not to worry about it.

And the next warning I had was about 5 after 8, when we received a call that there was an attack on.

General FRANK. What did you assume this was that was coming in? It might have been what?

Colonel TYLER. As far as I was concerned, it could. I thought it most probable that it would be the B-17's which were coming from the mainland.

General FRANK. You knew there was a flight of B-17's due in?

Colonel TYLER. I didn't have official information. You see, I had a friend who was a bomber pilot, and he told me, any time that they play this Hawaiian music all night long, it is a very good indication that our B-17's were coming over from the mainland, because they use it for homing; and when I had reported for duty at 4 o'clock in the morning, I listened to this Hawaiian music all the way into town, and so I figured then that we had a flight of B-17's coming in; so that came to my mind as soon as I got this call from him.

General FRANK. Did you give any thought to the fact that it might be planes from a navy carrier?

Colonel TYLER. Yes, sir. In fact, I thought that was just about an equal probability of the two.

General FRANK. What did you do, from then on?

Colonel TYLER. Well, there was nothing to do between the call, until the attack came.

General FRANK. Where were you when the attack came?

Colonel TYLER. I was awaiting relief. I was due at 8 o'clock to be relieved, and there being nothing going on, I just stepped outside of the door. There was an outside door, there, and I got a breath of fresh air, and I actually saw the planes coming down on Pearl Harbor; but even then, I thought they were Navy planes; and I saw antiaircraft shooting, which I thought was practicing antiaircraft.

General FRANK. The last connection that you had with this station was when you told the operator up at Opana to "forget it," so to speak?

Colonel TYLER. Yes, sir.

General RUSSELL. How long had you been in the Air Corps, then, Colonel?

Colonel TYLER. I was first commissioned in 1937. I had it, just a little over four years, sir, at that time.

General RUSSELL. You knew something about the mission of fighter airplanes, did you?

Colonel TYLER. Yes, sir.

General RUSSELL. And you knew the only thing you had to do was to get in touch with the people who could put those planes up, isn't that true?

Colonel TYLER. That is not exactly true, sir, because we had nothing on the alert. We had no planes.

General RUSSELL. Well, if you had had some planes on the alert, then your job was to call for the commander of those planes and tell him, "Here come some enemy planes—go get them!" Wasn't that your job, as the pursuit officer?

Colonel TYLER. That would be my job if I had any way of telling. There was no means of identifying.

General RUSSELL. There seemed to be a lot of mystery about a pursuit officer and you not being trained as a pursuit officer, and I am trying to see if I can solve that mystery. You had a telephone in that place, on which you could talk to the commanders of the aircraft on the Island?

Colonel TYLER. Well, my next higher, the first one there called would have been Major Bergquist. I would have called him in his quarters, I presume.

General RUSSELL. Then he was to tell the people to get into the planes and go get the enemy?

Colonel TYLER. That was his duty; yes, sir.

General RUSSELL. So it was a rather simple job, after all, wasn't it, Colonel?

Colonel TYLER. That's right; it would have been.

General RUSSELL. The only mystery about it was the fact that you did not know that there were any Jap planes coming in, there?

Colonel TYLER. Yes, sir.

General RUSSELL. And you had the information from this boy at the Opana radar station that he had picked up the biggest flight that he had ever picked up, is that right?

Colonel TYLER. Yes, sir.

General RUSSELL. Did he appear somewhat excited over the flight that was coming in?

Colonel TYLER. I would say that he seemed more than normal. Of course, I didn't know the fellow up there, but he seemed— I would say he was interested in it, all right, sir.

General RUSSELL. He had found something out there, that had impressed him to quite an extent?

Colonel TYLER. Yes, sir.

General RUSSELL. And you said, "Don't worry about it—don't bother"? That was your decision, is that right?

Colonel TYLER. Yes, sir.

General RUSSELL. Now, to go back to these other people who had been there, and who had folded up and gone away at 7 o'clock. It was their job, as I understand this information center, to evaluate the incoming information?

Colonel TYLER. No, sir; their job was to present it to the Board for evaluation by them.

General RUSSELL. Who was the man, there, to evaluate that information?

Colonel TYLER. The Navy liaison officer and the bomber liaison officers.

General RUSSELL. They were the people who would evaluate any information from one of these operating stations out on the Island?

Colonel TYLER. Yes, sir.

General RUSSELL. Were they there at all that morning?

Colonel TYLER. No, sir.

General RUSSELL. They had never been?

Colonel TYLER. No, sir.

General RUSSELL. So there wasn't anybody there whose job it was, or whose duty it was, to evaluate this incoming information?

Colonel TYLER. That's right, sir.

General RUSSELL. Well, why were you up there, at all?

Colonel TYLER. I really don't know.

General RUSSELL. You were not to go into action as the pursuit officer, until these other people, who were going to evaluate the information, had evaluated it and told you that hostile aircraft was en route to the Island; that is the situation, isn't it?

Colonel TYLER. That is right, sir.

General RUSSELL. Therefore, it wasn't your job to evaluate this information at all?

Colonel TYLER. No, sir; it wasn't.

General RUSSELL. I was interested, merely as a matter of information, in what you said as to the report this chap out at that station, that he had "a big" something, and I missed that part.

Colonel TYLER. I don't know whether he said "a large flight of planes," or "an indication," or "a large blip on his radar."

That is the word that is used, and that I have used considerably, since then, so I am not sure whether he said "blip."

General RUSSELL.   "A large blip" indicated a lot of planes?

Colonel TYLER.   Yes, sir. It means one and the same thing, sir.

General RUSSELL.   That is all.

.   .   .   .

The first actual contact between American and Japanese forces occurred in the early morning hours of December 7, 1941, when the U. S. S. *Ward* fired upon an unknown submarine. The following documents consist of excerpts from the testimony of Captain William W. Outerbridge of the *Ward,* who fired the first shot; Lieutenant Commander Harold Kaminski, the duty officer at headquarters to whom Outerbridge reported his action, and Captain John B. Earle, Chief of Staff, 14th Naval District. Lieutenant Commander Kaminski's testimony was taken by the Roberts Commission, the others', by the Hewitt Inquiry.

Pearl Harbor Attack, XXXVI, 55-59; ibid., XXIII, 1034-1038; ibid., XXXVI, 267-270.

Testimony Of
Captain William W. Outerbridge, USN,
Before The Hewitt Inquiry,
Navy Department, May 21, 1945

. . . .

Admiral Hewitt. State your name and rank.
Captain Outerbridge. William W. Outerbridge, Captain, U.S. Navy.
Admiral Hewitt. You were the commanding officer of the *WARD* on the morning of 7 December 1941?
Captain Outerbridge. Yes, sir.
Admiral Hewitt. And during the early hours of that morning, you had several actual contacts with submarines? Is that so?
Captain Outerbridge. Several actual contacts?
Admiral Hewitt. Well, reported contacts.
Captain Outerbridge. Yes, sir. We had one alert and one actual contact and then later, after the attack, we had several outside.

Admiral HEWITT. There has been reported and logged the conversation which you had with the *CONDOR* along about 0520 Honolulu time and later there is in evidence the report of your actual attack on the submarine. Will you give me your story of the events of the morning, beginning with the report from the *CONDOR* about 0400?

Captain OUTERBRIDGE. That doesn't appear on this record, but she signalled us by flashing light that she believed she had seen an object that looked like a submarine proceeding to the westward, and I believe she had just come out in the channel, but she said, "The submarine is standing to the westward."

Admiral HEWITT. What was her location?

Captain OUTERBRIDGE. Outside of the actual channel, sweeping with her magnetic sweeps.

Admiral HEWITT. The approach channel to Pearl Harbor?

Captain OUTERBRIDGE. Outside of the actual channel, between the reefs, but on the approach channel to Pearl Harbor.

Admiral HEWITT. Swept channel?

Captain OUTERBRIDGE. Swept channel, yes, and we went to General Quarters and proceeded to her position, as close as we could get to her without fouling her sweeping gear, and then we stood to the westward, slowed to ten knots, and searched. It was a sonar search. We couldn't see anything.

Admiral HEWITT. About what time did you get that signal?

Captain OUTERBRIDGE. We got that signal about 0358, visual signal about 0358, and we searched for about an hour and didn't find anything; so I got in contact with her again and asked her for a verification. Then she said—this is in the record here. We asked her first, "What was the approximate distance and course of the submarine that you sighted?" and she said, "the course was about what we were steering at the time 020 magnetic and about 1000 yards from the entrance apparently heading for the entrance." Well, I knew then that we had been searching in the wrong direction. We went to westward, and, of course, there was still doubt as to whether she had actually seen a submarine because there hadn't been any other conversation, except by flashing light with us, and I wondered whether they were sure or not; so I did ask them, "Do you have any additional information on the sub?" and they said, "No additional information," and I asked them, "When was the last time approximately that you saw the submarine?" and they said, "Approximate time 0350 and he was apparently heading for the entrance." Then we thanked them for their information and asked them to notify us if they had any more information and then we just kept on searching in our area, in the restricted area outside of the buoys. That was the end of this incident for the first search.

Admiral HEWITT. You made no report of that to higher authority?

Captain OUTERBRIDGE. No, sir, I didn't make any report of it.

Admiral HEWITT. What was your evaluation of that?

Captain OUTERBRIDGE. Well, at the time I thought perhaps it wasn't a submarine, because they didn't report it. This conversation was taken over another circuit entirely. This is not in either his log or mine. They didn't report it and I thought if he didn't report it, he must not think it is a submarine. It was his initial report and I thought it may not be. It may have been anything; it may have been a buoy. Since then, I don't believe it was a buoy. I believe the Commanding Officer of the *CONDOR* saw a submarine. I don't know where he is, I think he was killed, killed in action. But at that time I didn't know whether or not it was a submarine.

Admiral HEWITT. You say you think the Commanding Officer of the *CONDOR* was killed?

Captain OUTERBRIDGE. I believe he was killed.

Admiral HEWITT. Do you remember his name?

Captain OUTERBRIDGE. No, sir, I don't know, but I met some people who told me about him.

Admiral HEWITT. Well, now about the later contact.

Captain OUTERBRIDGE. The later contact—I turned in again and was sleeping in the emergency cabin, as usual, and Lieutenant Goepner had the deck. He was a j. g. He called me and said, "Captain, come on the bridge." The helmsman was the first one to sight this object and he saw this thing moving. It looked like a buoy to him, but they watched it and after they had watched it for a while, they decided probably it was a conning tower of a submarine, although we didn't have anything that looked like it in our Navy, and they had never seen anything like it. I came on the bridge as fast as I could and took a look at it. I don't know where it appeared to them at first, but at that time it appeared to me to be following the *ANTARES* in. The *ANTARES* had been reported to me and at that time I thought the *ANTARES* had been heading into the harbor. She also had a tow, towing a lighter, and it appeared to me the submarine was following astern of the tow.

Admiral HEWITT. Astern of the tow?

Captain OUTERBRIDGE. Yes, sir. It may or may not have been. I think other people can testify it was standing in to Honolulu. To me it appeared to be following the *ANTARES* in and I thought, "She is going to follow the *ANTARES* in, whatever it is." It was going fairly fast. I thought she was making about twelve knots. It seemed to be a little fast to me. I was convinced it was a submarine. I was convinced it couldn't be anything else. It must be a submarine and it wasn't anything that we had and we also had a message that any submarine operating in the restricted area—not operating in the submarine areas and not escorted—should be attacked. We had that message; so there was no doubt at all in my mind what to do. So, we went to General Quarters again and attacked. That was 0740-0640.

Admiral HEWITT. And you attacked and you reported, I believe that—

Captain OUTERBRIDGE. Yes, sir, we reported.

Admiral HEWITT. Will you identify those exchanges of messages? Will you identify the messages on the radio log?

Captain OUTERBRIDGE. Yes, sir. The Executive Officer was on the bridge at the time. We made the attack and dropped depth charges in front of the submarine. The first report was, "We have dropped depth charges upon sub operating in defensive sea area." I thought, "Well, now, maybe I had better be more definite," because we did fire and if we said we fired, people would know it was on the surface, because saying it was a sub and dropping depth charges, they may have said it might have been a blackfish or a whale. So I said, "We have attacked fired upon and dropped depth charges upon submarine operating in defensive sea area," so they would feel, well, he shot at something. We sent the message at 0653, the second one.

(The radio log of the Naval Radio Station, Bishop's Point, Oahu, containing the conversation between the *WARD* and the *CONDOR* and the *WARD's* report of attack upon a submarine, was received and marked, "Exhibit 18.")

Admiral HEWITT. What do you feel was the effect of your attack?

Captain OUTERBRIDGE. I think we sank the submarine.

Admiral HEWITT. What do you base that on?

Captain OUTERBRIDGE. On the gun hit, only on the gun hit.

Admiral HEWITT. There was a gun hit on it?

Captain OUTERBRIDGE. There was a gun hit on it, and I looked these submarines over and there is no hatch between the conning tower and the tube of the submarine, where I believe it was hit, right at the waterline, the base of the conning tower.

Admiral HEWITT. And the submarine disappeared after that?

Captain OUTERBRIDGE. Yes, sir, it disappeared.

Admiral HEWITT. That was before you made the depth charge attack?

Captain OUTERBRIDGE. Yes, sir, we fired at the submarine before we made the depth charge attack, and as she was going under the stern, we dropped over the depth charges.

Admiral HEWITT. Your depth charges were close to her?

Captain OUTERBRIDGE. Yes, sir.

Admiral HEWITT. Definitely?

Captain OUTERBRIDGE. Definitely, they were there. I didn't claim a kill—

Admiral HEWITT. Whom were those reports addressed to?

Captain OUTERBRIDGE. I believe it was Commander Inshore Patrol. We were working for inshore patrol, but the interpretation is here—

Admiral HEWITT. You got the calls?

Captain OUTERBRIDGE. Yes, sir, we got the calls.

Admiral HEWITT. Do you remember what they mean?

Captain OUTERBRIDGE. No, sir.

Admiral HEWITT. Those were the only reports of that attack you made?

Captain OUTERBRIDGE. Yes, sir, two messages on that.

Admiral HEWITT. What was your action after the completion of that attack?

Captain OUTERBRIDGE. Well, I saw one of these large white sampans lying to out there in the defensive area.

Admiral HEWITT. Was that against regulation?

Captain OUTERBRIDGE. That was against standing rules. They weren't supposed to be in the defensive area, but he was in there. So, I turned around and went after him and we chased him out towards Barber's Point. He was going pretty fast.

Admiral HEWITT. He tried to get away from you?

Captain OUTERBRIDGE. It appeared that way to me. He could have stopped much sooner, but he appeared to be going around Barber's Point. When we did catch up to him, he came up waving a white flag. I thought that was funny. I thought, "We will just send for the Coast Guard." That was what we always did when we caught a sampan in the defensive area. We sent for the Coast Guard and they were very prompt. They sent a cutter out to take him in.

Admiral HEWITT. Will you identify for the record those two messages you sent about the sampan, which are on the Bishop's Point record?

Captain OUTERBRIDGE. "We have intercepted a sampan into Honolulu. Please have Coast Guard send cutter to relieve us of sampan." And, "We have intercepted sampan and escorting sampan into Honolulu. Please have cutter relieve us of sampan." We sent that. That is a little garbled, but that looks like it.

Admiral HEWITT. What was the time of it?

Captain OUTERBRIDGE. That was 0833 and 0835.

Admiral HEWITT. Well, then, I understand that several days later you saw a midget submarine which was recovered off Bellow's Field. Is that correct?

Captain OUTERBRIDGE. Yes, sir, that is correct.

Admiral HEWITT. Was the appearance of the conning tower similar to the one that you saw?

Captain OUTERBRIDGE. Yes, sir.

Admiral HEWITT. What was the condition of that submarine off Bellow's Field? Did it have its torpedoes?

Captain OUTERBRIDGE. Yes, sir, it was in good condition and I went inside and there was a torpedoman—I believe he was a chief torpedoman—working on the torpedoes, trying to get them out without exploding them, and I saw the torpedoes inside.

Admiral HEWITT. Well, I think, that is all I had planned to ask you. I am naturally interested in any information you can provide on this Pearl Harbor attack. Is there anything that you might think would be pertinent to this investigation that you can volunteer?

Captain OUTERBRIDGE. Well, I suppose it would be a matter of opinion, which probably wouldn't do you much good, but I was even a little surprised at the attack which followed. I mean I had no idea that the air attack was going to follow. We brought the sampan in and got another submarine attack. We dropped four depth charges on another submarine in the area. We got depth charges that morning and at 11 o'clock we ran out. When the attack started, we were still at General Quarters and we saw the planes coming in, but not until after the bombs began to fall, because the bombs were falling on Pearl Harbor, and the Exec and I were standing on the bridge. Lieutenant Commander Dowdy was the Exec and he said, "They are making a lot of noise over there this morning, Captain." I said, "Yes, I guess they are blasting the new road from Pearl to Honolulu." He said, "Look at those planes. They are coming straight down." I looked at them, and he said, "Gosh, they are having an attack over there." I said, "They certainly are," and that was the time the attack actually began.

Admiral HEWITT. That was about 0750?

Captain OUTERBRIDGE. 0750, yes, sir.

Testimony Of Lieutenant Commander Harold Kaminski, USNR, Before The Roberts Commission, January 8, 1942

. . . .

Admiral STANDLEY. What duty were you performing on the night of December 6 and the morning of December 7?

Commander KAMINSKI. I was District Watch Officer.

Admiral STANDLEY. From what time?

Commander KAMINSKI. I had the watch at 4 o'clock Saturday.

Admiral STANDLEY. Four p.m. Saturday?

Commander KAMINSKI. Yes.

Admiral STANDLEY. 1600?

Commander KAMINSKI. Yes, 1600 Saturday night. I stayed on continuously for three days after that.

Admiral STANDLEY. What was your tour of duty?

Commander KAMINSKI. My duty at that time was that I was the officer in charge of the net and boom defenses.

Admiral STANDLEY. I mean so far as your watch duty on that night was concerned. You went on watch at 1600?

Commander KAMINSKI. Yes.

Admiral STANDLEY. When would you be relieved, ordinarily?

Commander KAMINSKI. I would ordinarily be relieved at 1 o'clock the next morning, sir, Sunday morning.

Admiral STANDLEY. Were you the only officer on watch at that time?

Commander KAMINSKI. Yes, I was the only officer on duty in the district. However, they had the yard watch and then the security watch, but at that time I was the only officer on watch.

Admiral STANDLEY. What were your duties as a watch officer?

Commander KAMINSKI. Well, my duties as watch officer were to take care of anything that turned up pertaining to the district—any district activities.

Admiral STANDLEY. Had there been any calls made upon you as duty officer which could not be performed at any time prior to that time?

Commander KAMINSKI. I do not understand.
Admiral STANDLEY. Had you been standing watch prior to December 6?
Commander KAMINSKI. Yes.
Admiral STANDLEY. Had any occasion ever arisen when any matters came up which could not be handled?
Commander KAMINSKI. No, sir.
Admiral STANDLEY. When you went on watch you relieved the officer who was on duty?
Commander KAMINSKI. Yes.
Admiral STANDLEY. You understood what your duties were supposed to be?
Commander KAMINSKI. Yes.
Admiral STANDLEY. Did you have any idea that you could not perform them under any circumstances?
Commander KAMINSKI. I felt that the station could not function efficiently with just myself. I felt that before. I had complained about the man they had on the telephone watch, and they had Hawaiians there who were not able to speak plain English and they did not receive the proper instructions at the telephone. In fact, the man I had that morning was perfectly useless and had not been instructed, and they did not understand the teletype there, and I felt there was too much responsibility for one person, and I felt that the situation should be corrected and we should have more personnel and the teletype should be manned and not just one officer with one enlisted man.
Admiral STANDLEY. Did your instructions call for any increase of help in case of emergency?
Commander KAMINSKI. No, my instructions in case of emergency were to call the Commandant; to call his aide, as a matter of fact, and second, if I could—no, that is wrong.
My first instructions were to call the chief of staff and the Commandant's aide. Those were the first to call: The chief of staff and the Commandant's aide.
Admiral STANDLEY. Did you have other calls that you were required to make?
Commander KAMINSKI. Constantly we had various routine calls. For instance there might be a destroyer coming in or some-

thing with contagious diseases and there might be various inspections and dispatches coming in. It was a regular routine duty.

Admiral STANDLEY. You received a call that morning of the sinking of a submarine.

Commander KAMINSKI. Yes. I have the original dispatch and I initialed it.

Admiral STANDLEY. What was the time?

Commander KAMINSKI. The time I received it? I initialed it. I saved a copy of it and I have it in this file.

Admiral STANDLEY. What was the time?

Commander KAMINSKI. 0712 . . . .

Admiral STANDLEY. What did you do when you received that message?

Commander KAMINSKI. When I received that message I endeavored to get in touch with the Commandant's aide. I could not reach him on the telephone. I then got in touch with the Cincus's duty officer. I read the message to him. I then got in touch with the chief of staff.

I have it here in chronological order.

Admiral STANDLEY. Just tell us what you did. How long did it take you to get in touch with the chief of staff?

Commander KAMINSKI. It took me quite a while to get him. I have some other message in here.

These are the reconstructed notes of the next morning. During the morning of December 7 at 0712 I received that dispatch from the *WARD* . . . . Upon receiving that dispatch, I immediately endeavored to raise the Commandant's aide and could not contact him. I called and contacted Cincpac Duty Officer and read him the dispatch.

Admiral STANDLEY. Do you have the time when that call was made?

Commander KAMINSKI. No, because it was practically the same time. I did not waste much time. It was right after I got it—I did that next.

General MCCOY. It was all within a few minutes?

Commander KAMINSKI. Yes.

I called and contacted the Cincpac Duty Officer and read him the dispatch. I sent the message to ready duty destroyer *MAHAN*.

THE EVENTS AT PEARL HARBOR 113

I have in here the *MAHAN*, but it was the *MONAGHAN* and they got it.

It was, "Get under way immediately and contact U.S.S. *WARD* in defensive sea area."

Admiral STANDLEY. Just a minute. Did you send that message on your own responsibility?

Commander KAMINSKI. Yes.

Admiral STANDLEY. Do you have instructions that that is what you are to do?

Commander KAMINSKI. I had instructions, yes, to use my own judgment. I knew it was a ready duty destroyer, so I sent that message out. It was by visual . . . . I then called the chief of staff, Captain Earle, notifying him of the *WARD's* message. . . . . He requested confirmation from the *WARD*, which I relayed to the *WARD* and never received an answer; but I received a second dispatch in the interim about the time which I will give to you. It was between 0712 and 0720 that I received this dispatch. That dispatch is:

> We have intercepted a sampan. We are escorting this sampan into Honolulu. Please inform Coast Guard to send cutter for relieve us of sampan.

That should be "to relieve us of sampan" instead of "for relieve us of sampan." That is garbled.

Admiral STANDLEY. That came in from the *WARD?*

Commander KAMINSKI. Yes, the U.S.S. *WARD*.

Admiral STANDLEY. Then what happened?

Commander KAMINSKI. I got in touch with the Coast Guard and found that they had received a communication practically simultaneous with mine; they had picked it up, so I dropped it.

Then I called the War Plans Officer, Commander Momsen, because after I called Captain Earle, he was quite astounded and he said he could not believe it. He asked for this confirmation. He asked to send him that confirmation, and he made several remarks at that time that he was astounded and that it was unbelievable, and made various other remarks. He asked me to notify the Commandant. I asked him if he would please notify the Commandant because I had other messages to put through. He said he would . . . . He notified the Commandant.

He suggested about calling Commander Momsen. I called the War Plans Officer, Commander Momsen, and was ordered to call Ensign Logan. He arrived at approximately 0725. Of course, these times are approximate and were reconstructed, and they are accurate to the best of my ability.

I called Commander Momsen around 0720, sir. I called Ensign Logan immediately after, in about five minutes.

It was 0725 that I received the message from the *WARD*. That is the sampan message. All these things were almost simultaneous.

A minute later, I got the Coast Guard . . . . Commander Momsen arrived in the operations office a few minutes after Ensign Logan. I then called my own commanding officer. After that, with the assistance of the lady at the switchboard I started to call all the department heads, after arranging with the telephone office to keep the lines open.

. . . .

TESTIMONY OF CAPTAIN JOHN B. EARLE
BEFORE THE HEWITT INQUIRY,
JUNE 19, 1945

. . . .

Mr. SONNETT. State your name and rank, please.
Captain EARLE. John B. Earle, Captain, USN.
Mr. SONNETT. What was your assignment on December 7, 1941, Captain?
Captain EARLE. Chief of Staff, Fourteenth Naval District.

. . . .

Mr. SONNETT. You testified previously, as I recall it, Captain, that in the several months preceding the attack on Pearl Harbor you had about ten or fifteen reports of submarines sighted around Pearl Harbor. Can you recall what those reports were?
Captain EARLE. Very indefinitely. They generally came from

sampans—from fishing boats; occasionally from Army lookout posts; and now and then from planes.

. . . .

Mr. SONNETT. Can you recall, Captain, whether any report prior to December 7, 1941, involved firing upon a submarine or a suspected submarine?

Captain EARLE. I am almost certain that there was no such report.

. . . .

Mr. SONNETT. You will note . . . Captain, a report by the *WARD* of its attack upon a submarine. That report did come to your attention prior to the attack, as I understand your previous testimony.

Captain EARLE. That report did come to my attention but not in the wording that it is included in the log of the section base.

Mr. SONNETT. Would you state, Captain, the report of that conversation which was received by you on December 7, 1941, and state the time approximately at which you received it?

Captain EARLE. About 0710 I was informed by the Operations Duty Officer, Lieutenant Commander Kaminski, that he had received a message from the *WARD* to the effect that "We have attacked and fired on a submarine."

Admiral HEWITT. Nothing about depth charges?

Captain EARLE. No, sir.

Mr. SONNETT. That report, Captain, was a more specific report, was it not, than any previous report concerning submarine contact which had been received by you?

Captain EARLE. Yes.

Mr. SONNETT. What action was taken on the report?

Captain EARLE. As I recall it, I immediately told the watch officer to inform the Commander-in-Chief's Operation Officer and to take steps to get the relief destroyer ready to proceed out of the harbor, to get the message checked and verified and attempt to find out what further action was being taken by the *WARD*. I then called the Commandant of the Fourteenth Naval District, Admiral Bloch, informed him of what had been done, and talked the situation over with him for some time with a view to deciding what other action should be taken. Our reaction was that it was probably a mistake as we had had numerous reports of sighting of submarines, but that if it were not a mistake, the *WARD* could take care of the situation and the relief destroyer could lend a hand, while the Commander-in-Chief had the necessary power to undertake any other action which might be desired. Mainly we were trying to definitely determine what had happened.

Mr. SONNETT. I take it, Captain, that no further action was taken on that report prior to the air attack on December 7th?

Captain EARLE. No other action was taken by me. I believe that in addition to that, that Commander Momsen, who was the Operations Officer, was contacted and told to take station. We were vaguely alarmed but could see no specific threat involved except that by the possible position of an enemy submarine in that area.

Mr. SONNETT. Captain, I show you exhibit 8 of the Naval Court of Inquiry, which is Pacific Fleet Confidential Letter number 2CL-41 (Revised), dated October 14, 1941, and ask whether you saw that and were familiar with that prior to December 7, 1941?

Captain EARLE. It is my recollection that I saw this before December 7, 1941.

. . . .

Mr. SONNETT. Now, Captain, coming back to the previous question, it appears, does it not, that one of the assumptions of the security letter was that a declaration of war might be preceded by a surprise Japanese attack? Having that in mind and turning to the statement that you previously read concerning the presence of a submarine, will you state why, on the morning of December 7, 1941, upon receipt of the report from the *WARD*, it was not believed that a large Japanese force might be in the offing and why appropriate action was not taken on that belief?

Captain EARLE. In the first place, we were not sure of this supposed contact. It still seemed to have a possibility of being in error. This was particularly strengthened by a later report received from the *WARD* which said that she was proceeding to escort a sampan toward Honolulu. We couldn't imagine that the *WARD*, having actually attacked a submarine, would leave her post to proceed to Honolulu if it were a real attack. In the second place, we had no force immediately available to resist any attack as far as the District was concerned, except the relief destroyer, and we felt that by referring the matter to the Commander-in-Chief, that we had done all that we possibly could even if the attack were real.

.   .   .   .

PART TWO

The Events in Washington

The Events in Washington

The actions of the authorities in Washington on the eve of America's entry into World War II constitute one of the most important keys to an understanding of the background of the Pearl Harbor attack. The following document consists of excerpts from a sworn statement given to the Joint Congressional Committee investigating the Pearl Harbor attack by former Secretary of War Henry Stimson with attached excerpts from a diary he kept in November and December 1941.

Pearl Harbor Attack, XI, 5416-5438, explanatory notes omitted.

STATEMENT BY HENRY L. STIMSON, FORMER SECRETARY OF WAR, TO THE JOINT COMMITTEE ON THE INVESTIGATION OF THE PEARL HARBOR ATTACK, S. CON. RES. 27, WITH APPENDIX, MARCH 1946

. . . .

The evidence which I am able to give the committee comes not only from my recollection of the events which transpired preceding the Pearl Harbor attack, but I am able to refresh my recollection from a contemporaneous record which I kept from day to day for my own personal use. As I explained to the Army board, I had a dictograph at my house at which I dictated these memoranda each morning before going to the War Department . . . . I am attaching to this statement as an appendix copies of my notes . . . of matters relevant to the Far Eastern situation and the events leading up to the attack on Pearl Harbor. Although these extracts speak largely for themselves, they were made roughly and hastily and were not revised when dictated. They therefore naturally need some addition to tie them in as a connected story and to give the whole picture as I saw it. It is for this reason that I am accompanying them with this statement.

No accurate understanding can be had of the situation which existed in the weeks preceding the Pearl Harbor attack or of the conduct of the various individuals concerned unless they are viewed in the light of the historical events which had been going on for some time and which ultimately led to the crisis that occurred in December and the war of the United States with the Axis powers. From some of the comments which have been made and given wide publicity, one receives the impression that many people have already forgotten the trend of events which were coming to a head in the autumn of 1941 and the threat to our safety which had unmistakenly developed in the actions of the two great aggressor nations, Germany and Japan, who already in the preceding months and years had begun spreading destruction and terror throughout a large portion of the civilized world.

Japan had started on her current path of aggression in the Far East as early as September 1931. She then attacked the Chinese in Manchuria and overran that territory, flouting her obligations under the Pact of Paris and the Nine Power Treaty. There then followed her attacks on the Chinese in Shanghai. She invaded China in 1937, after the conclusion of the Anti-comintern Pact with Germany. The brutal and barbarous type of military aggression for which she stood was typified by the outrages committed by her Army in the occupation of Nanking and similar incidents, which by 1941 had become notorious events of history. In September 1940, after Germany had set out on her temporarily triumphal path toward the subjugation of the nations of Europe, Japan concluded a military alliance with Germany and Italy and placed herself formally in the camp of the Axis powers.

By the summer of 1941, the Japanese intentions in the Far East became very clear. After Germany attacked Russia in June of that year, Japan began extensive military preparations—

among other things, calling an additional 2,000,000 men to the colors. The utterances of her war lords became increasingly threatening. She extended her military operations into southern French Indo-China. That she was headed toward the ultimate occupation of Singapore and the Netherlands East Indies, and thence the domination of entire Southeast Asia, was evident not only from her overt act and announcements but from certain of her intercepted diplomatic messages in which her intentions were expressed in more detail.

All this presented a great threat to our safety and interests. If Singapore and the Netherlands Indies should be occupied, Japan would be strengthened by the acquisition of a great fortress and a great source of natural resources in rubber and oil, which would help her greatly to carry on her program of depredation. The Philippines, which lay between Japan and these British and Dutch targets, would inevitably be the next victim, and at her mercy. China might easily be forced to capitulate and taken out of the war. Our military advisers had given the President their formal advice that, if Japan attacked British Malaya or the Dutch East Indies or moved her forces west of a certain line in Indo-China, we would have to fight for the sake of our own security.

On the other side of the world, we were faced with a situation which was even more critical. Hitler, having seized Norway, France, Belgium, Denmark, and Holland, had just attacked Russia in June of 1941 and the Russians were fighting a desperate battle to stop the German Army from overrunning a large portion of her territory and her capital. In the meantime, the Germans were maintaining large forces deployed on the north coast of Europe as a continual threat of an invasion of England which, as we know, was ill prepared to meet it. As we now know from the evidence presented at the trial of the German war criminals in Nuremburg, Hitler was planning ultimately to attack the United States and was conspiring with the Japanese to aid them while they attacked us in the meantime. It was then very apparent to everyone who had carefully followed the course of events that we would sooner or later have to meet the threat to civilization which these aggressor nations were presenting to the world, and the great danger was that the nations who were then fighting desperately and gallantly to stem this threat would be knocked out of the war one by one before our turn came and that we would ultimately be left to face the onslaught alone. . . .

From some of the comments quoted in the public press, one would get the impression that the imminent threat of war in October and November 1941 was a deep secret, known only to the authorities in Washington who kept it mysteriously to themselves. Nothing could be further from the truth. At least one of our destroyers had been attacked by German war vessels. Aside from the war warnings which were sent to our military and naval commanders in the various theaters of danger, the imminence of war with Japan was a matter of public knowledge and the people were being warned time and time again of the danger which was approaching. One need only read the headlines of the newspapers during this period. . . .

In mid-October the Japanese Konoye cabinet fell and a new cabinet under General Tojo came into power, which all expected would be even more aggressive and warlike.

. . . .

On Friday, November 7, we had the usual weekly Cabinet meeting. The Far Eastern situation was uppermost in many of our minds. Mr. Hull informed us that relations had become extremely critical and that we should be on the outlook for an attack by Japan at any time. Our military advisers, while desirous of delay, had urged military action if Japan attacked territory whose security was vital to us and in this connection specified American, British, or Dutch territory. The President at the meeting undertook to take an informal vote of the Cabinet as to whether it was thought the American people would back us up if it became necessary to strike at Japan, in case she should attack England in Malaya or the Dutch in the East Indies. The Cabinet was unanimous in the feeling that the country would support such a move. The Cabinet voted this way even though only Mr. Hull and the President knew of the efforts which we had been making to reinforce the Philippines with the big bombers and which we in the Army felt could be effective support in case any attack should be made on the British or Dutch in southeastern Asia. On November 10 at a staff meeting, General Marshall, among other things, read us a long letter from General MacArthur in the Philippines, telling us of hopeful progress in the reorganization of the Philippine Army and the construction of airports throughout the islands.

Between November 10 and 21, talks were commenced in Washington between Nomura and Kurusu on the one hand, and the President and Mr. Hull on the other. During this period a very serious crisis developed by reason of the threatened strike of the coal miners, which would have been a most serious obstacle to our preparations for defense. Not only was the President occupied with this but we in the War Department during this period were obliged to make preparations for taking over and operating the coal mines in case the strike should eventuate. Much of my personal time was occupied during these days with these preparations. Fortunately, the strike was ultimately averted and the matter resolved shortly after November 20. My notes contain no reference to any developments in the Japanese situation during this period. It was during this period, on November 20, that Kurusu presented the Japanese proposals to Mr. Hull which, among other things, demanded that we should withdraw all material and moral support to China and at the same time resume supplying to Japan the oil she required to assist her in carrying on her war with China.

My notes recall to me the fact that on November 24 I had a good talk with General Olmstead, who had recently been promoted to be Chief Signal Officer. This department was of particular interest to me because I had been giving a great deal of personal attention during the past months to the development of radar by the Army. I had for some time become convinced of the importance of radar, both as an antiaircraft protection as well as its uses for installation in planes and ships for combat purposes. We had made every effort to get as much radar equipment to Hawaii as possible, particularly for antiaircraft protection; and, as the committee has undoubtedly heard, substantial amounts of this equipment of the movable type were in Hawaii and capable of operation.

On Tuesday, November 25, Secretary Knox and I met in Mr. Hull's office for our usual Tuesday morning meeting. Mr. Hull showed us a proposal that he had prepared, which he was considering laying before Nomura and Kurusu for a 3 months' truce.

At 12 o'clock on the same day, we three went to the White House, where we met with the President and also General Marshall and Admiral Stark. The President at once brought up the relations with the Japanese. Mr. Hull said the Japanese were poised for attack—that they might attack at any time. The President said the Japanese were notorious for making an attack without warning and stated that we might even be attacked, say next Monday, for example.

One problem troubled us very much. If you know that your enemy is going to strike you, it is not usually wise to wait until he gets the jump on you by taking the initiative. In spite of the risk involved, however, in letting the Japanese fire the first shot, we realized that in order to have the full support of the American people it was desirable to make sure that the Japanese be the ones to do this so that there should remain no doubt in anyone's mind as to who were the aggressors. We discussed at this meeting the basis on which this country's position could be most clearly explained to our own people and to the world, in case we had to go into the fight quickly because of some sudden move on the part of the Japanese. We discussed the possibility of a statement summarizing all the steps of aggression that the Japanese had already taken, the encirclement of our interests in the Philippines which was resulting and the threat to our vital supplies of rubber from Malaya. I reminded the President that on August 19 he had warned the Japanese Ambassador that if the steps which the Japanese were then taking continued across the border into Thailand, he would regard it as a matter affecting our safety, and suggested that he might point out that the moves the Japanese were now apparently on the point of making would be in fact a violation of a warning that had already been given.

When I got back to the War Department after this meeting on that same day, I found news from G-2 that was very disturbing. It indicated that the Japanese were embarking a large expeditionary force of 30, 40, or 50 ships at Shanghai and that this expedition was proceeding along the China coast south of Formosa. I at once telephoned Mr. Hull and also sent copies of the report to the President.

The next morning, November 26, Mr. Hull told me over the telephone that he had almost decided not to make the proposition of the three months' truce that he had discussed with Knox and me on November 25. The Chinese, for one thing, had pointed out strong objections to the proposal, particularly the effect on the morale of their own people. Mr. Hull stated that he felt the best thing to do was simply to tell the Japanese that he had no further action to propose.

I telephoned the President shortly thereafter and asked him whether he had received the news of the new expedition from Shanghai proceeding down the China coast toward Indo-China. He had not received it. He was shocked by it, and at once took it as further evidence of bad faith on the part of the Japanese, that while they were negotiating with him—negotiations in which we were asking for a withdrawal of their invading troops in China—they should be sending a further expedition down to Indo-China.

On Thursday morning, November 27, the news was still coming in of the movement of the large Japanese expeditionary force south from Shanghai and eventually headed toward Indo-China, with a possibility that it might be proceeding to the Philippines or to Burma to cut off the Burma Road, or to the Dutch East Indies. It seemed probable, however, that it was a concentration to move over into Thailand, from which they could be in a position to attack Singapore at the proper moment; or, as the President later pointed out, it might develop into an attack on Rangoon and thus effectually stop the Burma Road at its beginning.

Early that morning I had called up Mr. Hull to find out what his final word had been with the Japanese—whether he had handed them the proposal for 3 months' truce, or whether he had told them he had no other proposition to make. He told me that he had broken the whole matter off. His words were:

"I have washed my hands of it and it is now in the hands of you and Knox—the Army and the Navy." I then called up the President, who gave me a little different view. He said that it was true that the talks had been called off, but that they had ended up with a magnificent statement prepared by Mr. Hull. I found out afterwards that this was the fact and that the statement contained a reaffirmation of our constant and regular position without the suggestion of a threat of any kind. I personally was relieved that we had not backed down on any of the fundamental principles on which we had stood for so long and which I felt we could not give up without the sacrifice of our national honor and prestige in the world. I submit, however, that no impartial reading of this document can characterize it as being couched in the terms of an ultimatum, although the Japanese were of course only too quick to seize upon it and give it that designation for their own purposes.

Shortly after this General Arnold came in with proposed orders for the movement of two of our biggest planes from San Francisco out across the Mandated Islands to Manila. We were to arrange to have these fly high over the Mandated Islands, beyond the reach of their pursuit planes, and photograph them with the idea of trying to detect any naval concentrations that might be going on there.

Later Mr. Knox and Admiral Stark came over and conferred with me and General Gerow. General Gerow was Chief of the War Plans Division. General Marshall was absent, having left the Department to attend certain Army training maneuvers which were going on that day. Both Admiral Stark and General Gerow were urging that any crisis be postponed as long as possible, to enable our preparations to proceed. A memorandum had been prepared by General Marshall and Admiral Stark to the President on this subject. The opinion of our top military and naval advisers was that delay was very desirable, but nevertheless we must take military action if Japan attacked American, or British, or Dutch territory or moved her forces in Indo-China west of 100° east or south of 10° north. I told them, which was the fact, that I also would be glad to have time but I did not want it at the cost of humiliation of the United States or of backing down on any of our principles which would show a weakness on our part.

We then discussed the messages that might be sent to the commanding officers of the various theaters, including in particular General MacArthur, who was in the Philippines and in the forefront of the threatened area. We had already sent MacArthur a warning but I felt that the time had now come for a more definite warning. In talking with the President on the telephone that morning, I had suggested, and he had approved the idea, that we should send out a final alert, namely that they should be on the qui vive for any attack, and explaining the exact situation. Ordinarily, of course, there would be no reason for me to participate in the sending of any such message, which was the normal function of the military staff. As the President himself, however, had now actually directed the sending of the message, and as I wanted the message clearly to apprise the commanding officers in the various areas as to exactly what the diplomatic situation was, I undertook to participate in the framing of this message myself. In order that it should be strictly accurate, I called up Mr. Hull myself on the telephone and got his exact statement as to the status of the negotiations, which was then incorporated in the first sentence of the message. My papers also indicate that I inserted in the second sentence the words *"BUT HOSTILE ACTION POSSIBLE AT ANY MOMENT."*

This same message was sent to commanding officer, Hawaiian Department, and to the three other commanding officers of our Pacific theaters or outposts, viz: Panama, the Philippines, and the west coast which included Alaska, except that in the case of the message to General MacArthur in the Philippines there were omitted from the third sentence from the end the following words: *"BUT THESE MEASURES SHOULD BE CARRIED OUT SO AS NOT COMMA REPEAT NOT COMMA TO ALARM CIVILIAN POPULATION OR DISCLOSE INTENT."* The message as sent to General Short read as follows:

Commanding General, Hawaiian Department,
Fort Shafter, T. H.

Negotiations with Japan appear to be terminated to all practical purposes with only the barest possibilities that the Japanese Government might come back and offer to continue period Japanese future action unpredictable but hostile action possible at any moment period If hostilities cannot comma repeat cannot comma be avoided the United States desires that Japan commit the first overt act period This policy should not comma not repeat not comma be construed as restricting you to a course of action that might jeopardize your defense period Prior to hostile Japanese action you are directed to undertake such reconnaissance and other measures as you deem necessary but these measures should be carried out so as not comma repeat not comma to alarm civil population or disclose intent period Report measures taken period Should hostilities occur you will carry out the tasks assigned in Rainbow Five so far as they pertain to Japan period Limit dissemination this highly secret information to minimum essential officers.

MARSHALL

This message has been criticized as ambiguous and described as a "do-don't" message. The fact is that it presented with the utmost precision the situation with which we were all confronted and in the light of which all our commanding officers, as well as we ourselves in Washington, had to govern our conduct. The situation was admittedly delicate and critical. On the one hand, in view of the fact that we wanted more time, we did not want to precipitate war at this moment if it could be avoided. If there was to be war, moreover, we wanted the Japanese to commit the first overt act. On the other hand, the matter of defense against an attack by Japan was the first consideration. In Hawaii, because of the large numbers of Japanese inhabitants, it was felt desirable to issue a special warning so that nothing would be done, unless necessary to the defense, to alarm the civil population and thus possibly to precipitate an incident and give the Japanese an excuse to go to war and the chance to say that we had committed the first overt act.

All these considerations were placed before the commanding officers of their respective areas, and it was because they were thought competent to act in a situation of delicacy requiring judgment and skill that they had been placed in these high posts of command. One of the basic policies of the Army command, which has been adhered to throughout the entire war, and in most instances with complete success, has been to give the local commander his objective and mission but not to interfere with him in the performance of it. When General Short was informed on November 27 that "Japanese action unpredictable" and that "hostile action possible at any moment," and that the policy directed "should not comma repeat not comma be construed as restricting you to a course of action that might jeopardize your defense," we had a right to assume that he would competently perform this paramount duty entrusted to him. We assumed that when he had been warned that hostile action was possible at any moment, it would not be necessary to repeat that warning over and over again during the ensuing days. The fact was of course that General Short did receive, not only from Washington, but from other sources, repeated intelligence of the impending crisis.

You will notice that this message of November 27 specifically mentions that reconnaissance is to be undertaken. This to my mind was a very important part of the message, not only because of its obvious desirability but also because we had provided the Hawaiian Department with what I regarded as a most effective means of reconnaissance against air attack and one to which I had personally devoted a great deal of attention during the preceding months. I refer to the radar equipment with which the Hawaiian Department was then provided. This equipment permitted approaching planes to be seen at distances of approximately 100 miles; and to do so in darkness and storm as well as in clear daylight . . . . When we specifically directed the commanding officer at Hawaii, who had been warned that war was likely at any moment, to make reconnaissance, I assumed that all means of reconnaissance available to both the Army and Navy would be employed. . . .

I repeat that my participation in the drafting of this message of November 27 was unusual, since I do not believe it is advisable for the Secretary of War to meddle with military staff matters. As already stated, I did so on this occasion because I felt I was conveying a message from the President. The President had taken a momentous decision that day, namely to send what I call a final alert. The Chief of Staff was away for the day, and I wanted to make certain that the President's orders were carried out accurately.

You will note that my notes speak only of the message to General MacArthur. This is evidence of what was the fact—namely that we all felt in Washington that the first and most likely danger was an attack on the Philippines and that such an attack would be most difficult to meet. Such information as we had been able to gather as to the movements of the Japanese forces indicated a movement toward the south, which might easily be diverted either to Indo-China, Malay Peninsula, Dutch East Indies, or the Philippines. We were correct in this inference. Such an attack on the Philippines was being prepared and immediately followed the attack on Pearl Harbor. The movements of the fleet which attacked Pearl Harbor were entirely unknown to us. . . . .

The first thing in the morning of the next day—Friday, November 28—I received information from G-2 of such a formidable character with regard to the movements of the Japanese forces along the Asiatic coast that I decided to take it to the President before he got up. I saw him while he was still in bed, and we discussed the situation. He suggested that there were three alternatives, as my notes show: First, to do nothing; second, to make something in the nature of an ultimatum, stating a point beyond which we would fight; or, third, to fight at once. I said that I felt that to do nothing was out of the question and the President agreed with me. As to the other two alternatives, the desirable thing to do from the point of view of our own tactics and safety was to take the initiative and attack without further warning. It is axiomatic that the best defense is offense. It is always dangerous to wait and let the enemy make the first move. I was inclined to feel that the warning given in August by the President against further moves by the Japanese toward Thailand justified an attack without further warning, particularly as their new movement southward indicated that they were about to violate that warning. On the other hand, I realized that the situation could be made more cleancut from the point of view of public opinion if a further warning were given.

I went at 12 o'clock that day to a meeting of the so-called War-Cabinet—that is to say, the President, Mr. Hull, Mr. Knox, Admiral Stark, General Marshall, and myself. The President had been studying the latest report of G-2 as to the movements of the Japanese expeditionary force, and we discussed the various possibilities as to what it meant. The various alternatives mentioned were that it might develop into an attack on the Philippines, the landing of further troops in Indo-China, an attack on Thailand, on the Dutch Netherlands, or on Singapore, or that it might develop into an attack on Rangoon and thus cut off the Burma Road at the beginning. The possibility of an attack on Pearl Harbor was not discussed at the meeting, since our thoughts were all focused on this movement toward southeast Asia, which indicated a crisis in that direction. All agreed that if the expedition were permitted to land in the Gulf of Siam it would place a strong Japanese force in such a strategic position as to be a severe blow at all three of the powers in southeast Asia—the British at Singapore, the Netherlands in the Indies, and ourselves in the Philippines. We all agreed that it must not be allowed; that, if the Japanese got into the Isthmus of Kra, the British would fight; and, if the British fought, we would have to fight. We realized that if this expedition was allowed to round the southern point of Indo-China, this whole chain of disastrous events would be set on foot.

We decided, therefore, that we could not just sit still and do nothing. On the other hand, we also decided that we could not attack without a further warning to Japan, and we discussed what form the warning should take. The President suggested a special telegram from himself to the Emperor of Japan. After some discussion it was decided that he would send such a letter to the Emperor, which would not be made public, and that at the same time he would deliver a special message to Congress reporting on the danger and reporting what we would have to do if the danger happened. The President left after the meeting to keep his engagement at Warm Springs, where he was going to have Thanksgiving with the children. The rest of the week end was largely taken up with preparing a suggested draft of a message for the President to deliver to Congress, in which Secretary Knox and I cooperated with Mr. Hull and his associates in the State Department.

On Monday morning, December 1, the President returned to Washington. I recollect that in the meantime we had received evidence that the Japanese expedition which we had been watching was landing in Indo-China in the neighborhood of Saigon, rather than going on to the Peninsula and up into the Gulf of Siam. This appeared to give us a little respite, since it indicated that perhaps they were not going to invade Thailand at once. The Russians had also made a new counter-attack against the Germans at Rostov, and we thought that possibly this had given the Japanese some pause.

On Tuesday, December 2, Secretary Knox, Sumner Welles, and I met with the President, as Mr. Hull was laid up with a cold. The President went step by step over the situation, and I felt sure that he had made up his mind to go ahead with the message to Congress and possibly the message to the Emperor. We also learned that he had asked the Japanese through the State Department what they intended by this new occupation of southern Indo-China and had demanded a quick reply. We were watching the situation in the Far East very carefully. I was in frequent conference with General Marshall and General Miles of G-2 and also General Gerow of the War Plans Division of the General Staff. We were particularly concerned with supplies which were on the way to the Philippines and additional big bombers which we were trying to fly over there, some of which were scheduled to start at the end of the week. I gave up another engagement in order to stay in Washington over the week end.

On Sunday, December 7, Mr. Knox and I went to Secretary Hull's office at 10:30 in the morning and talked the whole matter over. This was the day on which we knew the Japanese were going to bring their answer, and Mr. Hull said he was certain that the Japanese were planning some deviltry and we were all wondering where the blow would strike. The messages we were receiving now indicated that the Japanese force was continuing on in the Gulf of Siam, and again we discussed whether we would not have to fight if Malaya or the Netherlands were attacked and the British or Dutch fought. We all three thought that we must fight if those nations fought. We realized that if Britain were eliminated it might well result in the destruction or capture of the British Fleet. Such a result would give the Nazi allies overwhelming power in the Atlantic Ocean and would make the defense of the American Republics enormously difficult if not impossible. All the reasons why it would be necessary for the United States to fight, in case the Japanese attacked either our British or Dutch neighbors in the Pacific, were discussed at length and at my request Mr. Hull and Mr. Knox dictated their views. . . . I returned to lunch at my home. At just about 2 o'clock, while I was sitting at lunch, the President called me on the phone and told me that the Japanese were bombing Hawaii. . . .

Summary Of My Views As To The Responsibility Of Members Of The Army

My views as to these responsibilities are stated at length in my final official report made under the Joint Resolution of Congress approved June 13, 1944 . . . . Many of the discussions on this subject indicated a failure to grasp the fundamental difference between the duties of an outpost command and those of the commander in chief of an army or nation and his military advisers. The outpost commander is like a sentinel on duty in the face of the enemy. His fundamental duties are clear and precise. He must assume that the enemy will attack at his particular post; and that the enemy will attack at the time and in the way in which it will be most difficult to defeat him. It is not the duty of the outpost commander to speculate or rely on the possibilities of the enemy attacking at some other outpost instead of his own. It is his duty to meet him at his post at any time and to make the best possible fight that can be made against him with the weapons with which he has been supplied.

On the other hand, the Commander in Chief of the Nation (and his advisers), particularly of a nation which has been as habitually neglectful of the possibility of war as our own, has much more difficult and complex duties to fulfill. Unlike the outpost commander, he must constantly watch, study, and estimate where the principal or most dangerous attack is most likely to come, in order that he may most effectively distribute his insufficient forces and munitions to meet it. He knows that his outposts are not all equally capable of defense. He knows also that from time to time they are of greatly varying importance to the grand strategy of the war.

For all these reasons he is compelled to give constant and close attention to the reports from all his intelligence agencies in order that he may satisfactorily solve the innumerable problems which are constantly arising in the performance of the foregoing duties.

During those days in November 1941 we at the War Department had been informed and believed that Hawaii had been more generously equipped from the Nation's inadequate supplies of men and munitions than either of the other three important Pacific outposts, and we believed that with the fleet at hand there it was more capable of defense. We also knew that the Philippines was by far the least capable of defense, although we were working vigorously to get it into a position to put up a hard fight. We also knew that a disaster there would have an incalculable bad moral effect on account of our relations to the Filipinos—well known throughout the Far East—and our pledges given for their protection. Finally, we had received these specific warnings of a Japanese expedition being on its way to a commanding position from which it would attack the Philippine Islands.

From the foregoing I believe that it was inevitable and proper that a far greater number of items of information coming through our Intelligence should be collected and considered and appraised by the General Staff at Washington than those which were transmitted to the commander of an outpost. General Short had been told the two essential facts: (1) A war with Japan is threatening. (2) Hostile action by Japan is possible at any moment. Given those two facts, both of which were stated without equivocation in the message of November 27, the outpost commander should be on the alert to make his fight. Even without any such message, the outpost commander should have been on the alert. If he did not know that the relations between Japan and the United States were strained and might be broken at any time, he must have been almost the only man in Hawaii who did not know it, for the radio and the newspapers were blazoning out those facts daily, and he had a chief of staff and an intelligence officer to tell him so. And if he did not know that the Japanese were likely to strike without warning, he could not have read his history of Japan or known the lessons taught in Army schools in respect to such matters. Under these circumstances which were of general knowledge and which he must have known, to cluster his airplanes in such groups and positions that in an emergency they could not take to the air for several hours, and to keep his antiaircraft ammunition so stored that it could not be promptly and immediately available, and to use his best reconnaissance system, the radar, only for a very small fraction of the day and night, in my opinion betrayed a misconception of his real duty which was almost beyond belief.

In the next place, having made these mistakes and disregarded the whole tenor of the warning message to him, he then sent a reply message to Washington which gave no adequate notice of what he had failed to do and which was susceptible of being taken, and was taken, as a general compliance with the main warning from Washington. My initials show that this message crossed my desk, and in spite of my keen interest in the situation it certainly gave me no intimation that the alert order against an enemy attack was not being carried out. Although it advised me that General Short was alert against sabotage, I had no idea that being "alerted to prevent sabotage" was in any way an express or implied denial of being alert against an attack by Japan's armed forces. The very purpose of a fortress such as Hawaii is to repel such an attack, and Short was the commander of that fortress. Furthermore, Short's statement in his message that "liaison" was being carried out with the Navy, coupled with the fact that our message of November 27 had specifically directed reconnaissance, naturally gave the impression that the various reconnaissance and other defensive measures in which the cooperation of the Army and Navy is necessary, were under way and a proper alert was in effect.

With the aid of "hindsight" I believe now that to a staff officer whose specific duty was to make dead sure that the warning order was being intelligently and thoroughly put into effect, the lack of detail in the reply should have suggested the importance of a follow-up inquiry and I have so stated in my final official report of August 1945.

With the further aid of such "hindsight" and in the same official report, I also reached the opinion that the War Plans Division of the General Staff would have placed itself and the safety of the country in a sounder position if it had transmitted to General Short more information than it did. The novelty of the imminence of war and the fact that our outpost commanders were untried in their positions now indicate that more details and repeated emphasis would have been a safer policy. Also there seems to have been a lack of coordination in the General Staff in respect to the method in which the warnings against sabotage were sent, which would not have occurred later in the war after the staff was fully organized.

Yet none of these things in my opinion alter in any material degree the responsibility of General Short for the complete absence of a real alert, which he had been directed to take in the message of November 27, and for the placing of his defense in a more helpless position than it was before that alert message was sent. After all, he was the man upon whom the country had a right to rely for the defense of Hawaii, and he had been sufficiently warned.

. . . .

Mr. Stimson's Notes—Appendix To Statement Of Henry L. Stimson

. . . .

Tuesday, November 25, 1941

This was a very full day indeed. At 9:30 Knox and I met in Hull's office for our meeting of Three. Hull showed us the proposal for a 3 months' truce, which he was going to lay before the Japanese today or tomorrow. It adequately safeguarded all our interests, I thought as we read it, but I don't think there is any chance of the Japanese accepting it, because it was so drastic. In return for the propositions which they were to do; namely; to at once evacuate and at once to stop all preparations or threats of action, and to take no aggressive action against any of her neighbors, etc., we were to give them open trade in sufficient quantities only for their civilian population. This restriction was particularly applicable to oil. We had a long talk over the general situation.

. . . .

Then at 12 o'clock we (viz, General Marshall and I) went to the White House, where we were until nearly half past one. At the meeting were Hull, Knox, Marshall, Stark, and myself. There the President, instead of bringing up the Victory Parade,[*] brought up entirely the relations with the Japanese. He brought up the event that we were likely to be attacked perhaps (as soon as) next Monday, for the Japanese are notorious for making an attack without warning, and the question was what we should do. The question was how we should maneuver them into the position of firing the first shot without allowing too much danger to ourselves. It was a difficult proposition. Hull laid out his general broad proposition on which the thing should be rested—the freedom of the seas and the fact that Japan was in alliance with Hitler and was carrying out his policy of world aggression. The others brought out the fact that any such expedition to the South as the Japanese were likely to take would

[*] This was an office nickname for the General Staff strategic plan of national action in case of war in Europe.

be an encirclement of our interests in the Philippines and cutting into our vital supplies of rubber from Malaysia. I pointed out to the President that he had already taken the first steps towards an ultimatum in notifying Japan way back last summer that if she crossed the border into Thailand she was violating our safety and that therefore he had only to point out (to Japan) that to follow any such expedition was a violation of a warning we had already given. So Hull is to go to work on preparing that. When I got back to the Department I found news from G-2 that an (a Japanese) expedition had started. Five divisions have come down from Shantung and Shansi to Shanghai and there they had embarked on ships—30, 40, or 50 ships—and have been sighted south of Formosa. I at once called up Hull and told him about it and sent copies to him and to the President of the message from G-2.

. . . .

Wednesday, November 26, 1941

Hull told me over the telephone this morning that he had about made up his mind not to give (make) the proposition that Knox and I passed on the other day to the Japanese but to kick the whole thing over—to tell them that he has no other proposition at all. The Chinese have objected to that proposition—when he showed it them; that is, to the proposition which he showed to Knox and me, because it involves giving to the Japanese the small modicum of oil for civilian use during the interval of the truce of the 3 months. Chiang Kai-shek had sent a special message to the effect that that would make a terrifically bad impression in China; that it would destroy all their courage and that they (it) would play into the hands of his, Chiang's enemies—and that the Japanese would use it. T. V. Soong had sent me this letter and has asked to see me and I called Hull up this morning to tell him so and ask him what he wanted me to do about it. He replied as I have just said above—that he had about made up his mind to give up the whole thing in respect to a truce and to simply tell the Japanese that he had no further action to propose.

A few minutes later I talked to the President over the telephone and I asked him whether he had received the paper which I had sent him over last night about the Japanese having started a new expedition from Shanghai down toward Indo-China. He fairly blew up—jumped into the air, so to speak, and said he hadn't seen it and that that changed the whole situation because it was an evidence of bad faith on the part of the Japanese that while they were negotiating for an entire truce—and entire withdrawal (from China)—they should be sending this expedition down there to Indo-China. I told him that it was a fact that had come to me through G-2 and through the Navy Secret Service and I at once got another copy of the paper I had sent last night and sent it over to him by special messenger.

. . . .

Thursday, November 27, 1941

A very tense, long day. News is coming in of a concentration and movement south by the Japanese of a large expeditionary force moving south from Shanghai and evidently headed toward Indo-China, with a possibility of going to the Philippines or to Burma, or to the Burma Road or to the Dutch East Indies, but probably a concentration to move over into Thailand and to hold a position from which they can attack Singapore when the moment arrives.

The first thing in the morning I called up Hull to find out what his finale had been with the Japanese—whether he had handed them the new proposal which we passed on 2 or 3 days ago or whether, as he suggested yesterday he would, he broke the whole matter off. He told me now that he had broken the whole matter off. As he put it, "I have washed my hands of it and it is now in the hands of you and Knox—the Army and the Navy." I then called up the President. The President gave me a little different view. He said they had ended up, but they ended up with a magnificent statement prepared by Hull. I found out afterward that this was not a reopening of the thing but a statement of our constant and regular position.

General Arnold came in to present the orders for the movement of two of our biggest planes out from San Francisco and across the Mandated Islands to Manila. There is a concentration going on by the Japanese in the Mandated Islands and these planes can fly high over them, beyond the reach of their pursuit planes and take photographs.

Knox and Admiral Stark came over and conferred with me and General Gerow. Marshall is down at the maneuvers today and I feel his absence very much. There was a tendency, not unnatural, on the part of Stark and Gerow to seek for more time. I said that I was glad to have time but I didn't want it at any cost of humility on the part of the United States or of reopening the thing which would show a weakness on our part. The main question has been over the message that we shall send to MacArthur. We have already sent him a quasi alert, or the first signal for an alert, and now, on talking with the President this morning over the telephone, I suggested and he approved the idea that we should send the final alert; namely, that he should be on the qui vive for any attack and telling him how the situation was. So Gerow and Stark and I went over the proposed message to him from Marshall very carefully; finally got it in shape and with the help of a telephone talk I had with Hull, I got the exact statement from him of what the situation was.

. . . .

Friday, November 28, 1941

Pursuant to my instructions G-2 had sent me a summary of the information in regard to the movements of the Japanese in the Far East and it amounted to such a formidable statement of dangerous possibilities that I decided to take it to the President before he got up. I told him there was an important coalition of facts and that I thought he ought to read it before his appointment which he had made for us at 12 o'clock, when the so-called War Cabinet was to meet him—Hull, Knox, myself with Stark and Marshall. He branched into an analysis of the situation himself as he sat there on his bed, saying there were three alternatives and only three that he could see before us. I told him I could see two. His alternatives were—first, to do nothing; second, to make something in the nature of an ultimatum again, stating a point beyond which we would fight;

third, to fight at once. I told him my only two were the last two, because I did not think anyone would do nothing in this situation, and he agreed with me. I said of the other two my choice was the latter one.

When we got back there at 12 o'clock he had read the paper that I had left with him. The main point of the paper was a study of what the expeditionary force, which we know has left Shanghai and is headed south, is going to do. G-2 pointed out that it might develop into an attack on the Philippines or a landing of further troops in Indo-China, or an attack on Thailand or an attack on the Dutch Netherlands, or on Singapore. After the President had read these aloud, he pointed out that there was one more. It might, by attacking the Kra Isthmus, develop into an attack on Rangoon, which lies only a short distance beyond the Kra Isthmus and the taking of which by the Japanese would effectively stop the Burma Road at its beginning. This, I think, was a very good suggestion on his part and a very likely one. It was the consensus that the present move—that there was an expeditionary force on the sea of about 25,000 Japanese troops aimed for a landing somewhere—completely changed the situation when we last discussed whether or not we could address an ultimatum to Japan about moving the troops which she already had on land in Indo-China. It was now the opinion of everyone that if this expedition was allowed to get around the southern point of Indo-China and go off and land in the Gulf of Siam, either at Bangkok or further west, it would be a terrific blow at all of the three Powers, Britain at Singapore, the Netherlands, and ourselves in the Philippines. It was the consensus of everybody that this must not be allowed. Then we discussed how to prevent it. It was agreed that if the Japanese got into the Isthmus of Kra, the British would fight. It was also agreed that if the British fought, we would have to fight. And it now seems clear that if this expedition was allowed to round the southern point of Indo-China, this whole chain of disastrous events would be set on foot of going.

It further became a consensus of views that rather than strike at the Force as it went by without any warning on the one hand, which we didn't think we could do; or sitting still and allowing it to go on, on the other, which we didn't think we could do—that the only thing for us to do was to address it a warning that if it reached a certain place, or a certain line, or a certain point, we should have to fight. The President's mind evidently was running towards a special telegram from himself to the Emperor of Japan. This he had done with good results at the time of the Panay incident, but for many reasons this did not seem to me to be the right thing now, and I pointed them out to the President. In the first place, a letter to the Emperor of Japan could not be couched in terms which contained an explicit warning. One does not warn an Emperor. In the second place it would not indicate to the people of the United States what the real nature of the danger was. Consequently I said there ought to be a message by the President to the people of the United States, and I thought that the best form of a message would be an address to Congress reporting the danger, reporting what we would have to do if the danger happened. The President accepted this idea of a message but he first thought of incorporating in it the terms of his letter to the Emperor. But again I pointed out that he could not publicize a letter to an Emperor in such a way; that he had better send his letter to the Emperor separate as one thing and a secret thing, and then make his speech to the Congress as a separate and more understandable thing to the people of the United States. This was the final decision at that time, and the President asked Hull and Knox and myself to try to draft such papers.

. . . .

Tuesday, December 2, 1941

I left for the White House conference at 12 o'clock, and there were present there just Knox, Sumner Welles and myself, as Hull is laid up with a cold. The President went step by step over the situation and I think has made up his mind to go ahead. He has asked the Japanese through Sumner Welles what they intend by this new occupation of southern Indo-China—just what they are going to do—and has demanded a quick reply. The President is still deliberating the possibility of a message to the Emperor, although all the rest of us are rather against it, but in addition to that he is quite settled, I think, that he will send a message to the Congress and will perhaps back that up with a speech to the country. He said that he was going to take the matters right up when he left us.

. . . .

Sunday, December 7, 1941

Today is the day that the Japanese are going to bring their answer to Hull, and everything in *MAGIC* indicated that they had been keeping the time back until now in order to accomplish something hanging in the air. Knox and I arranged a conference with Hull at 10:30 and we talked the whole matter over. Hull is very certain that the Japs are planning some deviltry and we are all wondering where the blow will strike. We three stayed together in conference until lunch time, going over the plans for what should be said or done. The remaining thing is to hold the main people who are interested in the Far East together—the British, ourselves, the Dutch, the Australians, the Chinese. Hull expressed his views, giving the broad picture of it, and I made him dictate it to a stenographer and I attach it to the end of this. Knox also had his views as to the importance of showing immediately how these different nations must stand together and I got him to dictate that and that is attached hereto. Hull was to see the Japanese envoys at 1 o'clock but they were delayed in keeping the appointment and did not come until later—as it turned out, till 2 o'clock or after. I returned to Woodley to lunch and just about 2 o'clock, while I was sitting at lunch, the President called me up on the telephone and in a rather excited voice asked me, "Have you heard the news?" I said, "Well, I have heard the telegrams which have been coming in about the Japanese advances in the Gulf of Siam." He said, "Oh, no. I don't mean that. They have attacked Hawaii. They are now bombing Hawaii." Well, that was an excitement indeed. The messages which we have been getting through Saturday and yesterday and this morning are messages which are brought by the British patrol south of Indo-China, showing that large Japanese forces were moving up into the Gulf of Siam. This itself was enough excitement and that was what we were at work on our papers about. The observer thought these forces were going to land probably either on the eastern side of the Gulf of Siam, where it would be still in Indo-China, or on the western side, where it would be the Kra Peninsula, or probably Malay. The British were very much excited about it and our efforts this morning in drawing our papers was to see whether or not we should all act together. The British will have to fight if they attack the Kra Peninsula. We three all thought that we must fight if the British fought. But now the Japs have solved the whole thing by attacking us directly in Hawaii.

. . . .

When the news first came that Japan had attacked us, my first feeling was of relief that the indecision was over and that a crisis had come in a way which would unite all our people. This continued to be my dominant feeling in spite of the news of catastrophes which quickly developed. For I feel that this country united has practically nothing to fear; while the apathy and divisions stirred up by unpatriotic men have been hitherto very discouraging.

. . . .

General George C. Marshall, the Chief of Staff at the time of the Pearl Harbor attack, was one of the principal witnesses before the Joint Congressional Committee investigating the Pearl Harbor attack. The following excerpts from his testimony and his examination by both Democratic and Republican members of the Committee on December 7, 8, 11, 12, and 13, 1945, show his side of the story. For purposes of clarification, a short excerpt from the testimony of General Sherman Miles, 1941 Assistant Chief of Staff, G-2, has also been included.

Pearl Harbor Attack, III, 1049, 1096-1113, 1146-1151, 1171-1176, 1319-1329, 1360-1362, 1429-1434, 1513-1515.

Testimony Of General Of The Armies George C. Marshall . . .

The CHAIRMAN. Counsel may proceed.

Mr. MITCHELL. General Marshall, when were you appointed Chief of Staff?

General MARSHALL. I was appointed Acting Chief of Staff on July 1, 1939, and formally appointed and confirmed Chief of Staff on the 1st of September 1939.

. . . .

Mr. MITCHELL. Now, I call your attention to this message (the warning message) that was sent to General Short over your signature on November 27. Were you in the city on the 27?

General MARSHALL. I was not, sir.

Mr. MITCHELL. Where were you?

General MARSHALL. I was in North Carolina.

Mr. MITCHELL. What was going on there?

General MARSHALL. General McNair was having a very large maneuver, I imagine about 300,000 troops, or thereabouts. It was a vital day, and I flew down on the afternoon of the 26th to see the operations on the 27th, and flew back late that evening, so that I appeared in the office on the early morning of the 28th.

Mr. MITCHELL. Before you left on the 26th, had this proposal to send a warning message out to the overseas outposts been discussed with you?

General MARSHALL. Yes, sir. My recollection of it, which is rather confirmed by the memorandum of General Gerow under date of the 27th, I believe that we had a considerable discussion on the joint board on the morning of the 26th, at which it was decided that an alert should be drafted and dispatched immediately.*

General Gerow had the task of drafting the alert. Whether or not he had a draft copy with him at the time or whether he was to prepare it after he returned to the War Plans Division I do not recall. I left in the afternoon following this meeting of the joint board in the morning. Present at the meeting was Admiral Stark, myself, the Deputy Chief of Staff of the Army, General Bryden, General Gerow, and I believe at that time the officers of the Air Corps, and their opposites were present from the Navy.

Mr. MITCHELL. The message was sent over your name then while you were away?

General MARSHALL. Yes, sir.

Mr. MITCHELL. When did you see the draft after you returned?

General MARSHALL. I saw it, the actual message, as it was sent, I think, the moment I reached my desk on the morning of the 28th.

Mr. MITCHELL. This memorandum referred to by General Gerow of November 27 is the one in which he states "The Secretary of War sent for me about 9:30 a.m. November 27, 1941," That is the one you refer to, is it?

General MARSHALL. Yes, sir.

Mr. MITCHELL. When you saw the message of the 27 to General Short after you returned from maneuvers, what was your reaction to its contents and sufficiency?

General MARSHALL. I concurred in the message and the manner in which it was drawn.

* See p. 130.

Mr. MITCHELL. Did you see at the same time the identical message sent to the Commander on the West coast?

General MARSHALL. I saw the message—

Mr. MITCHELL. To all the commanders?

General MARSHALL. Pacific commanders.

Mr. MITCHELL. Did you see General Short's response and the responses of the other commanders to the warning message that had been sent to them?

General MARSHALL. I assume I did. I find in looking at the copy I did not initial it. I assume I must have seen it.

. . . .

Mr. MITCHELL. How did you happen to route it to the Secretary of War?

General MARSHALL. Because I thought it was very important that he should see this particular message. It had been my custom always when there was anything up that was out of the ordinary that he might miss I always initialed it for him and had it taken directly to his room.

Mr. MITCHELL. The fact that he participated in your absence in the drafting of the message to which these were responses, did that have anything to do with your sending it to him?

General MARSHALL. It might have; I don't recall, sir.

Mr. MITCHELL. What do you remember now about your appraisement or reaction to General Short's message of the 28th?

General MARSHALL. I have not a clear-cut recollection at all because shortly after the attack—I presume about an hour and a half—I was in conversation with Colonel Bundy in regard to the measures we were then taking to reestablish ourselves on the west coast, to get the convoys straightened out, and see what other measures we had to take throughout the United States for security, and he mentioned this message, which he apparently had reexamined, and referred to the sabotage factor in it, and also referred to the implication he had gotten from the liaison with the Navy which is included in the message. . . .

Mr. MITCHELL. What was the date of that talk with Colonel Bundy?

General MARSHALL. I would say that was an hour and a half

or an hour, thereabouts, after the news of the attack on Pearl Harbor.

Mr. MITCHELL. On December 7?

General MARSHALL. Yes, sir.

Mr. MITCHELL. Well, then, at that time Colonel Bundy brought up with you the question of Short's report of November 28?

General MARSHALL. My recollection of it is that when we finished this business I had him in there for, he being the officer in immediate charge of all details relating to the Pacific, that was his subsection of the War Plans Division, or the section of the War Plans Division, he would be in charge, and so I was doing business with him direct as to what we were to do to reestablish the situation, and when we finished that, as I recall the incident, he was leaving the room and stopped about halfway out of the room and made a reference to the message which he evidently had looked back on it to see what was going on, and referred to this sabotage clause, and I have forgotten just what his reference to it was. I recall his reference to liaison with the Navy. He referred to that. They had gone ahead with the procedure.

Now, my difficulty in answering your question was it is very hard for me to associate myself with the statement about what came next because from that instant on I was completely involved in the most active period during the war, the next 6 weeks.

Mr. MITCHELL. Well, I was referring more especially to your appraisement or reactions to this message of Short's on November 28 when it was shown to you, or you saw it on the 28th?

General MARSHALL. Yes, sir.

Mr. MITCHELL. Did you notice the brevity of it or the difference in contents—

General MARSHALL. I have no recollection regarding it at all.

Mr. MITCHELL. (Continuing)—by comparison with any of the other reports that you received?

General MARSHALL. I have no recollection regarding it at all, other than the fact that I find the two messages together and that I signed the upper one.

Mr. MITCHELL. In the ordinary course of operations in the department of the General Staff where would the messages have gone for consideration?

General MARSHALL. It would have gone to the War Plans Division and by the Executive officer there would have been routed to the particular section that had that, which was Colonel Bundy's section.

Mr. MITCHELL. At no time between November 28 and the 7th of December did anybody ever come back to you and mention the Short report or question its sufficiency or anything of that kind?

General MARSHALL. I have no recollection of any comment.

Mr. MITCHELL. Had you any information that after the warning message was sent there was no air reconnaissance being conducted at Hawaii for any distance, any considerable distance?

General MARSHALL. No, sir; I had no intimation of that.

Mr. MITCHELL. Well, did you after November 27, when this warning was sent out, make any inquiry as to what measures were being taken at Hawaii?

General MARSHALL. None that I recall.

Mr. MITCHELL. Did you make any inquiry, any further inquiry about what measures were being taken at these other posts where the warning message had been received, or one like it?

General MARSHALL. None that I recall. We were deeply engaged in the business of trying to get our material rerouted to General MacArthur as rapidly as we possibly could and we had, as you will see, in *MAGIC*, picked up the fact of the report that he was unloading at night. I learned that from the Japanese. I did not learn that from MacArthur.

. . . .

Mr. MITCHELL. I think you told us that you currently saw these decoded intercepts of the Jap diplomatic messages.

General MARSHALL. Yes, sir.

Mr. MITCHELL. Did you also see these decoded intercepts of Jap messages relating to military installations and ship movements?

General MARSHALL. I would assume I would, yes, the same as the diplomatic.

. . . .

Mr. MITCHELL. Was there any regulation in the War Department that you established or knew about that forbade the people in the War Department, such as G-2 and War Plans Division, from sending of Hawaii not the test of any intercepted messages, nor a paraphrase of it, nor the fact that they had decoded it, but the substance of the information that they had derived by the intercept?

General MARSHALL. I am unaware of any regulation on that subject. As a matter of fact practically everything concerning *MAGIC* was oral rather than written, in my recollection.

Mr. MITCHELL. Did you know that G-2 was not sending out the gist of those intercepted messages in all cases?

General MARSHALL. Was not sending out the gist?

Mr. MITCHELL. Not sending out the gist. General Miles testified that he never, of course, sent a copy of a message, of an intercepted Jap decoded message to Hawaii and he would not send a paraphrase of it and he did not want to let them know at Hawaii that he was cracking the code and he went further, I understand, and I think said that the information derived in that way could not in a covered-up way be passed on to Hawaii. Was that your understanding of the practice?

General MARSHALL. I do not know as I got that understanding but I know that the G-2 of the War Department, whoever he was, General Miles, General Strong, General McCabe or Colonel McCabe, General Lee and later General Bissell, always were emphatic in their safeguarding of the source and not advertising anything that was done, to hazard the source.

The extent to which they might transmit the information was one that I am not familiar with, just what they did, because there was a continual passage of data from the G-2 of the War Department in the performance of his mission to the G-2's of the various overseas divisions and as the security factor was always ever present in the mind of the Assistant Chief of Staff,

G-2 of the Army, that thought that he would be reckless had never occurred to me. His fear was that I would be reckless.

Mr. MITCHELL. Do you remember ever seeing these intercepted Jap messages relating to dividing Pearl Harbor into area A, B, C, D, and E and locating the—

General MARSHALL. I do not recall the message. I know the one you are referring to.

Mr. MITCHELL. You have examined the book?

General MARSHALL. Yes, sir. I saw it in the book.

Mr. MITCHELL. And you have no recollection of ever seeing it?

General MARSHALL. I have no recollection of that.

Mr. MITCHELL. Are you familiar with the decoded Jap message of November 19, translated November 28, which appears in the book of diplomatic intercepts at page 154, which set up an emergency system of communication between the Japs and their foreign representatives by the use of certain words and weather broadcasts?

General MARSHALL. I remember seeing this winds message at the time it came through. This is the winds message I believe.

. . . .

Mr. MITCHELL. I want to inquire about a matter you testified to yesterday in connection with the so-called "winds" implementing message.

In reading over the transcript I am not so sure that it is as clear as it should be and I want to be sure it is clear. In the first place, I want to call your attention again to the message in Japanese code that we intercepted and translated appearing on page 151 of Exhibit 1, which is the intercepted diplomatic messages.

At the left hand bottom of the page it is dated November 19, 1941, translated November 28, 1941, and it read this way:

> Regarding the broadcast of a special message in an emergency.
>
> In case of emergency (danger of cutting off our diplomatic relations), and the cutting off of international communications, the following warning will be added in the

middle of the daily Japanese language short wave news broadcast.

(1) In case of Japan-U. S. relations in danger: *HIGASHI NO KAZEAME*," which . . . means "East wind—rain."

(2) Japan-U. S. S. R. relations: *KITANOKAZE KUMORI*," which . . . means "North wind—cloudy."

(3) Japan-British relations: *NISHI NO KAZE HARE*," which . . . means "West wind—clear."

The dispatch continues:

This signal will be given in the middle and at the end as a weather forecast and each sentence will be repeated twice. When this is heard please destroy all code papers, etc. This is as yet to be a completely secret arrangement.
Forward as urgent intelligence.

Now, I spoke of that as the message which set up the code system. You understood that, did you? And on the next page . . . there is a second message from Tokyo to Washington intercepted on November 19, 1941, translated November 26, 1941 . . . . That sets up a slightly different system of giving out this news. . . .

Now, those are what we call the initial messages which were received on the dates shown and in my questions I used the word "implementing" message which I intended to describe as any subsequent message in which the Japs were using this code, in which the Japs using this code had sent out these warnings.

Now, I notice when I was inquiring . . . that one of my questions was not clear.

I called your attention to the first message this way:

"Are you familiar with the decoded Jap message of November 19th, translated November 28th . . . which set up an emergency system of communication between the Japs and their foreign representatives by the use of certain words and weather broadcasts?

General MARSHALL. I remember seeing this winds message at the time it came through. This is the winds message, I believe."

.   .   .   .

Mr. MITCHELL. That is the message that established the code, the one on page 154. It is in Japanese there.

"General MARSHALL. Oh, I see. I do not remember exactly that. I am familiar with the specific winds message which would utilize this code, would it not?

"Mr. MITCHELL. Well, there are two. This is the message which came in on the 19th of November and was translated on November 28th.

Now, when I said "two" in that question I was referring to the one on the bottom of page 154 and the sceond one of the top of page 155.

General MARSHALL. Are you asking me now specifically did I see both of these messages?

Mr. MITCHELL. Well, having that statement I would like to know if you remember knowing about these two messages of November 19th which set up these code systems: The first one had the "winds" word in it and the second one did not.

General MARSHALL. I have no distinct recollection of the breakdown between the two messages.

Mr. MITCHELL. I see.

General MARSHALL. But I am quite certain I saw them both.

Mr. MITCHELL. Now, I think maybe we have been clear on this on the next page . . ., but I will ask you again:

Prior to December 7, 1941, did you ever see or hear of any later message in which the Japs in using this winds code sent out word that there was "East wind—rain," which meant trouble with the United States?"

General MARSHALL. I have no recollection of either seeing or hearing of such a message.

Mr. MITCHELL. Now, when we closed last evening I had just asked you a question. I will repeat it now:

"Do you remember this diplomatic message from Tokyo to their Ambassadors here, what we call for short the 14-part message and the 1 P.M. message?"*

Your answer was, "Yes, sir."

"Will you state in your own way just when you first knew about that and under what circumstances?"

* See pp. 225 ff.

And you got as far as saying: "I first was aware of this message when I reached the"—and then we adjourned.

Will you give us now the answer?

General MARSHALL. When I reached the office on the morning of Sunday, December the 7th.

On that particular morning I presumably had my breakfast at eight, and following the routine that I had carried out on previous Sundays, I went riding at some time thereafter.

I think in one of the previous statements I made in this investigation of Pearl Harbor incidents that I said I probably rode at 8:30. Discussions with the orderlies and also evidence that I had seen of other individuals leads me purely by induction and not by definite memory to think that I must have ridden later; just what time I do not know; but between 8 o'clock and the time I went to the War Department I ate my breakfast, I probably looked at the Sunday papers and I went for a ride.

Now, as to the probable duration of such a ride I can only say that there were very limited places to which one might ride unless you crossed from the Arlington side of the river up over Memorial Bridge and the park system on the Washington side, which I did not do but once, I think, in the previous 6 years. My rides took me almost invariably down to the site of the present Pentagon Building, which is the Government experimental farm.

On a few occasions I crossed the approaches to the Memorial Bridge, not the bridge itself, and rode along the Potomac about two-thirds of the way down to where the present National Airport is, but no further. The average length of my rides was about, the time period of my rides is about 50 minutes because I rode at a pretty lively gait, at a trot and a canter and at a full run down on the experimental farm where the Pentagon now is and returned to the house, so I would say that the high probability is that the ride was an hour or less, generally or certainly not longer.

My recollection beyond that is that while I was taking a shower, either as I went into the shower or while I was actually taking a shower, word came to me that Colonel Bratton had something important and wished to come out to Fort Myer.

I sent word that I was coming to the War Department, so I finished my shower, dressed and left for the War Department.

My average time of taking a shower and dressing would be about 10 minutes, possibly less. As to what time I arrived at the War Department is a matter of conjecture; I have no recollection.

On my arrival there Colonel Bratton handed me these intercepts which included the 14 sections of the Japanese message, and I started reading them through. You recall it is a rather lengthy document and of such a nature that there were portions of it that I read twice.

When I reached the end of the document the next sheet was the 1 o'clock message of December 7.

Mr. MITCHELL. That is the message that directed the Ambassadors to deliver this thing at 1:00 p.m. Sunday to the American Government?

General MARSHALL. Yes, sir, that message. That, of course, was indicative to me, and all the others who came into the room, of some very definite action at 1:00 o'clock, because that 1:00 o'clock was Sunday and was in Washington and involved the Secretary of State, all of which were rather unusual put together.

I think that I immediately called Admiral Stark on the phone, and found he had seen the message, and I proposed a message to our various commanders in the Pacific region, the Philippines, Hawaii, the Caribbean, that is the Panama Canal, and the west coast, which included Alaska. Admiral Stark felt that we might confuse them, because we had given them an alert and now we were adding something more to it.

I hung up the phone which was the White House phone, and in longhand wrote out the message. My recollection was that he called me back. I am told now that the White House telephone records show that I called him back. I had no recollection of reading the message to him. I thought, on the contrary, he called me just as I finished the message, saving the last sentence.

However, one way or the other, there was a call or conversation between Stark and myself, the effect of which was he wished me to add specifically "show this to your Naval officers," which I did in longhand.

I then directed Colonel Bratton to take it immediately to the message center and start it. There was a proposal then that we have it typed. The decision was there was no time for typing, and Colonel Bratton left with the message.

On his return I questioned him as to the length of time involved and I could not make out whether or not he was talking about the time of encoding as well as the time of dispatching and the time of receipt, so I sent him back accompanied by Colonel Bundy, the officer in charge of the immediate details of all Pacific affairs.

They came back and gave me the estimate of the time of deliveries in these various parts of the world. My recollection is that I sent at least Colonel Bundy back again, and I thought Colonel Bratton with him. I believe others state that there was no third trip. There were certainly two—my own recollection is there were three. However that may be, that was the procedure on the dispatching of the measure.

Do you wish me to go ahead?

Mr. MITCHELL. Yes.

General MARSHALL. The next information I had was the notification of the actual attack on Pearl Harbor. Of my own recollection I do not recall whether I was at the War Department or at the house. I am told on one side by the Secretary of the General Staff at that time, the Acting Secretary at that time, General Dean, that I had returned to the house. I am told, on the other hand by my orderly that I was at the War Department. I do not know where I was.

Anyway, shortly thereafter, if not immediately then, I was at the War Department, because it was a very quick drive, and on Sunday there was no traffic. It was a matter of about 7 minutes from my house to the Munitions building.

The information then came in in fuller detail, and telephone communication was established and I talked to General Short's Chief of Staff, Colonel Phillips. You could hear the explosions at the time. He was endeavoring to tell me what was actually happening.

My questioning, as I recall, was with relation to a report that had come from somewhere—and there were many reports of course at that time, rumors and authentic, confusion—that a Japanese landing was being attempted, as I recall, below Barber Point, and my recollection is my inquiry of Colonel Phillips was to the facts in regard to that.

I talked to Colonel Phillips because, as I recall, at that time General Short had gone to his command post and therefore was not able to talk to me directly.

The procedure on the dispatch of the messages did not come to my attention in detail until I was before the Roberts Board. The fact that the one message had been sent by the Western Union to San Francisco on a direct line, relayed by the RCA and presumably teletyped, which was not done in Hawaii, I did not know about that.

Admiral Stark tells me, and I am quite certain he is right—I do not recall it but he is undoubtedly right—that he asked me at the time of our second conversation that morning, or he said that they had rapid means of communication and if I wished to use it, and I told him no. That must be a fact—I do not recall—that must be a fact.

That, I think, covers the main details.

Mr. MITCHELL. Now, do you remember your movements on the evening of December 6, as to where you were?

General MARSHALL. I can only account for them by sort of circumstantial evidence. The only definite thing I have is that I had no dinner engagement. I found our engagement book, or Mrs. Marshall's engagement book, and between the 1st of November and the 7th of December I had one dinner engagement, that was the 2nd of December.

Also they checked on the post movie. It was about our only recourse for relaxation, and I had never seen the picture. So I was not there.

We were not calling. We were leading a rather monastic life. There was also in that record the affairs of the day for her, which involved, I think, an old clothes sale, I think, all day long, to raise money for one of these industries they had down there, so the probability is she was tired and we were home.

Mr. MITCHELL. You are sure you were not at the White House that evening?

General Marshall. No, sir; not at all.

. . . .

Mr. Mitchell. .... This is a record of telephone calls on December 7 by outside parties through using the White House exchange.

It says, and I will show it to you—the record says "11:40 A" which means "A.M.," I suppose.

General Marshall cld Ad'm Stark—O.K.

11:30 A—Gen. Marshall cld Ad'm Stark—O.K.

In that particular instance, according to the White House records, these hours are reversed. The 11:40 A is ahead of 11:30, which does not seem to be the practice, and we are not sure just what it means.

Will you look at it and see if it means anything to you? That is exactly what the record shows there, that the time 11:40 precedes the entry of the 11:30 message.

General Marshall. I would not know what the significance of that is.

Mr. Mitchell. You would not know anything about it?

General Marshall. No, sir. It does this, though. It gives the time one way or another of the 14-point thing and the preparation of this other message.

Mr. Mitchell. Then at least you did read the message and were in the act of preparing a warning by 11:30 or 11:40?

General Marshall. Yes, sir; 11:40 would be quite evidently the completion of it, because I had it all written except the last sentence.

Mr. Mitchell. I will offer now, as Exhibit 61, a photostat which reads as follows: "December 7, 1941." It is typed.

Memorandum For The Adjutant General
(Through Secretary, General Staff)

Subject: Far East Situation

The Secretary of War directs that the following first priority secret radiogram be sent to the Commanding General,

U. S. Army Forces in the Far East; Commanding General, Caribbean Defense Command; Commanding General, Hawaiian Department, Commanding General, Fourth Army;

and the message is this:

Japanese are presenting at one p.m. Eastern Standard time today what amounts to an ultimatum also they are under orders to destroy their code machine immediately stop Just what significance the hour set may have we do not know but be on alert accordingly stop Inform naval authorities of this communication.

MARSHALL

It has the signature of General Gerow on it. Has the committee a copy?

The CHAIRMAN. Yes.

Mr. MITCHELL. And the committee will note that underneath it is a record:

"Radios as follows dispatched 11:52 AM, 12-7-41 by Code Room, WDMC."

General MARSHALL. War Department Message Center.

Mr. MITCHELL. And another was dispatched 12:05 to Manila; another one to Hawaii at 12:17; the one to the Caribbean Command is blurred. It looks like 12:00 o'clock, and the one to the Fourth Army at San Francisco at 12:11.

. . . .

Mr. MITCHELL. Did you give any instructions to the Communications Center as to the means of transmitting this message to Hawaii?

General MARSHALL. No, sir. Their business was to dispatch it in the most efficient and rapid manner possible. This photostat of this document of General Gerow's should be read in the light that it was written after the event. The message was sent from a longhand pencil copy on an ordinary ruled sheet of paper, which, incidentally, was before the Roberts board.

Mr. MITCHELL. The original message was in your handwriting and you gave directions that it should not be typed?

General MARSHALL. Yes, sir. It was carried by hand by Colonel

Bratton, and then I thought there also should be a third trip by Colonel Bundy, but there was a difference of opinion on that.

Mr. MITCHELL. In the message center it was necessary to take your handwritten draft and encode it.

General MARSHALL. Yes, sir; encode it first.

Mr. MITCHELL. And then put it on the way?

General MARSHALL. Yes, sir.

Mr. MITCHELL. Was there any report made to you at that time that there was any difficulty in reaching Hawaii on the telephone?

General MARSHALL. No, sir.

Mr. MITCHELL. I mean before the attack?

General MARSHALL. No, sir. I did not ask the question.

Mr. MITCHELL. You didn't ask the question as to means of transportation?

General MARSHALL. I didn't ask the question about the telephone.

Mr. MITCHELL. What did they estimate to you would be the required time for delivery to Fort Shafter of the Hawaiian message?

General MARSHALL. I don't recollect, sir. I have a faint recollection of being told that it would take 8 minutes to get it through, but I think you will have positive testimony on that.

Mr. MITCHELL. You sent the message to all the commands without any special selection of Pearl Harbor?

General MARSHALL. Exactly. I sent each commander involved in the Pacific situation. The Western Defense Command, which is the Fourth Army, the Caribbean Command, the Philippine Command, and the Hawaiian Command.

Mr. MITCHELL. Did you make any inquiry of the communications people or your subordinates as to the prospective time of delivery of that message to Hawaii?

General MARSHALL. That was the reason I sent Colonel Bratton back with Colonel Bundy, to give me a clear picture of what the time involved was, because when I first questioned Colonel Bundy I couldn't tell whether he was including the time necessary to encipher the message, and so I sent him back to determine that for me.

Mr. MITCHELL. Well, what report did he make to you, do you remember, about that?

General MARSHALL. I do not recall the minutes. I think it is shown in one of the documents. I couldn't tell you off hand. I think they are prepared to give you that, sir.

Mr. MITCHELL. Did anybody in your office, when you were reading the 14-part message and the 1 p.m. supplement, on the morning of the 7th, make any mention of the fact that 1 p.m. in Washington would be about 7:30 a.m. in Honolulu?

General MARSHALL. There was no mention of the 1 p.m. message until I came across it at the end of the pile. I am quite clear about that, because I was very much taken back by the time I had spent on the preceding lengthy message in trying to understand its significance, and then arriving at this, to me, very critical one of 1 p.m.

Mr. MITCHELL. You thought you ought to have been shown the 1 p.m. part first?

General MARSHALL. I don't know about that. I am just talking about my own reaction.

Mr. MITCHELL. Well, was any discussion had when you saw the 1 p.m. message? Any discussion about the corresponding time of day in Honolulu or the Philippines?

General MARSHALL. I don't recall that. I don't recall that at all. The whole thing was, it was a significant message, and what would we tell these commanders, and I went ahead and wrote it out myself.

. . . .

The VICE CHAIRMAN. Now, Mr. Chairman, I would like to inquire briefly.

. . . .

Well, where did you think the first Japanese attack on the United States would occur?

General MARSHALL. I thought it would occur in the Philippines. I thought the first Japanese attack was going to be directly south towards Singapore, that that would be the main campaign, and the Philippines, of course, would become involved in it. Just when they would strike and their method of striking with landing forces rather than just air, I did not know, but the air strike might occur very early, which it did.

I assumed that Guam would fall almost immediately and I assumed that Wake would fall almost immediately.

The VICE CHAIRMAN. Did you think the first Japanese attack would be at Pearl Harbor?

General MARSHALL. I did not anticipate that. I thought they would not hazard that. That of course, was a raiding attack, to strike a crippling blow, which did not involve any landing, or any possible landing.

Their campaign was headed south through the China Sea. It was to cover their flank with that strike. Those same carriers appeared quite quickly in the China Sea operations.

The VICE CHAIRMAN. I do not want to detain you too long, General, because I know other members of the committee want to ask you questions, but I have one or two questions, if I may, about what occurred immediately before the attack.

I understood you to state that you were out of Washington on November 27.

General MARSHALL. Yes, sir, I was down in North Carolina.

The VICE CHAIRMAN. Reviewing maneuvers in North Carolina?

General MARSHALL. Yes, sir.

The VICE CHAIRMAN. And the message about which you have been examined here at some length, which was sent over your name on November 27 to the Commanding General, Hawaiian Department, and the other Commanders mentioned—that message of November 27, 1941, to the Commanding General, Hawaiian Department, was brought to your attention early the next morning, the 28th, when you returned?

General MARSHALL. I saw it about 8 o'clock on the morning of the 28th.

The VICE CHAIRMAN. Did you consider that message an adequate warning to the Commanding General, Hawaiian Department?

General MARSHALL. I did, sir.

The VICE CHAIRMAN. Was there ever any doubt in you mind at any time—

General MARSHALL. There was not.
The VICE CHAIRMAN. That that was adequate warning?
General MARSHALL. That is correct.

. . . .

The VICE CHAIRMAN. I believe you stated, in response to a question by the Chairman, that certainly in view of subsequent events, you recognized that the message from General Short was not an adequate response to the message of November 27.

General MARSHALL. That is correct, sir.

The VICE CHAIRMAN. But you do not recall that that was checked on any further, or any further messages sent?

General MARSHALL. I am quite certain there was no further message sent. I might say here, Mr. Congressman, that the people working with him had sent an alert direction which all in the War Department then and now, I think, thought was a sufficient directive, and the comment out there, as far as we knew, from all our communications, had been insistent on measures to meet an air attack and submarine attack.

The thought of merely expecting an alert direction for sabotage was not in anybody's mind at all, which undoubtedly, in my opinion, may account for the fact that that word did not register, and when they spoke of liaison with the Navy that did register as to the assumption that the reconnaissance was one. That is merely conjecture.

. . . .

Mr. GEARHART. Now, referring to your warning message which was sent in slightly different forms to Manila, Hawaii, Panama, and other places, that warning message required the addressees to report to you, didn't it?

General MARSHALL. Require—

Mr. GEARHART. The addressees to report to you?

General MARSHALL. Yes, sir.

Mr. GEARHART. What they had done in response to your directions?

General MARSHALL. Yes, sir.

Mr. GEARHART. General Short reported that he had taken

steps in accordance with your part of your directions against sabotage, in his message of November 28?

General MARSHALL. Yes, sir.

Mr. GEARHART. You received that report, did you not?

General MARSHALL. I testified in regard to that, sir. The presumption is I did. The War Department received it and the presumption is that I read it . . . . I do not remember and I did not initial the report.

Mr. GEARHART. You heard, or were you present in this room when General Gerow testified and accepted full responsibility for not having acted on the inadequacy, as he called it, of this report?

General MARSHALL. I was not present in the room and I admire very much his attitude.

. . . .

Mr. GEARHART. Well, can you give any reason now why you did not take exception yourself to the message of General Short's of November 28?

General MARSHALL. I can only say, sir, that that was my opportunity to intervene and have a further check made and I did not take it. Just why I do not know.

Mr. GEARHART. You expected immediate attention to be given to your message of November 27 by the various addressees to whom you had sent it, didn't you?

General MARSHALL. Yes, sir. That was a command direction for alert against a state of war.

Mr. GEARHART. Yes. Did you expect General Short to take immediate action?

General MARSHALL. I did, sir.

Mr. GEARHART. Then will you explain how he could have taken immediate action and ordered a No. 3 alert instantly without creating alarm among the people and disclosing the intention of the United States?

General MARSHALL. I think he could have, sir. We had done such things before out there. We had done it the previous summer. There are a good many ways to get at that.

The reconnaissance, for example by air over water—that was

a naval directive responsibility—could not in any way have alarmed the population.

The issue where the people came most closely in contact with the military might be as a change of attitude related to sabotage because that required the posting of a great many detachments in order to avoid action being taken.

I would like to say, in regard to this right now, it was necessary, we felt, specifically necessary, to include that particular direction regarding the public, both as to Hawaii and as to the west coast, because it was the strong desire of, I will say, the War Cabinet, certainly of the Army and Navy officials and I am quite certain of the President of the United States, that the Japanese be given no opportunity whatever to claim that we had taken some overt act which forced a state of war upon them.

The feeling was—I am now speaking as Chief of Staff only, from the point of view I could obtain as Chief of Staff—the feeling was at that time that if the Japanese could have created a situation, however unjustified, however illogical, in which they could have led at least a portion of the people to believe that our overt action had forced them into an act of war and we would have had a divided country, which would have been a terrible tragedy in a war situation. Therefore, each move we made had to be taken carefully into account to avoid the possibility that the Japanese would instantly make a claim that we had forced the issue, that we had really made the overt act and they were forced to fight us.

.   .   .   .

Mr. GEARHART. The evidence shows that the 13 parts and the pilot message were received and decoded on December 6, 1941. All this became available on Saturday night. The President, the Secretary of War, the Secretary of State, and the Secretary of the Navy had it, your subordinates Miles and Bratton had it.

How do you explain the fact that none of it was given to your attention on Saturday, December 6, 1941?

General MARSHALL. As I recall—of course, the message itself will show—the first 13 parts were not of the nature of a vital threat as the 14th part. That was a message of direct importance to the Secretary of State and of related importance, of course, to the Secretary of War and the Secretary of the Navy who had been collaborating with him in his relationship in the dealings with Japan. The fact of the matter was it was not brought to my attention.

Mr. GEARHART. Do you now feel that General Short was not entitled to have information of that character to guide him in setting up the degree of alert that it was essential to have done?

General MARSHALL. Yes, sir, that was my view. He was issued a command and directed to do something. Now, if the directive was so written that he could not understand it, that is a matter for judgment. Once you issue an order, amendments or, you might say, codicils, are very dangerous business when it is an operational order. In most instances it is far better to cancel the entire order and start anew. The transmission of information from the G-2, for example, of the War Department to G-2, for example, under General Short is another matter. That is informational and that is not directional.

. . . .

Senator FERGUSON. On page 249, General, we get a message—it is No. 910, from Tokyo to Washington, December 7, 1941. It is marked "Extremely urgent":

After deciphering part 14 of my #902a and also #907b, #908c and #909d, please destroy at once the remaining cipher machine and all machine codes. Dispose in like manner also secret documents.

When did that first come to your attention?

General MARSHALL. I will have to check up here to see if—what is the message that had the 1 o'clock hour in it? How do I find that?

Mr. MITCHELL. That is 907.

General MARSHALL. I see it now.

That message must have come to my attention on the morning of the 7th of December, because in my draft in longhand from which the message was sent to the overseas theaters in the Pacific, I mentioned the fact regarding the destruction of codes.

. . . .

Senator FERGUSON. General, going to page 238, the message we had been referring to as a pilot message, the first paragraph, No. 844. . . .

That message, General, read the first paragraph.

General MARSHALL (reading):

1. The Government has deliberated deeply on the American proposal of the 26th of November and as a result we have drawn up a memorandum for the United States contained in my separate message #902b (in English).

Senator FERGUSON. That would indicate that the message is going to come in English and it is going to be coded, and also that it is an answer to the message of the 26?

General MARSHALL. Yes, sir.

Senator FERGUSON. Now, "this separate message" will you read further?

General MARSHALL (reading):

This separate message is a very long one. I will send it in fourteen parts and I imagine you will receive it tomorrow. However, I am not sure. The situation is extremely delicate, and when you receive it, I want you to please keep it secret for the time being.

Senator FERGUSON. The date of the 6th, that is the 5th here, that is on Friday, is it not?

General MARSHALL. Yes, sir.

Senator FERGUSON. Read the next sentence.

General MARSHALL (reading):

Concerning the time of presenting this memorandum to the United States, I will wire you in a separate message. However, I want you, in the meantime, to put it in nicely drafted form and make every preparation to present it to the Americans just as soon as you receive instructions.

Senator FERGUSON. Now, General, doesn't that message [indicate] that there is going to be a zero time as far as the delivery of that message to the United States Government is concerned?

General MARSHALL. That is correct, sir.

Senator FERGUSON. Now, that being true, and having all these other messages and all this information, how do you account for the fact that that message when translated, when decoded on the 6th, was not delivered to you? The importance of that message is clear, is it not?

General MARSHALL. Yes, sir.

Senator FERGUSON. How do you account for it not being delivered to you on the 6th?

General MARSHALL. The only way I can account for that, Senator, is that the first thirteen parts, as I have been told, and I read, as I say, hurriedly here, the other day, most of that portion did not have the critical phase of the message included, which showed in the fourteenth part, and, as I have been told, I am not the authoritative witness on this,—that fourteenth part didn't come in too available, workable, or readable form, until sometime during the night, possibly was not available until the next morning.

The data will show that. Therefore, I presume the assumption was as it did not include the critical statements, that is, the first to the thirteenth part, it was not thought necessary to bring that to my immediate attention.

Senator FERGUSON. General, this message is not part of the fourteen-part message. This is a separate, short, independent message, giving a zero hour or a zero date, or time of the delivery of the message.

Now as I recall, going back through these intercepts, I find no other, and I want you to correct me if you know of any other, where a message was to be delivered at a particular time, and there was a pilot message before, indicating that there would be a zero time for delivery.

. . . .

Senator FERGUSON. How do you account for the fact that that message was not delivered to you?

General MARSHALL. I can give you nothing further than what I have said.

. . . .

Senator FERGUSON. Was there anyone alerted that could have received that particular message?

General MARSHALL. Well, there was someone on duty in the office of the Chief of Staff, there was someone on duty in the office of the War Plans Division, there was someone on duty in the office of G-2.

Senator FERGUSON. Was there anyone that could have acted?

General MARSHALL. Presumably so, yes, sir.

. . . .

Senator FERGUSON. Who had authority to actually receive magic as far as the Chief of Staff was concerned? It had to come to him in a locked pouch.

General MARSHALL. Yes, sir.

Senator FERGUSON. Did anyone have the key to the locked pouch other than you?

General MARSHALL. No, sir.

Senator FERGUSON. Therefore the only one in Washington so far as the Chief of Staff was concerned was the Chief of Staff himself who had the authority to receive it?

General MARSHALL. That is correct.

Senator FERGUSON. Now, was there anyone authorized to take the pouch and deliver it to you in your office?

General MARSHALL. In my office?

Senator FERGUSON. Yes, in your office, was there anyone actually able to receive the pouch? He didn't have the key to it, but receive the pouch?

General MARSHALL. It would be received in the office of the Secretary of the General Staff and delivered to me. Everything came through there unless it was brought in to me directly by the Assistant Chief of Staff.

Senator FERGUSON. Who was the Secretary on the 6th?

General MARSHALL. General Bedell Smith was the Secretary.

. . . .

Senator FERGUSON. He would have authority to take the actual pouch, would he not?

General MARSHALL. He would have authority, or anybody else on duty in his office, of taking the pouch in to me.

Senator FERGUSON. Was he alerted so that if the pouch would have come to him on the day of the 6th he would have immediately got to you?

General Marshall. I don't know that any special instructions were given Colonel Smith at all.

Senator Ferguson. Well, did you anticipate any messages? The message before said there would be a reply in 2 or 3 days.

General Marshall. Yes, sir.

Senator Ferguson. Now, was that of sufficient importance, and these other messages, to indicate that someone should have been alerted to receive this message and get it to you?

General Marshall. Senator, these were messages to the Secretary of State, these were diplomatic messages, all of which concerned important things. The delivery to Mr. Hull was the important direct requirement of the procedure. We deduced what we could out of the particular messages but the delivery to the Secretary of State of a diplomatic message from the Japanese was the issue of the moment.

. . . .

Senator Ferguson. And, now, have you ever made—personally, as I understand it, you conducted no examination or no inquiry as to why the parts were not delivered to you on Saturday that were completed and why one message, the pilot message, was not delivered to you?

General Marshall. I had no investigation of that; no, sir.

Senator Ferguson. And you haven't any other knowledge than what you have given here?

General Marshall. No, sir.

Senator Ferguson. Did Bedell Smith get in touch with you Saturday night?

General Marshall. Not to my knowledge.

Senator Ferguson. You were at home Saturday night?

General Marshall. The presumption is that I was at home.

Senator Ferguson. You mean to say now that you were?

General Marshall. I have not read my testimony through but think I saw in a paper something that may mean my testimony is not as I intended to give it.

Senator Ferguson. Well, do you want to change it? Not that you want to change your testimony, but do you want to reiterate what you said?

General MARSHALL. I want to repeat what I said, that I found an engagement book for the family that shows I only had one evening engagement, a dinner, between the 1st of November—the newsmen said the 1st of December—between the the 1st of November and the 7th of December and that was on the night of the 3rd of December.

Senator FERGUSON. If you left the house, for instance, on the night of the 6th of December was there someone there to answer the telephone?

General MARSHALL. Yes, sir; there was an orderly there.

Senator FERGUSON. An orderly?

General MARSHALL. Yes.

Senator FERGUSON. And he was in the Army in effect?

General MARSHALL. Yes, sir. I had three orderlies that rotated that duty at that time and for about a year thereafter they stayed until 10 o'clock, until I returned if I went out to the movies. That is the only place I went to.

. . . .

Senator FERGUSON. So that if Bedell Smith desired to get you that night there wasn't any reason why he should not have been able to get you?

General MARSHALL. I could have been obtainable.

Senator FERGUSON. And would that same thing be true with General Miles and Colonel Bratton?

General MARSHALL. Yes, sir; I would say it would.

. . . .

TESTIMONY OF MAJOR GENERAL SHERMAN MILES

(General Sherman Miles was the G-2 in Washington and had testified before.)

General MILES. Mr. Chairman, on reading the transcript of my testimony on Tuesday, December 4, I find certain inferences that I think should be clarified. I request the indulgence of the committee for about 5 minutes for that.

The CHAIRMAN. Proceed.

. . . .

General MILES. On Saturday, December 6, we were at peace with Japan; we were maintaining diplomatic relations with her; we were holding a diplomatic conference with her. We believed that the diplomatic conference would be broken as a result of Japanese refusal to accept our note of November 26. We also had serious reasons to fear, because of code burnings and other indications, that Japan might break diplomatic relations and go to war with the United States. But we had no proof of this.

Obviously, Japan had the option of agreeing to disagree, of breaking up the conference, of going ahead with her plans of conquest and putting it up to us to go to war in defense of the British, the Dutch, or the Siamese.

. . . .

General MILES. And that would have been a difficult thing to have done in the winter of 1941. That was another reason that we talked to the last about Thailand. That was probably one reason discussions were being held about a line beyond which Japan could not go without war.

In the meanwhile, 9 days before, our Pacific commands had been warned that hostile action by Japan was possible at any moment. They also knew that the Japanese were burning certain codes. We had nothing definite as to the time or place to add to that.

There we stood on the afternoon of the 6th when the pilot message came in. That told us that a 14-part reply to our note of November 26 would come in, that it would be long, that it was to be put in nice shape for delivery but not delivered until further notice. Certainly no indication here of anything threatening on the next day, Sunday.

Late on the night of the 6th the first 13 parts of the Japanese reply came in. It repeated their well worn arguments that it was all our fault, not theirs, and it concluded only that they could not accept our note of November 26 as a basis of negotiations. So far, so good—nothing unexpected in this. The fourteenth part would tell the story.

Some time between 8:30 and 9 on the morning of the 7th the fourteenth part came in from the Military Intelligence Division. It formally ruptured the conference but it went no further than that. Simultaneously the delivery message came in, 1 p.m. on a Sunday, a startling hour. It meant trouble somewhere, against someone, but still not necessarily against the United States. However, we knew something at last, not where and against whom, but when.

The action taken by the Chief of Staff, though unfortunately delayed, covered that situation perfectly.

Such was the information received successively on the 6th and the 7th, on which decision had to be taken. We could not look into the future as we can now look into the past. We had to deal with what we then had.

It seems to me that magic has been overstressed in one important aspect or respect. It was a priceless asset but its value in bringing to our Pacific garrisons a realization of impending war can be overemphasized.

It is highly significant that General MacArthur, who had magic, could not identify as having seen any of the most important magic messages and yet stated categorically that the War Department dispatches, which were not magic, were ample and complete for the purpose of alerting his command for war. It is also significant that the war warning dispatch of November 27 was not, apparently, based primarily on magic, but on our own decision of the previous day as to our position *vis-a-vis* the Japanese Government. Magic need not have been, and indeed was not, necessary to a true comprehension of the situation. . . .

Testimony Of General George C. Marshall
(Resumed)

. . . .

Mr. KEEFE. Now, at this point in the hearing, General Marshall, we get into the realm of some conflict.

Testimony has been read into the record here of Colonel Bratton given before the Army Board as to the delivery of this 13-part message, and the pilot message in the locked pouch which was very specific, very direct that he delivered it on the evening of the 6th to Col. Bedell Smith, Secretary to the Chief of Staff, and later in the Clausen investigation, a different situation developed.

I understood General Miles to testify that in view of the fact that there was to be a 14th part to this message, that perhaps that was the reason that Colonel Bratton did not deliver the 13 parts, and the pilot message, that night to you.

Now, I do not know what the fact is. I am simply trying to get the facts. At least as far as you know, General Marshall, there was no change in the orders to the Chief of G-2 by you?

General MARSHALL. No change by me.

Mr. KEEFE. And if an important message came in, it was the duty of G-2, and its courier, to see to it that that important message was brought to your attention immediately?

General MARSHALL. I would say so, sir.

Mr. KEEFE. All right.

Now, the fact is, as I think is undisputed, that you personally did not get this 13-part message on Saturday night.

General MARSHALL. That is correct, sir.

Mr. KEEFE. Nobody called you about it?

General MARSHALL. Not to my recollection.

.   .   .   .

Mr. KEEFE. Well, so far as you are concerned, General Marshall, you went to bed that night without any knowledge that the Japs were sending in any reply at all?

General MARSHALL. That is correct, sir.

Mr. KEEFE. And you got up in the morning without any such knowledge?

General MARSHALL. That is correct, sir.

Mr. KEEFE. And performed your Sunday morning functions as usual?

General MARSHALL. That is correct, sir.

Mr. KEEFE. In entire ignorance that this message had come in to the final fourteenth part, and instructions to deliver at 1 o'clock?

General MARSHALL. That is correct, sir.

Mr. KEEFE. So you went out for your morning horseback ride?

General Marshall. Correct, sir.

Mr. Keefe. And you have indicated that you got back to your house, and during or right after your shower there was a telephone call.

General Marshall. Yes, sir; I think during the shower.

Mr. Keefe. That was from Colonel Bratton?

General Marshall. That was from Colonel Bratton as I recall, wishing to come out to see me there, and I sent in word I would be right out to the War Department.

. . . .

Mr. Keefe. Well, the evidence seems to indicate that you got in your office about 11:25.

General Marshall. I think that evidence indicates the time we were preparing this message. Prior to that I had read this fourteen part message.

Mr. Keefe. I only go by the testimony of Colonel Bratton, whose testimony I have studied rather carefully, and I think he said 11:25.

General Marshall. I do not think that is correct. I think it is more nearly 11.

Mr. Keefe. Well, at least when you read the message, as has been indicated, it was getting pretty close to noon, wasn't it?

General Marshall. Yes, sir.

Mr. Keefe. You called up Stark, didn't you?

General Marshall. Yes.

Mr. Keefe. And talked with him.

General Marshall. Yes, sir; I called him up on the telephone.

Mr. Keefe. He wanted to know if you wanted to use the Navy radio to send the message out.

General Marshall. He asked me if I wanted to use the Navy radio. I first spoke to him about sending the message. I do not think he spoke in that first telephone conversation about the Navy radio. I think it is probable that that came in the second message, the second conversation 10 minutes later.

Mr. Keefe. At any event, in one of the conversations before the message was sent to your message center, you talked to Stark and he wanted to know if you wanted to use the Navy radio?

General Marshall. That is correct, sir.

Mr. Keefe. And you did not accept it?

General Marshall. I did not accept it.

Mr. Keefe. Well, when you were before the Army Board, General Marshall, there were some questions asked you at that time as to why you did not use the telephone, and you gave quite a long answer, if you recall, and in your answer you referred to the fact that, oh, it would have required getting those fellows out of bed out there in Hawaii at that hour. Do you remember that?

General Marshall. Well, I was talking about the time involved, and I was multiplying it by the number of places involved.

Mr. Keefe. And was that one of the reasons why you decided not to use the telephone, that perhaps it would take time getting the fellows out of bed in Hawaii?

General Marshall. I think you are giving a considerable emphasis to the "bed." I was talking about the time required to get the people on the phone and giving them the communication at the hour the communication would come in.

. . . .

Mr. Keefe. Yes.

Now, as a matter of fact, what sort of telephone service did you have to Hawaii at that time?

General Marshall. We had no special lines, but I think we had a scrambler. I know I had a scrambler on mine, and I think we had a scrambler on the phone.

Mr. Keefe. Did you have to use the ordinary commercial telephone service?

General Marshall. I think so, yes.

Mr. Keefe. Put in a call and ask to get somebody out there?

General Marshall. Well, as far as I recall, that was the situation at that particular time.

Mr. Keefe. You got a call that morning from somebody out there, and they got you out there right when the bombs were dropping?

General Marshall. I think I put in that call.

Mr. KEEFE. You may have put in the call later on that morning?
General MARSHALL. Yes, sir.
Mr. KEEFE. Whom did you call?
General MARSHALL. I called General Short, and I got his Chief of Staff, Colonel Phillips.
Mr. KEEFE. How long did it take you to get it?
General MARSHALL. I do not recall.
Mr. KEEFE. You got it right when the raid was in progress?
General MARSHALL. Yes, when the bombs fell.
Mr. KEEFE. There will be testimony from Mr. Shivers, the chief of the FBI out there, calling Mr. Hoover right when this was in progress without any difficulty at all, and he talked with him a short time on the telephone.
General MARSHALL. Yes.
Mr. KEEFE. Were you aware of the fact that the FBI had direct radio communications with Hawaii?
General MARSHALL. I was not, sir.
Mr. KEEFE. Did not the FBI let you know or tell you they had a radio communication tower over here at Bainbridge connected with San Diego and direct to Honolulu?
General MARSHALL. I have no doubt the War Department knew that, but I individually did not.
Mr. KEEFE. Did not anybody in this conference that morning on the 7th suggest that they could get word out there quickly by using either the Navy or the FBI radio?
General MARSHALL. I think everyone in that conference thought the Army radio would get word out there as quickly as any other, and it did, I believe, everywhere but Hawaii.
Mr. KEEFE. This message went by Western Union, did it not?
General MARSHALL. Yes, sir, I am told it went by Western Union, then RCA, and then a boy.
Mr. KEEFE. Did you have direct radio communications with Hawaii at that time, that is, the Army?
General MARSHALL. The reason it was sent that way at that time is they could not raise Hawaii on their radio, and they did not turn to anything else but sent it the way I described.

Mr. KEEFE. Do you understand that the Army Signal Corps tried to get into contact with somebody and raise them up there at Hawaii?

General MARSHALL. As I understand it—and that can be testified to directly—they proceeded on the basis of a radio message to each place. They were unable to raise Hawaii. They raised the Philippines and they raised the Caribbean, but they did not raise Hawaii, and then they turned to this other method of sending the message through.

Mr. KEEFE. Did anybody ever try to find out what was the matter out there that they could not raise them?

General MARSHALL. I do not know whether it was static or what it was, but I have been told since that the Navy radio was a more powerful set than the Army radio.

Mr. KEEFE. And the message got there after the raid had started?

General MARSHALL. That is right, sir.

. . . .

Mr. KEEFE. Do I understand, General Marshall, and is it fair to conclude from your testimony, that you fix responsibility for this disaster upon General Short so far as the Army is concerned?

General MARSHALL. I have never made that statement, sir.

I feel that General Short was given a command instruction to put his command on the alert against a possible hostile attack by the Japanese. The command was not so alerted.

Mr. KEEFE. Well, I will ask the same question, from a full and complete knowledge of the situation and the responsibility involved, do you assume any responsibility for this disaster at Pearl Harbor?

General MARSHALL. I assume the responsibility, as I already stated, in connection with Short's acknowledgment of the alert message, in not detecting that that did not indicate a full alert but merely a sabotage alert.

. . . .

Mr. GEARHART. Don't you think the specific inquiry from Tokyo in reference to ship movements in Honolulu and in

Pearl Harbor was not sufficiently important to convey to the commanders in Hawaii?

General MARSHALL. I can only answer that, Mr. Gearhart, by repeating again what I am saying, that this information was coming in regarding many points in the world. It is very significant in the light of the knowledge of what the Japs actually did, it is very significant as to that, but at the time there were a great many messages about a great many places, and there were a great many people involved in evaluating those messages. Certainly none of them, certainly no one of them, was endeavoring to avoid an evident indication of just where the Japanese were going to strike, if they were going to strike. That did not so register; that did not so register.

Mr. GEARHART. General, you do not justify yourself for not sending specific information to Admiral Kimmel and General Short to which they were entitled simply because you failed to send to other commanders and other generals in other areas information to which they were entitled?

General MARSHALL. Will you repeat that, please?

(The question was read by the reporter.)

General MARSHALL. No, sir. I am speaking about the evaluation of that, as to what it meant, what its significance was at the time the messages came in.

Mr. GEARHART. If there had been a specific inquiry from Tokyo intercepted by us in respect to ship dispositions in Panama, would it not have been your duty, as the possessor of that information, to advise the commanders of Panama that the Japanese were showing an inordinate interest in the situation there, and tell them what that interest reflected?

General MARSHALL. If it did not seem to be a portion of their routine inquiries regarding our shipping and our fleet, wherever the shipping was, or wherever the fleet was.

Mr. GEARHART. In the light of the fact that Hawaii had been bombed, with a terrific result, don't you think now, that you should have sent the information in these seven intercepts in respect to Japan's inquiry into the shipping arrangements at Hawaii?

General MARSHALL. That is asking a very definite backsight.

I do not necessarily think so. I am still in the position of feeling that when you give a command to a high officer you expect to have it executed.

Mr. GEARHART. But don't you think that you were withholding vital information from Admiral Kimmel and General Short when you did not advise them of these particular seven messages?

General MARSHALL. It did not appear vital at that time. It appeared to be a portion of a general resume by the Japanese doing what we eventually thought they would do all over the world.

Mr. GEARHART. Will you tell us now, General, why, at that time that information did not impress you as vital?

General MARSHALL. I could not answer that, sir. As a matter of fact, I testified that I did not have a definite recollection of these particular messages. I must assume that I saw them. They did not register on my mind according to your reaction as stated here by you.

Just what their reaction was I do not know. There was no evaluation of them brought to me by G-2 of the character that you have indicated.

. . . .

Mr. GEARHART. Then your answer is as you gave it first, that if these messages had been transmitted to General Short and Admiral Kimmel at the time they were received, things might have been different at Hawaii?

General MARSHALL. Things might have been different. The same instructions, however, were sent literally to the Philippines, and they were sent also to Panama, and the alerts were executed, and the additional information was not sent.

. . . .

THE EVENTS IN WASHINGTON

American intelligence agencies had broken the Japanese code long before Pearl Harbor. Whether or not proper use was made of these "magic" intercepts, especially the final fourteen-part message from Tokyo, and whether or not the so-called "winds execute" message was heard in Washington became an object of intense scrutiny in the various investigations. The following excerpts consist of testimony of Captain Laurence F. Safford, who headed the Navy Department Communications Intelligence Unit; Captain Alwin D. Kramer, who did the actual translating, and Commander Lester R. Schulz, who delivered the final message to the President. The fourteen parts and related messages have been included.

Pearl Harbor Attack, VIII, 3555-3563; 3567-3586; 3601, 3893-3912; *ibid.,* IX, 3935-3936; *ibid.,* X, 4659-4664 (Testimony before the Joint Congressional Committee on the Investigation of the Pearl Harbor Attack, February 1, 2, 6, 7, and 15, 1946); *Pearl Harbor Attack,* XII, 238-245, 248, Exhibit 1 (14-part and related messages).

Testimony Of Capt. Laurence Frye Safford, United States Navy

Pearl Harbor Attack, VIII, 3555-3563; 3567-3586, 3601.

(Having been duly sworn by the Vice Chairman.)

Mr. RICHARDSON. Captain Safford, will you give your full name and age to the reporter?

Captain SAFFORD. Laurence Frye Safford. Age 53 years.

. . . .

Mr. RICHARDSON. Will you detail in a general way to the committee, Captain, just what your naval experience has been, the general work that you have done and the present position which you occupy?

Captain SAFFORD. After graduation from the Naval Academy

I served in battleships, destroyers, submarines, mine craft, cruisers, and battleships. I have had a total of 14 years' sea duty, the last 3 of which being spent as gunnery officer on the battleship *New Mexico*.

I was in charge of the Antiaircraft Gunnery School in the summer of 1935, which was fairly successful.

All my shore duty has been spent in my specialty as a cipher expert and radio intelligence expert. I came ashore to assume this duty in charge of the Navy Department Communications Intelligence Unit in May 1936, and remained on that duty until February 15, 1942, at which time I was removed by the orders of Admiral Horne.

. . . .

Mr. RICHARDSON. Are you on active service in the Navy now?

Captain SAFFORD. At the present time I am on active service in the Navy and am called the Assistant Director of Naval Communications for cryptographic research.

. . . .

Mr. RICHARDSON. You recall in a general way that it was a message which came into this country from Japan in 13—first a pilot message that was followed by a 13-part message.

Now will you tell me when you first heard of anything with reference to what turned out to be the 14th part message?*

Captain SAFFORD. I probably heard of the pilot message in the early afternoon of Saturday, December 6, 1941, although I cannot recall it.

. . . .

Mr. RICHARDSON. Why would you think that would be a particularly important message?

Captain SAFFORD. Because it gave information that the long-awaited reply to the Secretary of State note of the 26th of November was about to be transmitted.

. . . .

Mr. RICHARDSON. When this message began to come in was

---

* See pp. 225 ff.

there any attempt made to make any delivery of any portion of it prior to the reception of the first 13 parts?

Captain SAFFORD. No, sir; not to my knowledge, except that Commander McCollum, who was the head of the Japanese section, Naval Intelligence, knew that the message was in and coming in and being worked on when it was partially in. I think he knew that around 3 or 4 o'clock in the afternoon.

Mr. RICHARDSON. But there was no delivery outside of your office of this message so that anyone could read it or see it or know of it or act on it or deliver it until the first 13 parts had come in, was there?

Captain SAFFORD. The message was not ready for delivery until about 9 o'clock in the evening. It might have been ready for delivery a little earlier on a limited scale.

Mr. RICHARDSON. Now, by "the message" you refer to the first 13 parts?

Captain SAFFORD. I mean the first 13 parts.

Mr. RICHARDSON. Did you consider the first 13 parts as a complete message for the purpose of delivery?

Captain SAFFORD. I never saw the first 13 parts until Monday morning.

Mr. RICHARDSON. When did you last see or hear anything of the message of Saturday, December 6th?

Captain SAFFORD. I left the office at the close of working hours, 4:30 p.m. on Saturday, December 6th. It was the first time in 2 weeks that I had observed normal working hours.

At that time Commander Linn had come on and was re-working the message. There had been a mistake in the key which was set up on the machine which decoded the message and the whole entire part which we had in there was badly garbled and because of its importance Linn thought it was better to check the key first and find out the mistake and produce perfect copy rather than to clear the garble by guess and maybe make mistakes at critical points in the message. This would take quite a little bit of time and we simply had to throw away all the work that had been done before.

Linn was my best man on the watch side. Normally I do not expect watches from a man in charge of a section. He was taking the place of a man whom we had let go on Christmas eve and we were hoping that we would be able to get somebody else to take his place.

Kramer was standing by to deliver the message. As soon as it was completed McCollum knew about it.

Mr. RICHARDSON. Were you there?

Captain SAFFORD. I was there until 4:30. I checked it and said:

There is nothing I can do but get in your way and make you nervous. I am going home.

Mr. RICHARDSON. Then after 4:30 you knew nothing of your own knowledge as to what happened to the 13-part message?

Captain SAFFORD. Until Monday morning, when I got the reports from Linn and Kramer on it.

. . . .

Mr. RICHARDSON. I now want to ask you some questions, Captain, about what is known as the winds code. . . .

. . . when you were called, you knew you were going to be a witness here, you prepared a written statement indicating what you wished to present to the committee on the winds code?*

Captain SAFFORD. That is correct.

. . . .

Mr. RICHARDSON. With the Committee's permission, I would ask him to read it.

The CHAIRMAN. Without objection, it will be read.

. . . .

Will you go ahead, Captain?

Captain SAFFORD. Yes, sir. The statement regarding the winds message will start with—

PREVIEW

There was a Winds Message. It meant War—and we knew it meant War. By the best estimate that can be made from my recollection and the circumstantial evidence now available, the

* See p. 153.

"Winds Message" was part of a Japanese Overseas "News" Broadcast from Station JAP (Tokyo) on 11980 kilocycles beginning at 1330 Greenwich Civil Time on Thursday, December 4, 1941. This time corresponded to 10:30 p.m. Tokyo time and 8:30 a.m. Washington time, December 4, 1941. The broadcast was probably in Japanese Morse code, and was originally written in the Kata-Kana form of written, plain language Japanese. It was intercepted by the U. S. Navy at the big radio receiving station at Cheltenham, Maryland, which served the Navy Department. It was recorded on a special typewriter, developed by the Navy, which types the Roman-letter equivalents of the Japanese characters.

. . . .

The Winds Message broadcast was forwarded to the Navy Department by TWX (teletypewriter exchange) from the teletype-transmitter in the "Intercept" receiving room at Cheltenham to "WA91," the page printer located beside the GY Watch Officer's desk, in the Navy Department Communication Intelligence Unit under my command. I saw the Winds Message typed in page form on yellow teletype paper, with the translation written below. I immediately forwarded this message to my Commanding Officer (Rear Admiral Leigh Noyes, USN), thus fully discharging my responsibility in the matter.

. . . .

When I first saw the Winds Message, it had already been translated by Lieutenant Commander Kramer, in charge of the Translation Section of the Navy Department Communication Intelligence Unit. Kramer had underscored all three "code phrases" on the original incoming teletype sheet. Below the printed message was written in pencil or colored crayon in Kramer's handwriting, the following free translations:

War with England (including NEI, etc.)
War with the U. S.
Peace with Russia.

I am not sure of the order; but it was the same as in the broadcast and I think England appeared first. I think Kramer used "U. S." rather than "United States." It is possible that the words "No war," instead of "Peace," were used to describe Japan's intentions with regards to Russia.

"This is *it!*" said Kramer as he handed me the Winds Message. This was the broadcast we had strained every nerve to intercept. This was the feather in our cap. This was the tip-off which would prevent the U. S. Pacific Fleet being surprised at Pearl Harbor the way the Russians had been surprised at Port Arthur. This was what the Navy Communication Intelligence had been preparing for since its establishment in 1924—*War with Japan!*

. . . .

Mr. RICHARDSON. Now, Captain, I want you to know that I do not care a tinker's damn whether the winds execute message came in or whether it did not. I am only interested in whether there should be reviewed by the committee all of the reliable facts that can be adduced so they can reach a conclusion.

I do not want to mislead you or browbeat you, if I talk rather loudly. It is because I am a rather loud talking individual.

I just want to make it clear that when you started, in the fall of 1943 to prepare yourself as a witness, your whole recollection was exceedingly hazy as to what had happened 2 years before, wasn't it?

Captain SAFFORD. There were a few outstanding facts and the details linking them together were very hazy.

Mr. RICHARDSON. Now, let me read you what you testified to on that point in the Hewitt investigation, at page 112:

Captain SAFFORD. In the fall of 1943, it appeared there was going to be a trial, a court martial of Admiral Kimmel. It was hinted in the newspapers and various people in the Navy Department were getting testimony ready for it. I realized I would be one of the important witnesses that my memory was very vague, and I began looking around to get everything that I could to prepare a written statement which I could follow as testimony.

That was the time when I studied the Roberts report carefully for the first time, and noted no reference to the winds message, or to the message which McCollum had written, and which I had seen, and which I thought had been sent, and then I began talking to everybody who had been around at the time and who knew I had been mixed up in it, to see what they could remember to straighten me out on the thing, and give me leads to follow down to where I got my hands on official messages, and things so it would be a matter of fact and not a matter of memory. . . . .

The investigation was conducted, if you call it that, for the purpose of preparing myself to take the stand as a witness in a prospective court-martial of Admiral Kimmel.

Now, you regard that today, do you not, Captain, as a fair statement of how you brought your mind to a factual conclusion as to what happened during that period, that week prior to Pearl Harbor, in the fall of 1943?

Captain SAFFORD. That is correct.

. . . .

Mr. RICHARDSON. Now, Captain, you were exceedingly anxious to get hold of an execute message to the winds code, were you not?

Captain SAFFORD. I first looked for the—

Mr. RICHARDSON. (interposing). No, no. I am asking you as to your mental condition. You were very anxious, while you waited to see what the monitoring stations would send in to see when an execute code would come in?

Captain SAFFORD. That is correct.

. . . .

Mr. RICHARDSON. All right.

Now, were the words *"HIGASHI NO KAZEAME"* in the middle of the broadcast?

Captain SAFFORD. That is the place they were underscored.

Mr. RICHARDSON. Were they also at the end?

Captain SAFFORD. I do not know now. They were not underscored at the end if they were there.

Mr. RICHARDSON. That would be a very important item in order to ascertain whether this was intended to be an execute of 2353, would it not?

Captain SAFFORD. Not necessarily. They would be repeated at the end only as a precaution so that if they missed the early part of the broadcast, they could pick it up at the last and not lose it.

Mr. RICHARDSON. Just a minute, Captain. Don't you think you are extending your authority a little when you interpret what the Japanese meant in a code direction? Did not you tell me a few minutes ago that every one of those directions that were contained in 2353 were important to be considered in determining whether or not a given message was an execute message?

Captain SAFFORD. I said they were important, that is correct.

Mr. RICHARDSON. Well, you did not even look to find out whether these three sets of words that had been translated were also at the end of the message, did you?

Captain SAFFORD. I never made such a statement.

Mr. RICHARDSON. Well, you did not?

Captain SAFFORD. I said I cannot remember whether they were repeated at the end or not. I was well satisfied that that message was authentic, an authentic signal of the execute given by the Japanese Government.

Mr. RICHARDSON. Captain, I am not the least interested in whether you are satisfied or not. I am only interested in ascertaining whether, when you saw the message, you endeavored to ascertain, as a careful, trained Intelligence man, whether it was an execute of the winds code message 2353, and consequently I asked you, first, was it in the middle and you said "yes"; and I then asked you, was it at the end, and you said you did not look.

Now, third, was each sentence repeated twice?

Captain SAFFORD. I did not say I did not look. I said I could not tell you from present memory.

. . . .

Mr. RICHARDSON. . . . .

You know, do you not, Captain, now that Kramer has three times in his sworn testimony heretofore, denied that he saw anything in this message with reference to Japanese words relating to the United States, and says that the only thing there was in the message he saw had reference to Russia. You know that, don't you?

Captain SAFFORD. I did not know that.

. . . .

Mr. RICHARDSON. Now, Captain, will you take a look again at Exhibit 142 and turn over to the dispatch from the commander in chief of the Army forces in the Pacific under date of November 13, 1945? . . . . Now, from your experience in this message and intelligence work wouldn't you construe that message from MacArthur as indicating that the Japanese never sent out an implementing message?

Captain SAFFORD. I would not.

Mr. RICHARDSON. Why not?

Captain SAFFORD. It says here:

> Interrogation of authorities so far has resulted in absolute denial of transmission of such an implementing message and existence of any prearranged instructions which would permit transmission of such an implementing signal.

In other words, the Japanese authorities denied ever having sent Tokyo circular 2343 and 2354.

. . . .

Mr. RICHARDSON. All right. Now, turning over to the dispatch from MacArthur of November 21, how do you interpret the language used:

> That signal implementing circular 2353 and 2354 was probably not transmitted prior to 8 December, Tokyo time, but was transmitted by radio voice at some hour after 0230, 8 December, Tokyo time. Exact hour unknown.

How would yon interpret that language?

Captain SAFFORD. That they had not found anybody who knew it or admitted it but MacArthur was not certain and, therefore, he said "probably" "probably not then transmitted."

. . . .

Mr. RICHARDSON. Now, turn over to the dispatch of the 24th, the next following, the language reading:

> Only use of Winds code (either voice or radio telegraph) shown here by available contemporaneous records is voice broadcast from Tokyo between 0902 and 0935 on 8 December.

That also indicates that the response from the Japanese records further was negative on this execute, doesn't it?

Captain SAFFORD. I do not agree with that, sir.

. . . .

Mr. RICHARDSON. All right. Now, go on over to the one of the 27th from MacArthur where he says that:

> Persons who conducted interrogation had no knowledge that prior to interrogation United States had information establishing use of Winds code on 8 December Tokyo time.

Making it certain that the people who were doing the interrogating did not know what they did it for would be important, wouldn't it?

Captain SAFFORD. That is correct.

Mr. RICHARDSON. Well, turn over now to the document entitled, "U. S. Naval Technical Mission to Japan," one or two pages following the one I just read from. Do you have that before you?

Captain SAFFORD. I have that before me.

Mr. RICHARDSON. Now, look at the last paragraph on that page where the person making the document says:

> He stated that he would have known of it if a message such as that described as being broadcast December 4 had been transmitted and that he had no recollection at all of any "east wind rain" report or any similar phrase being broadcast prior to December 8.

That would also indicate that they did not know out there if the man was telling the truth that there had been any winds execute message until December 8, doesn't it?

Captain SAFFORD. I would not consider that conclusive.

. . . .

Testimony Of Capt. Alwin Dalton Kramer, United States Navy

Pearl Harbor Attack, VIII, 3895-3912; *ibid.,* IX, 3935-3936.

(Having been first duly sworn by the Chairman.)

The CHAIRMAN. Counsel will proceed.

Mr. RICHARDSON. If the chair permits, I shall follow the same course of conduct with Captain Kramer that I did with Captain Safford because Captain Kramer's testimony, like that of Captain Safford, applies to two main evidentiary issues in this hearing, first with reference to the 14-part message, with which he was intimately connected, and second with reference to the asserted winds execute message which has been recently discussed with Captain Safford.

Captain, will you give your name in full to the reporter?

Captain KRAMER. Captain Alwin Dalton Kramer, United States Navy.

. . . .

Mr. RICHARDSON. Do you speak Japanese?

Captain KRAMER. I do, sir.

Mr. RICHARDSON. Fluently?

Captain KRAMER. I will leave that to my betters to judge.

Mr. RICHARDSON. Were you supposed to be a fluent Japanese linguist?

Captain KRAMER. I presume I was supposed to be.

Mr. RICHARDSON. What were your duties, Captain, during the months of November and December 1941 in a detailed way, if you will describe them to us?

Captain KRAMER. I was in charge of a section in the Division of Naval Communications which was a subsection under then Commander Safford, known as the Communications Security Group.

GZ was the subsection concerned with the translation of decrypted ciphers and the recovery of Japanese codes. My permanent assignment was to the Far East Section of the Division of Naval Intelligence.

As a subordinate of the Director of Naval Intelligence I was given the further duty of disseminating at the direction of the Director of Naval Intelligence or my immediate superior, the head of the Far East section, translations produced in my section.

. . . .

Mr. RICHARDSON. Now, do you recall the fact of what has been referred here as the incident relating to the so-called 14-part message?*

Captain KRAMER. I am not certain what incident you refer to, sir.

Mr. RICHARDSON. I mean the entire incident of there having been a 14-part message.

Captain KRAMER. I believe I am thoroughly familiar; yes, sir.

Mr. RICHARDSON. Now, when was the first thing that brought into existence in your mind what later turned out to be this incident that I refer to?

Captain KRAMER. I am as certain as I can be, sir, that the first knowledge I had that the Japanese note was being sent to the United States was around 3 or shortly after 3 p.m. Saturday, December 6, 1941.

The issue of that time arose from this circumstance: Because of traffic on hand at noontime on Saturday, December 6, I requested certain of the translators to remain on past the regular working hours, about a quarter of 1, to clean it up. They were still there at about 3 p.m. Before releasing them for the afternoon I made a final check with the teletype and the GY watch officer to see if anything were coming in on the Tokyo-to-Washington circuit, in other words, dispatches originating in Tokyo addressed to Washington, which might by any chance either be such a note in reply to Secretary Hull's note of November 26 or which might bear on these negotiations.

When I made that check there was something coming in on the teletype so addressed. I therefore requested the translators to hold on for a while longer, until we broke down that message coming in.

Within, I recollect, one-half hour or less the first part of a message we broke down was broken to the extent of reading

* See pp. 225 ff.

the first few lines of the text of the message, specifically the first part of the first line, which is an internal indicator of how many parts there are to that message. That was standard Japanese practice and procedure.

The first part we broke down I rather distinctly recollect was part 8 of a 14-part message.* After about the third line, as I recollect, it went into English text with many insertions of three letter code groups, indicating statements of various kinds.

Does that answer your question, sir?

Mr. RICHARDSON. Proceed and carry through what happened with reference to that message during the afternoon while you were there.

Captain KRAMER. Well, then—

Mr. KEEFE. Mr. Chairman, might I ask before counsel starts on this line, whether or not the 3 or 3:15 message refers to the pilot message or the first 13 parts?

Mr. RICHARDSON. Was there, Captain, what may be called a preliminary pilot message a part of this incident?

Captain KRAMER. I believe, Mr. Counsellor, that you are referring to Tokyo Serial 901 on page 238 of Exhibit 1. I have no recollection of seeing that message until later in the afternoon, although it is possible that the Army delivered it to my section earlier in the afternoon.

I would like to invite your attention to the fact that at the foot of that message there is indicated as a file number, "J. D. 7149"; that at the foot of each of the parts of the 14-part note is "File No. 7143," six numbers earlier. I stated that I was uncertain whether that came in earlier in the afternoon or not. In any case, it was not stamped with a file number until approximately 8:30 that evening for dissemination.

Mr. RICHARDSON. When had the first 13 parts finished coming in?

Captain KRAMER. My recollection is that the last of the first 13 parts was coming in about 7:30 that evening.

Mr. RICHARDSON. Did you make a more or less detailed examination of those 13 parts?

* See p. 231.

Captain KRAMER. Yes, sir.

Mr. RICHARDSON. From your experience in the matter and your familiarity with other dispatches, particularly the intercepts between Tokyo and the United States, were you impressed with anything unusual about these 13 parts as you read them?

Captain KRAMER. I have stated that the first part I recollect seeing is part 8. If you will refer to that you will see that there is nothing in that part—in fact, the last half of that part quotes the United States note—that was materially different than the general tenor of previous notes back and forth between the United States and Japan.

When the first 13 parts were complete I did, however, have that distinct impression, that this note was far and appreciably stronger language than earlier notes had been and that indicated a strong probability that the Japanese were concluding any further negotiations.

Mr. RICHARDSON. That was the impression you had?

Captain KRAMER. Yes, sir.

Mr. RICHARDSON. Now, was the message translated and in shape for delivery further into the Navy Department by 7:30 in the evening?

Captain KRAMER. It was not, no, sir.

Mr. RICHARDSON. When, as near as you can recall—and bear in mind, Captain, that everyone here recognizes that recollections are only recollections.

Captain KRAMER. Yes, sir.

Mr. RICHARDSON. About what time do you think this 13-part message was ready for delivery?

Captain KRAMER. I am quite certain regarding my times that that was ready for delivery. Briefly it is as follows:

The folders for delivery to the usual recipients of this traffic were in process of preparation about between 8:30 and a quarter of 9 Saturday evening. At about a quarter of 9 I commenced my usual practice of phoning to the probable locations of these usual recipients.

Mr. RICHARDSON. And who would those recipients normally be?

Captain KRAMER. The Secretary of the Navy, Mr. Knox;

Chief of Naval Operations, Admiral Stark, or his flag secretary, then Commander Wellborn; Director of Naval Intelligence, Admiral Wilkinson; the head of the Far East section of the Division of Naval Intelligence, then Commander McCollum; the Director of War Plans Division, Admiral Turner; and either the White House directly or the naval aide to the President, then Captain Beardall.

Mr. RICHARDSON. Would there be any distribution made to the Army?

Captain KRAMER. Distribution was automatically made to the Army of all messages typed by my section. Within a matter of minutes or at most a couple of hours after they were typed.

Mr. RICHARDSON. And to whom would they go as representing the Army?

Captain KRAMER. To the parallel section to mine in the Signal Intelligence Section of the Army.

Mr. RICHARDSON. Who was in charge of that, if you recall?

Captain KRAMER. I believe then Captain Doud, or Major Doud, was in charge of that section.

Mr. RICHARDSON. But you had no further duty with respect to dissemination of any such message within the Army beyond the delivery to the Doud section?

Captain KRAMER. That is correct, sir.

Mr. RICHARDSON. But it was your duty, as I understand your testimony, to arrange for the delivery of the message to the individuals connected with the naval establishment whom you have just identified in your testimony?

Captain KRAMER. In general, that is correct, sir. My responsibility in that regard was as a subordinate of the Director of Naval Intelligence. In carrying out those responsibilities I was acting for him. I could, and on a number of occasions did, make special deliveries on his direction.

Mr. RICHARDSON. Did you physically make any deliveries yourself of such messages?

Captain KRAMER. In most cases I physically made the deliveries myself.

Mr. RICHARDSON. Well, when the first 13 parts of this message we are talking about had been completed and had been translated, and was in shape to be delivered, did you deliver it?

Captain KRAMER. I began to describe what I was doing at a quarter of 9. If I may continue I think it will answer your question.

Mr. RICHARDSON. Go ahead.

Captain KRAMER. I phoned the usual recipients I have already named at their offices or homes in order to locate them. As I have indicated, that was my usual practice day or night.

Mr. RICHARDSON. Well, now, you will pardon me if I interrupt you as you go along, because I have to get it into my head my way. When you telephoned a recipient would you give that recipient over the telephone any information as to why you were telephoning him and what you proposed to tell him?

Captain KRAMER. In cryptic language, yes. Generally it was in such terms as, "I have something important that I believe you should see at once," or something of that nature.

Mr. RICHARDSON. Well, now, go ahead with your narration as to what occurred on Saturday night.

Captain KRAMER. I phoned the quarters of Admiral Stark on Observatory Circle on Massachusetts Avenue, but could not reach him. He was apparently not at home. I similarly phoned Admiral Turner's home. I phoned the situation room at the White House.

Mr. RICHARDSON. What do you mean by the "situation room"?

Captain KRAMER. It was a room on the ground floor, south side, in the center of the White House which the naval aide, Captain Beardall, had set up a month or two before, equipped with maps to follow the war in Europe and to assist, presumably, the President with those maps and to have a center to handle any messages or traffic of intelligence from the Navy Department.

Mr. RICHARDSON. Who was Beardall?

Captain KRAMER. Naval aide to the President.

Mr. RICHARDSON. And who was under him in that work at the White House?

Captain KRAMER. When that room was set up my recollection is that there was initially one Army and one Navy junior officer as assistants. Other assistants were brought in later. I believe at about the time of Pearl Harbor a classmate of mine at the Naval Academy, then Lieutenant Commander Leahy, was put in charge of those assistants to the situation room.

Mr. RICHARDSON. Now proceed with what you did by way of handling this message, the 13 parts message.

Captain KRAMER. I further phoned then Commander McCollum at his home in Alexandria, indicating what had come in in cryptic terms on the phone, and after completing these various phone calls then phoned Admiral Wilkinson at his home in Arlington to inform him of whom I had been able to contact.

First I informed him of the nature of what I had that I felt should be delivered at once, and further informed him what I proposed to do in the way of delivery. He approved my proposals, which consisted of delivery to the White House, to Mr. Knox, who, incidentally, I had also phoned, and then to his home.

Mr. RICHARDSON. Whose home?

Captain KRAMER. Admiral Wilkinson's home.

Mr. RICHARDSON. Yes, well, at about what time did you start out to make these deliveries?

Captain KRAMER. There was one other phone call I made and that was to my own home, to my wife, asking her to be my chauffeur.

Mr. RICHARDSON. I thought, Captain, you were going to ask permission. Proceed.

Captain KRAMER. She very graciously complied and did act as my chauffeur during the evening.

We reached the White House, I should say, about 9:15, where, as I recollect it, one of these junior aides to Captain Beardall was on duty. I do not recall whether it was the Army or the naval aide; in fact, they may both have been there. I left rather categorical instructions with him to get that folder to the President as quickly as possible.

Mr. RICHARDSON. Would you mind telling us the exact language as near as you can remember it?

Captain KRAMER. I said in approximately these terms that "there was something in this folder"—which, incidentally was inside a locked pouch—"that the President should see as quickly as possible." I was given to understand that the President was entertaining at the moment. I learned only within the last couple of months that Mrs. Roosevelt was entertaining rather than the President. I learned only the last few days who was being entertained, when Captain Safford testified—and told him that when I had phoned Admiral Wilkinson I was informed that the naval aide, Captain Beardall, was at dinner at Admiral Wilkinson's home. I therefore told this assistant of Captain Beardall's that I would show it to him, that I would show it to the aide when I reached Admiral Wilkinson's home and that very likely he would get in touch with him at that time to find out whether Mr. Roosevelt had seen this traffic. From there—

Mr. RICHARDSON. Now, you said that this message was in a locked pouch. Was it customary when you delivered messages that they be kept in a locked pouch?

Captain KRAMER. Invariably; yes, sir.

Mr. RICHARDSON. Who had the key to the pouch?

Captain KRAMER. The recipients and my section only.

Mr. RICHARDSON. The pouch then, as I take it, was not opened until you reached the recipient who was to receive the message?

Captain KRAMER. That is correct, sir.

.   .   .   .

Mr. RICHARDSON. Did you deliver a copy of this 13-part section to the aide in charge at the White House on this evening around 9:15?

Captain KRAMER. That is correct, sir.

Mr. RICHARDSON. And where did you go after leaving the White House?

Captain KRAMER. To the Wardman Park Hotel on Connecticut Avenue.

Mr. RICHARDSON. Whom did you see there?

Captain KRAMER. Mr. Knox, the Secretary of the Navy.

Mr. RICHARDSON. Did you have any conversation with the Secretary?

Captain KRAMER. Yes, sir, I did.

Mr. RICHARDSON. What was the nature of it?

Captain KRAMER. The first twenty minutes or so of my presence in his apartment, where there were also incidentally Mrs. Knox and a civilian business associate of Mr. Knox, I believe acting manager of the Chicago Daily News, whom I had seen on frequent occasions in his outer office in the Navy Department—Mr. Knox read the dispatches for the first 20 minutes or so. During that time there was very little said. During that time I sat near him in a corner of the room part of the time, the rest of the time engaged in general conversation with the other two people present.

Mr. RICHARDSON. Was there anything said after the Secretary completed his examination of the document?

Captain KRAMER. Not specifically bearing on this traffic in the folder he was reading. Mr. Knox was very security-minded and had been since he was indoctrinated, if I may use that term, into the security features and identified in handling this traffic and I do not believe customarily discussed this decrypted traffic with either his wife or his business associates.

Mr. RICHARDSON. Was there anything said by the Secretary with respect to taking any action on the message which he had read?

Captain KRAMER. There was not, sir.

Mr. RICHARDSON. Now, about what time do you think you left the Wardman Park?

Captain KRAMER. Between 9:45 and quarter of 10 I should say.

Mr. RICHARDSON. Whither did you go?

Captain KRAMER. To Arlington, Va., the home of Admiral Wilkinson.

Mr. RICHARDSON. Now, when you arrived at the home of Admiral Wilkinson who in respect to the Naval Establishment did you find there?

Captain KRAMER. Admiral Wilkinson was present, also Captain Beardall. I have had my memory refreshed only quite recently to the effect that General Miles was also present.

Mr. RICHARDSON. Was Admiral Wilkinson there?

Captain KRAMER. Admiral Wilkinson was there; yes, sir.

Mr. RICHARDSON. To whom did you make delivery at the Wilkinson home?

Captain KRAMER. To Admiral Wilkinson in the first instance. Captain Beardall also read the traffic from an extra folder I had. General Miles also perused it.

Mr. RICHARDSON. Was there any discussion of it while they were perusing it or following the perusal?

Captain KRAMER. Yes, sir; there was.

Mr. RICHARDSON. Can you give us the general nature of it?

Captain KRAMER. The general nature of it was to the effect that it certainly looked as though the Japanese were terminating negotiations with the United States. Other than that I can recall no specific phraseology used.

Mr. RICHARDSON. Was there anything said in that conversation by any of them with respect to sending any message or taking any action based on this traffic?

Captain KRAMER. No, sir; there was not.

Mr. RICHARDSON. About what time do you think you left the Wilkinson home?

Captain KRAMER. It was about 12:30; after midnight.

Mr. RICHARDSON. And did you attempt to make any further deliveries that night?

Captain KRAMER. I did not.

Mr. RICHARDSON. You went home, I presume, from the Wilkinson home?

Captain KRAMER. No, sir. I never took these folders with encrypted traffic to my home. They were returned—speaking specifically of the copies shown Mr. Knox and Admiral Wilkinson and the extra copy I had—to my safe in section GZ in the Navy Department.

Mr. RICHARDSON. Then when you returned to your office where your safe was, were all of the copies of this message that you had started out to deliver returned to your safe or did certain copies remain with certain recipients?

Captain KRAMER. The only copy that remained out that I recollect was the one left in the situation room at the White House in a locked pouch.

Mr. RICHARDSON. How long did you remain in your office upon your return there when you put these documents in your safe?

Captain KRAMER. Probably 10 or 15 minutes, checking with the GY watch officer to see if anything new of interest or importance had come in.

Mr. RICHARDSON. Did you have reason to believe at that time that there was still another part of this message to come in?

Captain KRAMER. I had positive knowledge that there was another part. There were 14 parts indicated as the number of parts of this message, and we still had only 13 parts.

Mr. RICHARDSON. Did you inquire from your staff there as to whether the fourteenth part had come in?

Captain KRAMER. That was one of the things I specifically inquired about.

Mr. RICHARDSON. And you ascertained what as to that fact?

Captain KRAMER. There was still no fourteenth part, or anything that looked as though it might be the fourteenth part.

Mr. RICHARDSON. Then sometime between half-past 12 and 1 you left your office and returned home.

Captain KRAMER. That is correct, sir.

Mr. RICHARDSON. Now, how early did you go to the office the next morning?

Captain KRAMER. My recollection is it was very shortly after 7:30 that I arrived at my office the following morning.

Mr. RICHARDSON. What was your customary hour of arrival in your office?

Captain KRAMER. The normal office hours commenced at 8 o'clock. I customarily arrived about that time.

Mr. RICHARDSON. Have you any recollection, Captain, that you went to your office earlier the next morning than usual?

Captain KRAMER. Yes, sir; I do.

Mr. RICHARDSON. Have you any recollection of having any reason for going there earlier than usual?

Captain KRAMER. Aside from the fourteenth part, there were other messages of a minor nature that had come in before I left the office the previous night, and I further wanted to be at the office earlier that morning than usual because of the likelihood that I would have to make earlier disseminations that morning than usual.

By that I mean that normally the folders during the course

of 1941 were disseminated in the latter part of the morning and another dissemination was frequently made in the afternoon, and others at odd times. I had a specific appointment to be at the State Department by 10 that morning, on instructions from Secretary Knox. I gathered from conversation with Admiral Wilkinson that Admiral Stark would very likely be in Sunday morning, which was not a usual practice.

Mr. RICHARDSON. Well, now, let me get these threads together.

Captain KRAMER. Those are various reasons influencing my arrival earlier that morning.

Mr. RICHARDSON. And those reasons were connected with the dispatch of business that was waiting for you in your office?

Captain KRAMER. That is correct, sir.

Mr. RICHARDSON. Among which would be matters that might be involved in the receipt of the fourteenth part of this message?

Captain KRAMER. Aside from the fourteenth part, probably my principal objective in arriving early was to make sure that anything that might have come in in the early morning would be in shape for delivery for Mr. Knox or for Admiral Stark.

Mr. RICHARDSON. Was there any arrangement, Captain, in connection with your conversation at Admiral Wilkinson's house on late Saturday night, with reference to having a conference the next morning?

Captain KRAMER. No, sir; there was not.

Mr. RICHARDSON. They did not then speak of having a conference or of arranging one, that you can recall?

Captain KRAMER. There is not only no recollection of a conference mentioned but it was an unusual thing for Admiral Stark to be there on Sunday morning. On a number of occasions that fall on Sunday morning I had delivered folders to his home and had been received in his study on the second deck, he being in pajamas and dressing gown on one occasion having breakfast. I recollect that because I was offered some coffee.

Mr. RICHARDSON. Well, now, having reference, Captain, to Wilkinson, and Turner, and Beardall in the Wilkinson home, there was nothing said there about having an early Sunday morning meeting?

Captain KRAMER. Not a conference; no, sir. My recollection is that Admiral Wilkinson had indicated that Admiral Stark would probably be in the office early the next morning.

Mr. RICHARDSON. Now you got in your office around 7 o'clock on Sunday morning?

Captain KRAMER. Shortly after 7:30, is my best recollection.

Mr. RICHARDSON. When you got there did you find that the fourteenth part of the message had come in?*

Captain KRAMER. I do not distinctly recollect in what shape it was then. By that I mean whether it was still being broken down or had been broken down, or was being translated, but my recollection is that the fourteenth part was there shortly after I got in that morning, or possibly when I got in that morning.

Mr. RICHARDSON. Was there anyone there who could translate such a message from Japanese into English?

Captain KRAMER. Not in my office; no, sir. That interpretation "no one there" should be modified, I feel, by stating, as I have previously indicated, that I was on a 24-hour basis, and my translators were also. I had on at least two dozen occasions, during the course of 1941, been called to my ofice at odd hours of the night, sometimes 2 and 3 in the morning. I had standing instructions with the GY watch officer to call me any time they felt a translator was required.

On a number of occasions that general instruction was emphasized with specific instructions before I left my office in the evening to call me if anything on a particular circuit came in. I was the nearest translator to my office, only 5 minutes away in Arlington, my home being near Fort Myer, I therefore put myself in the status of being the first one called rather than one of the translators whose homes were in outlying districts.

Mr. RICHARDSON. Do you know who received the fourteenth part from the wire?

Captain KRAMER. From first-hand knowledge I do not, sir.

Mr. RICHARDSON. Who translated it? The fourteenth part, I mean now.

* See p. 236.

Captain Kramer. At the foot of the fourteenth part, before the expression "Navy translation," is the parenthetical letter (M). That means me.

Mr. Richardson. Your answer would be then that you translated the fourteenth part?

Captain Kramer. I have no recollection, but by looking at this part of the message on page 245 of Exhibit 1 it would indicate I was the translator.

Mr. Richardson. Now, when that message was translated, was it put in the shape of a separate dispatch by itself?

Captain Kramer. Yes, sir; it was. That, however, was contrary to the usual practice in my section. It was done because the evening before one of the various other parts of this note were coming in, and we called on the Army at about 6 o'clock, as I recall it—

Mr. Richardson. P.m?

Captain Kramer. Six p.m.—for assistance, primarily the assistance of their purple machine in breaking down these parts which were beginning to pile up on our machine.

It was almost invariably the practice in my section to include all parts of a multipart message under one heading 1 and 2, to assign the same file number to all those parts, but that was contrary to the Army practice which assigned a separate file number to each part of multipart messages.

The exception to our usual practice was made in the case of this code, because we proceeded to type up each part as they were finished in rough form.

Some of these parts were finished in rough form, long hand, by Army and sent over to us. They were all typed in my section in finished form.

Mr. Richardson. Well, was a delivery made on Sunday morning of the fourteenth part?

Captain Kramer. Yes, sir; it was; in its proper place, accompanying the first 13 parts.

Mr. Richardson. When the delivery was made on Sunday morning then the entire 14-part message was delivered as one message.

Captain Kramer. That is correct, sir.

Mr. RICHARDSON. So that there would have been, in effect, a duplication in delivery, so far as the first 13 parts were concerned?

Captain KRAMER. That was frequently the case.

Mr. RICHARDSON. Did you make delivery Sunday morning?

Captain KRAMER. I did, sir.

Mr. RICHARDSON. Now, will you tell the committee just what you did, whom you saw, how you made delivery, and what time it was?

Captain KRAMER. Some details of delivery between 8 and 9 o'clock I have only in the last month or so had my memory refreshed on, in conversation with other officers.

The first delivery, to my present best recollection, was made to Commander McCollum, head of the Far Eastern Section, Navy Intelligence.

Mr. RICHARDSON. Where and about what time?

Captain KRAMER. It was probably about 8 or a few minutes after.

Mr. RICHARDSON. At his office in the Navy Building?

Captain KRAMER. That is correct, sir.

Mr. RICHARDSON. Well, proceed.

Captain KRAMER. Another delivery was made, I believe, about a quarter of 9 to Captain McCollum, also, or Commander McCollum then, when I was informed that Admiral Wilkinson had arrived at his office, and I therefore automatically delivered another copy to Admiral Wilkinson. It was about that time, or shortly afterward, that another copy was delivered to Admiral Stark's office.

Mr. RICHARDSON. Now, at the time of delivery to Admiral Stark's office, who delivered it? Did you?

Captain KRAMER. That first delivery to Admiral Stark's office, I believe, was done by either Admiral Wilkinson or Captain McCollum.

Mr. RICHARDSON. Did you see that delivery made?

Captain KRAMER. My recollection is not positive in that regard. If it was made by Admiral Wilkinson or Captain McCollum, I would not have seen it.

Mr. RICHARDSON. How early was the first time you saw Admiral Stark on Sunday morning, as nearly as you can recall?

Captain KRAMER. My first positive recollection of seeing Admiral Stark is when I was on my way to the State Department to keep my 10 o'clock appointment when I left a copy of some of the other traffic that had come in in Admiral Stark's outer office. That was probably 9:30 or 9:40.

Mr. RICHARDSON. Was there anything said at that time by you to Admiral Stark with reference to this 14-part message?

Captain KRAMER. There was not, sir.

Mr. RICHARDSON. What was this 10 o'clock appointment you had with the State Department?

Captain KRAMER. The previous evening when I was in Secretary Knox's apartment, after he had read the folder of traffic, he directed me to be at the State Department at 10 o'clock the following morning where there would be a meeting between he, Mr. Hull, and, I gathered, Mr. Stimson.

Mr. RICHARDSON. Did you attend such a meeting?

Captain KRAMER. I did not attend such a meeting.

Mr. RICHARDSON. Did you make any delivery to the State Department on Sunday morning of the whole 14-part message?

Captain KRAMER. Yes, sir; I was at the State Department almost exactly 10 minutes of 10.

Mr. RICHARDSON. And to whom did you make delivery actually?

Captain KRAMER. Actually to Mr. Knox directly. He came in, as I recollect, about 5 minutes of 10, a few minutes after I got there, and went into the conference room, Mr. Hull's office.

Mr. RICHARDSON. Did you have any discussion on the matter with Secretary Knox?

Captain KRAMER. Only to the extent of pointing out what new traffic was in the folder which he had not seen the night before.

Mr. RICHARDSON. But nothing with reference to the details of the 14-part message?

Captain KRAMER. No, sir.

Mr. RICHARDSON. How long were you at the State Department making your delivery?

Captain KRAMER. There was a brief discussion between myself, the Army courier, and Mr. Hull's private secretary in Mr. Hull's outer office. It lasted probably not more than 3 or 4 minutes, and then I headed back for the Navy Department.

Mr. RICHARDSON. What time did you return to the Navy Department?

Captain KRAMER. My best recollection is about 10:20.

Mr. RICHARDSON. Have you any recollection as to what you did upon your return there at 10:20?

Captain KRAMER. On my arrival there at 10:20, the most striking recollection I have is the first sighting of that message from Tokyo directing the delivery of this note from Tokyo at 1 o'clock p.m., December 7, Washington time.

Mr. RICHARDSON. Now, that was in a separate dispatch, was it not?

Captain KRAMER. Yes, sir.

Mr. RICHARDSON. It came in separately?

Captain KRAMER. Yes, sir.

Mr. RICHARDSON. Was it in the same character of code transmission that the fourteenth part had been?

Captain KRAMER. The same general character; yes, sir.

Mr. RICHARDSON. It had come in by the time you returned from the State Department?

Captain KRAMER. Yes, sir.

Mr. RICHARDSON. Now, Captain, when you came to your office at 7:30 that morning, who was in your office carrying on business there?

Captain KRAMER. My only positive recollection is that the then Chief Yeoman Bryant was there. I have a somewhat vaguer recollection that two of the translators were also there. There may only have been one.

Mr. RICHARDSON. Who was at your office, if you can recall, when you returned from the State Department and found the 1 o'clock section of the message?*

Captain KRAMER. It was probably Dr. Hoffman, one of my chief translators.

---

* See p. 237.

Mr. RICHARDSON. What did you do, if anything, with this 1 o'clock section?

Captain KRAMER. I immediately instructed my chief yeoman to prepare another set of folders so I could make immediate delivery of them.

Mr. RICHARDSON. He did so?

Captain KRAMER. In the course of 5 minutes or so.

Mr. RICHARDSON. And what did you do then with respect to delivering that section?

Captain KRAMER. In that folder I mentioned, there were several other short messages, some of which appear in Exhibit 1. Just as I was about to leave the office, a plain language Japanese message was sent in to my office by the GY watch officer that carried, I believe, the hidden word message on page 251 of Exhibit 1. I recognized it as such from an external indicator, namely, the word "Stop" at the end, and recognized the first word as being one of the code words referring to England. In scanning the rest of the message, as I recollect, the sixth or seventh word had another code word, which incidentally, were all proper names. The word was "Hattori" which, although I recognized as a code word, I did not immediately recall the meaning of, and hastily referred to the list of such code words . . . referring—or rather, interpreted as "relations between Japan and (blank) country," to be inserted, was not in accordance with expectations.

I dictated to my chief yeoman the sense of that message, which now appears in Exhibit 1.

I took time to insert those in the folders that were made up and was on my way.

Mr. RICHARDSON. Where did you go?

Captain KRAMER. I stopped off at Admiral Stark's office, and then hurried first to the State Department.

Mr. RICHARDSON. Did you find Stark there?

Captain KRAMER. Admiral Stark was in his office.

Mr. RICHARDSON. To whom did you make delivery?

Captain KRAMER. The office door was closed when I arrived at his outer office. Word was sent in with one of the people there—I do not recollect who it was—that I had something for him.

My impressions earlier have been that it was his Flag Secretary, then Commander Wellborn. That has only quite recently been corrected on that score since I am informed that Wellborn was not there that morning at all. My recollections were fully refreshed in a conversation only in the last few days with Captain McCollum to the effect that he was the one who came to the door. I distinctly recollect that now.

I further recollect pointing out to Captain McCollum the tie-up of the time, 1 o'clock Washington, with the scheme that had been developing for the past week or so in the Southwest Pacific with reference to Malaya and the Kra Peninsula.

Captain McCollum reacted instantaneously to my pointing that out. His reactions, I believe, were identical with mine. I do not believe our conversation lasted more than 10 seconds or so, and then I headed for the State Department.

Mr. RICHARDSON. Now, at what time do you think it was that delivery was made at Stark's office, as you have testified?

Captain KRAMER. I should say it was between 10:30 and 10:35.

Mr. RICHARDSON. Are you able to state, Captain, when the 1 o'clock message was ready for delivery out of your office?

Captain KRAMER. It was ready for delivery when I returned to my office about 10:20, to the extent of its being completely translated.

Mr. RICHARDSON. Now, what time did you arrive at the State Department?

Captain KRAMER. Within probably 10 minutes after I left Admiral Stark's office.

Mr. RICHARDSON. To whom did you make delivery there?

Captain KRAMER. To one of the private Secretaries of Mr. Hull, who was the normal recipient for Mr. Hull.

Mr. RICHARDSON. Did anything else transpire there after you made the delivery?

Captain KRAMER. Before that folder was taken in to Mr. Hull, there was a brief conversation of the identical nature that I had had with Captain McCollum at Admiral Stark's door, pointing out the tie-up of the time 1 o'clock Washington, with the situation in the Southwest Pacific.

Mr. RICHARDSON. One o'clock Washington meant dawn in Hawaii, did it not?

Captain KRAMER. It was 7:30 in Hawaii, yes, sir.

Mr. RICHARDSON. And was that fact pointed out in your conversations with McCollum, and at the State Department?

Captain KRAMER. It was mentioned in passing, yes, sir.

Mr. RICHARDSON. Now, proceed.

Captain KRAMER. I should like to amplify that further, since such an issue has been made of that.

I earlier indicated, in outlining my naval career, that for about 2 years I was operating out of Pearl Harbor. I was executive officer and navigator of a destroyer based at the submarine base at Pearl Harbor.

I had had earlier experience as a navigator, namely, in Central America, in fact navigation was a hobby of mine.

Pearl Harbor uses a time zone which is rather unusual in the Navy in that it is not an even time zone, but is time zone 10½.

It is customary for navigators to draw time circles in working out navigation problems. I had made such a time circle in the few minutes I was in the Navy Department between 10:20 and 10:30 that morning, to get a picture of how this 1 o'clock Washington tied up with the movement of the big Japanese convoy down on the coast of French Indo-China; in other words, to get an idea of whether it was evening or midnight or early morning around Kota Bharu.

Incidentally, in drawing that time circle, that is figuring out roughly those times, I did not take the time to check to see what the actual time zone was. The 10½ time zone at Pearl Harbor was part of that time circle.

Furthermore, 7:30 Sunday morning at Pearl Harbor, at the time I was out there, and at other times during fleet problems, was probably the quietest time of the week aboard ship at Pearl Harbor.

I am not presuming to state what the situation was in 1941—7:30 is the normal time for the piping of the crew to breakfast.

There would, therefore, normally be only top side out of the living quarters, only those men on watch.

Furthermore, it was customary over week ends when I was serving out there for a larger percentage of the crew to be ashore on Sunday than other days of the week when ships were in port.

Those were all factors bearing on this idea of mine that 7:30 Sunday morning was a quiet time of the week.

Mr. RICHARDSON. What would be the significance of that to you as a Navy man?

Captain KRAMER. Nothing more than I have already indicated, that it would probably be the time of the week when there would be the fewest people aboard ship, when there would be less ship's work going on.

Mr. RICHARDSON. When you got to the State Department did you see Secretary Knox?

Captain KRAMER. I did not see him myself, except when the door was open to the conference room, Mr. Hull's office.

Mr. RICHARDSON. There was no communication then between you and Secretary Knox in any way?

Captain KRAMER. No, sir.

Mr. RICHARDSON. Now after you made delivery at the State Department, where did you go then?

Captain KRAMER. I went to the White House to deliver that same set of traffic.

Mr. RICHARDSON. To whom did you deliver at the White House?

Captain KRAMER. I do not recall the individual, but the delivery was made, to the best of my recollection—in fact I can state rather unequivocally I cannot conceive I would have delivered to any other place than the room I had previously described.

Mr. RICHARDSON. What time?

Captain KRAMER. Within 10 minutes of the time I left the State Department.

Mr. RICHARDSON. Where did you go from the White House?

Captain KRAMER. Back to the Navy Department.

. . . .

Mr. RICHARDSON. When you were at the State Department, you said when the door opened, you saw Knox. You did not send him a note, or have any intercourse with him at all that morning?

Captain KRAMER. Most emphatically not.

Mr. RICHARDSON. I have a note that rather indicated to me that there was an explanation of the 1 o'clock message sent by you to Knox on this theory of yours as to what was meant.

Captain KRAMER. There was only one verbal explanation, which I may not have fully explained due to interruptions with the foreign service officer, Mr. Hull's private secretary.

Mr. RICHARDSON. What was that?

Captain KRAMER. The identical tenor and nature that I described in the case of Captain McCollum.

Mr. RICHARDSON. The significance of the 1 o'clock date?

Captain KRAMER. That is correct, sir.

Mr. RICHARDSON. Well, now, I really would like to have you, since you discussed it with McCollum, and you discussed it with the private secretary of the Secretary of State—

Captain KRAMER (interposing). There was also a conversation with the Army courier who was there at the same time with the same set of traffic for Mr. Stimson.

Mr. RICHARDSON. All right. Now then, give the committee as detailed an account as you can of just what that conversation was and what its significance was, what you were talking about, what you had in mind, and what you feared, or expected, or anticipated, as the result of that 1 o'clock date.

Captain KRAMER. The primary point of that was the conviction, at least in my mind, that the Japanese intended to carry out their plans against Kota Bharu, with the intention and purpose of forcing the hand of the Thai Premier, Pibul, who had been maintaining, for some time past, the position that his country was neutral, that any foreign nation that invaded his quarters would be considered an enemy, and that the moment such an invasion took place he would call on the other party for assistance. By "other party" I refer to Japan or to Britain.

Mr. RICHARDSON. Was there any discussion that the 1 o'clock

date had any significance in connection with any attack at Pearl Harbor?

Captain KRAMER. Absolutely none, sir.

Mr. RICHARDSON. That was not in your mind primarily in connection with this 1 o'clock date at all?

Captain KRAMER. No, sir; it was not. It was mentioned only in passing; it was incidental to our general conversation.

. . . .

The VICE CHAIRMAN. Now, with respect to the so-called winds execute message, Captain, just a few questions in connection with that.

I have before me page 12 of the statement read to this committee by Captain Safford. I assume counsel can supply you with a copy of it, if you do not have it.

Captain KRAMER. I have one.

The VICE CHAIRMAN. I ask you to please turn to page 12 of Captain Safford's prepared statement, which he read to this committee about the middle of the page, and I invite your attention to the paragraph beginning:

> When I first saw the winds message, it had already been translated by Lieutenant Commander Kramer, in charge of the Translation Section of the Navy Department Communications Intelligence Unit. Kramer had underscored all three "code phrases" on the original incoming teletype sheet. Below the printed message was written in pencil or colored crayon in Kramer's handwriting the following three translations:
>
> "War with England (including NEI, etc).
> "War with the U. S.
> "Peace with Russia."
>
> I am not sure of the order; but it was the same in the broadcast, and I think England appeared first. I think Kramer used "U. S." rather than "United States." It is possible that the words "No war" instead of "Peace" were used to describe Japan's intentions with regard to Russia.

Now, having read that part of Captain Safford's testimony, Captain, are you prepared to give this committee information bearing on that?

Captain KRAMER. I think the testimony I have given already covers most of this point. I can only reiterate those statements. Anything appearing in one of those winds broadcasts indicating a negative form, in other words, as interpreted on this page, peace with someone would have immediately discarded it in my mind as being a signal in the winds system.

I might further comment along that line that I think it would be a very strange sort of disguising on the part of the Japanese to have said "No north wind."

The winds set-up was to be ostensibly an authentic weather broadcast.

I would like to comment further, that there were at least six or eight false alarms on this weather broadcast.

. . . .

The specific piece of teletype that was shown me and which I accompanied the watch officer with to Captain Safford's office, was a short piece of teletype paper torn off the teletype machine. My presumption at the time was that the GY watch officer had determined that it fitted the general conditions required by this weather broadcast, namely that it appeared in its proper location in the text of a news broadcast, either at the beginning or at the end or both, and that it had been repeated the required number of times.

That was part of the function of the GY watch officer, not only on this particular weather system but on all systems. They were the break-down people, they identified systems; they turned into my section only the final Japanese text.

That applies to everything except incompletely recovered codes in which the coded Japanese text would be turned into my section.

I therefore personally, in the case of this Friday morning so-called winds message, had no occasion to check on these points the question of whether it appeared in its proper context of a news broadcast or whether it was repeated the proper number of times. It may have been repeated the proper number of times on the piece of teletype paper. I am not positive as to the precise wording of that.

In the last few weeks, I have had occasion to see some interrogations conducted by General MacArthur's headquarters in Japan of high Japanese officials who were concerned with these broadcasts.

In view of their statements that no such weather signal was made, it is my present belief, in the light of my recollections on this matter, as well, that what I was receiving Friday morning in December before Pearl Harbor was also a false alarm on this winds system. It was, nevertheless, definitely my conception at the time that it was an authentic broadcast of that nature. I am still of that opinion, that it used that precise wording, keeping in mind, as I indicated this morning, that my recollections on that are that only one country was involved.

The Vice Chairman. What country was that?

Captain Kramer. To the best of my recollection, it was England.

I would like to point out one other item in connection therewith.

I have already indicated that the first time the question of what country appeared on that winds broadcast came up in conversation or anything that we had in connection with this matter, was when that one question was asked me by the court of inquiry at Pearl Harbor.

My first reaction was, without having thought about it since December 1941, that it was the United States, because of the fact we were at war with Japan, so of course, it must have been the United States.

I would like, however, to invite the committee's attention to the fact that later on, in the course of questioning me at Pearl Harbor, . . . I made the statement that through the latter part of that week and until the attack on Pearl Harbor there was still nothing whatsoever in this traffic to indicate any overt intentions of the Japanese directed at the United States. That

I believe appreciably modifies my first hasty reactions to the first time the question was propounded to me.

. . . .

Senator Lucas. Well, now, Captain, we have spent a good long time about this so-called winds execute message and assuming that this winds execute message had been a genuine one, what would that have added to what you already had as far as the tenseness of the situation is concerned between Japan and this country?

Captain Kramer. It would have added considerably to the already tense situation between Washington and this country because it would have indicated a contemplated break with this country. To date and up until December 7, the time of the attack, there was still no indication that the Japanese definitely contemplated a complete break in relations with this country, to say nothing about the slightest indication of any intention to attack this country.

Senator Lucas. Well, is the so-called execute winds message, if it had been a genuine one and if it had been understood, more important than the 14-point message?

Captain Kramer. No, sir; it is not.

Senator Lucas. In other words, the so-called winds execute message did not say when war was going to break out?

Captain Kramer. No, sir.

Senator Lucas. It did not say where war was going to break out?

Captain Kramer. No, sir.

. . . .

Senator Lucas. And nobody knew where the attacks were going to—where the Japs were going to attack the United States if they attacked us at all?

Captain Kramer. No, sir; or that they would attack the United States. In fact, I am speaking from my own personal recollections, but I believe that it was the consensus of the opinion of my associates and many of the high officials in Washington, that it was very illogical and foolish on the part of Japan to undertake open warfare with the United States, that it was almost inconceivable that they would in view of the fact that it was very likely that they could get everything that they wanted and as they had got in French Indo-China and what they wanted in the south of French Indo-China, without any action being taken by the United States.

. . . .

Testimony Of Commander Lester Robert Schulz, United States Navy

Pearl Harbor Attack, X, 4659-4664.

(Having been first duly sworn by the Chairman.)

Mr. RICHARDSON. Will you state your full name, please?

Commander SCHULZ. Lester Robert Schulz.

. . . .

Mr. RICHARDSON. Were you in Washington during November and December 1941?

Commander SCHULZ. Yes, sir; I was.

Mr. RICHARDSON. What was your assignment for duty in Washington during the first week of December?

Commander SCHULZ. I was under instruction in the Office of Naval Communications for communication intelligence. That was my permanent assignment. However, I was on temporary duty under verbal orders at the White House as a communications assistant to the Naval Aide, then Captain Beardall. Also, I had gone to Warm Springs in the same capacity the previous week end. Thus, my return to Washington. I believe, was Tuesday of that week.

. . . .

Mr. RICHARDSON. Were you on duty at the White House in Admiral Beardall's office there on the night of December 6, 1941?

Commander SCHULZ. I was on duty in the White House. Admiral Beardall had no fixed office in the White House at that time. He conducted his business for the most part in the Navy Department in the Navy Building and I was given a small office in the corner of the mail room, a closed office, but it was not a place used by Admiral Beardall.

Mr. RICHARDSON. That was at the White House?

Commander SCHULZ. Yes, sir; it was.

Mr. RICHARDSON. Do you recall Captain Kramer coming to the White House on the evening of December 6 to deliver any papers?

Commander SCHULZ. Yes, sir; I do.

Mr. RICHARDSON. About what time did he come?

Commander SCHULZ. Between 9 and 10; I should say about 9:30.

Mr. RICHARDSON. In the evening?

Commander SCHULZ. In the evening; yes sir.

Mr. RICHARDSON. Who was there besides you?

Commander SCHULZ. No one else of the Navy.

Mr. RICHARDSON. To whom, if anyone, did Captain Kramer hand his papers?

Commander SCHULZ. He handed them to me. They were in a locked pouch.

Mr. RICHARDSON. Was that the customary way in which dispatches that were being delivered there were delivered?

Commander SCHULZ. Material of that category was so delivered.

Mr. RICHARDSON. What did you do with the locked pouch when it was handed to you?

Commander SCHULZ. I took it from the mail room, which is in the office building, over to the White House proper and obtained permission to go up on the second floor and took it to the President's study.

Mr. RICHARDSON. Did you go alone?

Commander SCHULZ. I was accompanied by someone from the usher's office and announced to the President. However, then I was alone.

Mr. RICHARDSON. But Captain Kramer did not go with you?

Commander SCHULZ. That is correct, sir.

Mr. RICHARDSON. How long from the time the papers were placed in your hands by Captain Kramer was it before you went to the President's study?

Commander SCHULZ. About 5 minutes, I would say.

Mr. RICHARDSON. Whom did you find in the study when you arrived there?

Commander SCHULZ. The President was there seated at his desk, and Mr. Hopkins was there.

Mr. RICHARDSON. That is Mr. Harry Hopkins?

Commander SCHULZ. Yes, sir; that is correct.

Mr. RICHARDSON. You knew him?

Commander SCHULZ. Yes, sir. I had met him the previous day.

Mr. RICHARDSON. And you knew the President?

Commander SCHULZ. Yes, sir.

Mr. RICHARDSON. Was the pouch still locked?

Commander SCHULZ. I had a key to the pouch. I don't recall just when I unlocked it. In all likelihood it was after I was in the study, however.

Mr. RICHARDSON. What did you do after you entered the study?

Commander SCHULZ. I was announced and I informed the President that I had the material which Captain Kramer had brought and I took it out of the pouch.

Mr. RICHARDSON. Did you make any further statement at the time with reference to the material, as to your having been told that it was important or not?

Commander SCHULZ. That I do not recall, sir, but I believe that the President was expecting it. As I recall, he was.

Mr. RICHARDSON. Why? What makes you believe that? Was there anything said, I mean, that would indicate that?

Commander SCHULZ. When Admiral Beardall instructed me to stay and meet Captain Kramer and receive the material, he told me of its important nature.

Mr. RICHARDSON. Now, wait just a moment there.

Commander SCHULZ. And my recollection was also that it was of such importance that the President expected to receive it.

Mr. RICHARDSON. Before Captain Kramer came did you have a talk with Admiral Beardall with reference to the possibility of papers being delivered in the immediate future?

Commander SCHULZ. Yes, sir; I did. That is why I stayed.

Mr. RICHARDSON. What did Admiral Beardall say to you?

Commander SCHULZ. He told me that during the evening Captain Kramer would bring up some magic material and that I was to take it and give it immediately to the President and he gave me the key to the pouch so that I could take it out and deliver it.

Mr. RICHARDSON. That is the substance of your conversation with Admiral Beardall?

Comander SCHULZ. Yes, sir; that is right.

Mr. RICHARDSON. Well, now, when you presented the material to the President, was it in the pouch?

Commander SCHULZ. To the best of my recollection I took it out of the pouch and handed it to him. The papers were clipped together. There were perhaps 15 typewritten pages and they were fastened together in a sheaf and I took them out of the pouch and handed them to the President personally.

Mr. RICHARDSON. You know now what we mean when we talk of the first 13 parts of the 14-part message; you know what I am talking about?

Commander SCHULZ. Yes, sir.

Mr. RICHARDSON. Are you able to state now whether among the papers which were delivered to the President there were this 13 parts of what was eventually the 14-part message?

Commander SCHULZ. No, sir; I cannot. I did not read the message. I have only learned of its substance through information that has been divulged during this inquiry, from newspapers and so on.

Mr. RICHARDSON. All right. Now, what happened when you delivered these papers to the President? You remained there?

Commander SCHULZ. Yes, sir; I remained in the room.

Mr. RICHARDSON. What happened?

Commander SCHULZ. The President read the papers, which took perhaps 10 minutes. Then he handed them to Mr. Hopkins.

Mr. RICHARDSON. How far away from the President was Mr. Hopkins sitting?

Commander SCHULZ. He was standing up, pacing back and forth slowly, not more than 10 feet away.

Mr. RICHARDSON. Did the President read out loud when he was reading the papers?

Commander SCHULZ. I do not recall that he did.

Mr. RICHARDSON. All right. Now go ahead and give us in detail just what occurred there, if you please, Commander.

Commander SCHULZ. Mr. Hopkins then read the papers and handed them back to the President. The President then turned toward Mr. Hopkins and said in substance—I am not sure of the exact words, but in substance—"This means war." Mr. Hopkins agreed, and they discussed then, for perhaps 5 minutes, the situation of the Japanese forces, that is their deployment and—

Mr. RICHARDSON. Can you recall what either of them said?

Commander SCHULZ. In substance I can. There are only a few words that I can definitely say I am sure of, but the substance of it was that—I believe Mr. Hopkins mentioned it first—that since war was imminent, that the Japanese intended to strike when they were ready, at a moment when all was most opportune for them—

The CHAIRMAN. When all was what?

Commander SCHULZ. When all was most opportune for them. That is, when their forces were most properly deployed for their advantage. Indo-China in particular was mentioned, because the Japanese forces had already landed there and there were implications of where they should move next.

The President mentioned a message that he had sent to the Japanese Emperor concerning the presence of Japanese troops in Indo-China, in effect requesting their withdrawal.

Mr. Hopkins then expressed a view that since war was undoubtedly going to come at the convenience of the Japanese, it was too bad that we could not strike the first blow and prevent any sort of surprise. The President nodded and then said in effect, "No, we can't do that. We are a democracy and a peaceful people." Then he raised his voice, and this much I remember definitely. He said, "But we have a good record."

The impression that I got was that we would have to stand on that record, we could not make the first overt move. We would have to wait until it came.

During this discussion there was no mention of Pearl Harbor. The only geographic name I recall was Indo-China. The time at which war might begin was not discussed, but from the manner of the discussion there was no indication that tomorrow was necessarily the day. I carried that impression away because it contributed to my personal surprise when the news did come.

Mr. RICHARDSON. Was there anything said, Commander, with reference to the subject of notice or notification as a result of the papers that were being read?

Commander SCHULZ. There was no mention made of sending any further warning or alert. However, having concluded this discussion about the war going to begin at the Japanese convenience, then the President said that he believed he would talk to Admiral Stark. He started to get Admiral Stark on the telephone. It was then determined—I do not recall exactly, but I believe the White House operator told the President that Admiral Stark could be reached at the National Theater.

Mr. RICHARDSON. Now, was it from what was said there that you draw the conclusion that that was what the White House operator reported?

Commander SCHULZ. Yes, sir. I did not hear what the operator said, but the National Theater was mentioned in my presence, and the President went on to state, in substance, that he would reach the admiral later, that he did not want to cause public alarm by having the admiral paged or otherwise when in the theater, where, I believe, the fact that he had a box reserved was mentioned and that if he had left suddenly he would surely have been seen because of the position which he held and undue alarm might be caused, and the President did not wish that to happen because he could get him within perhaps another half an hour in any case.

Mr. RICHARDSON. Was there anything said about telephoning anybody else except Stark?

Commander SCHULZ. No, sir; there was not.

Mr. RICHARDSON. How did he refer to Admiral Stark?

Commander SCHULZ. When he first mentioned calling him, he referred to him as "Betty."

Mr. RICHARDSON. Was there any further discussion there before you left?

Commander SCHULZ. No, sir. To the best of my knowledge

that is all that was discussed. The President returned the papers to me, and I left the study.

. . . .

THE FOURTEEN-PART AND RELATED MESSAGES INTERCEPTED BY MAGIC CODE

Pearl Harbor Attack, XII, 238-245, 248.

(Secret)

From: Tokyo
To: Washington
December 6, 1941
Purple
#901

Re my #844a.

1. The Government has deliberated deeply on the American proposal of the 26th of November and as a result we have drawn up a memorandum for the United States contained in my separate message #902b (in English).

2. This separate message is a very long one. I will send it in fourteen parts and I imagine you will receive it tomorrow. However, I am not sure. The situation is extremely delicate, and when you receive it I want you to please keep it secret for the time being.

3. Concerning the time of presenting this memorandum to the United States, I will wire you in a separate message. However, I want you in the meantime to put it in nicely drafted form and make every preparation to present it to the Americans just as soon as you receive instructions.

Army 25838
JD: 7149   Trans. 12-6-41 (S)

(Secret)

From: Tokyo
To: Washington
December 6, 1941
Purple
#902 (Part 1 of 14) Separate telegram

Memorandum

1. The Government of Japan, prompted by a genuine desire to come to an amicable understanding with the Government of the United States in order that the two countries by their joint efforts may secure the peace of the Pacific area and thereby contribute toward the realization of world peace, has continued negotiations with the utmost sincerity since April last with the Government of the United States regarding the adjustment and advancement of Japanese-American relations and the stabilization of the Pacific area.

The Japanese Government has the honor to state frankly its views, concerning the claims the American Government has persistently maintained as well as the measures the United States and Great Britain have taken toward Japan during these eight months.

2. It is the immutable policy of the Japanese Government to insure the stability of East Asia and to promote world peace, and thereby to enable all nations to find each its proper place in the world.

Ever since the China Affair broke out owing to the failure on the part of China to comprehend Japan's true intentions, the Japanese Government has striven for the restoration of peace and it has consistently exerted its best efforts to prevent the extention of war-like disturbances. It was also to that end that in September last year Japan concluded the Tri Partite Pact with Germany and Italy.

JD-1: 71143
25843   Navy Trans. 12-6-41 (S)

From: Tokyo
To: Washington
December 6, 1941
Purple
#902 (Part 2 of 14)

However, both the United States and Great Britain have resorted to every measure to assist the Chungking regime so as to obstruct the establishment of a general peace between Japan and China, interfering with Japan's constructive endeavours toward the stabilization of East Asia, exerting pressure on the Netherlands East Indies, or menacing French Indo-China, they have attempted to frustrate Japan's aspiration to realize the ideal of common prosperity in cooperation with these regions. Furthermore, when Japan in accordance with its protocol with France took measures of joint defense of French Indo-China, both American and British governments, wilfully misinterpreted it as a threat to their own possession and inducing the Netherlands government to follow suit, they enforced the assets freezing order, thus severing economic relations with Japan. While manifesting thus an obviously hostile attitude, these countries have strengthened their military preparations perfecting an encirclement of Japan, and have brought about a situation which endangers the very existence of the empire.

JD-1: 7143
25843   Navy Trans. 12-6-41 (S)

From: Tokyo
To: Washington
December 6, 1941
Purple
#902 (Part 3 of 14)

Nevertheless, facilitate a speedy settlement, the Premier of Japan proposed, in August last, to meet the President of the United States for a discussion of important problems between the two countries covering the entire Pacific area. However, while accepting in principle the Japanese proposal, insisted that the meeting should take place after an agreement of view had been reached on fundamental— (75 letters garbled)—The Japanese government submitted a proposal based on the formula proposed by the American government, taking fully into consideration past American claims and also incorporating Japanese views. Repeated discussions proved of no avail in producing readily an agreement of view. The present cabinet, therefore, submitted a revised proposal, moderating still further the Japanese claims regarding the principal points of difficulty in the negotiation and endeavored strenuously to reach a settlement. But the American government, adhering steadfastly to its original proposal, failed to display in the slightest degree a spirit of conciliation. The negotiation made no progress.

JD-1: 7143
25843   Navy Trans. 12-6-41 (S)

From: Tokyo
To: Washington
December 6, 1941
Purple
#902 (Part 4 of 14)

Thereupon, the Japanese Government, with a view to doing its utmost for averting a crisis in Japanese-American relations, submitted on November 20th still another proposal in order to arrive at an equitable solution of the more essential and urgent questions which, simplifying its previous proposal, stipulated the following points:

(1) The Governments of Japan and the United States undertake not to dispatch armed forces into any of the regions, excepting French Indo-China, in the Southeastern Asia and the Southern Pacific area.

(2) Both Governments shall cooperate with a view to securing the acquisition in the Netherlands East Indies of those goods and commodities of which the two countries are in need.

(3) Both Governments mutually undertake to restore commerical relations to those prevailing prior to the freezing of assets.

The Government of the United States shall supply Japan the required quantity of oil.

(4) The Government of the United States undertakes not to resort to measures and actions prejudicial to the endeavours for the restoration of general peace between Japan and China.

(5) The Japanese Government undertakes to withdraw troops now stationed in French Indo-China upon either the restoration of peace between Japan and China or the establishment of an equitable peace in the Pacific area; and it is prepared to remove the Japanese troops in the southern part of French Indo-China to the northern part upon the conclusion of the present agreement.

JD-1: 7143
25843   Navy Trans. 12-6-41 (S)

(Secret)

From: Tokyo
To: Washington
December 6, 1941
Purple
#902 (Part 5 of 14)

As regards China, the Japanese Government, while expressing its readiness to accept the offer of the President of the United States to act as "Introducer" of peace between Japan and China as was previously suggested, asked for an undertaking on the part of the United States to do nothing prejudicial to the restoration of Sino-Japanese peace when the two parties have commenced direct negotiations.

The American government not only rejected the above-mentioned new proposal, but made known its intention to continue its aid to Chiang Kai-Shek; and in spite of its suggestion mentioned above, withdrew the offer of the President to act as the so-called "Introducer" of peace between Japan and China, pleading that time was not yet ripe for it. Finally, on November 26th, in an attitude to impose upon the Japanese government those principles it has persistently maintained, the American government made a proposal totally ignoring

Japanese claims, which is a source of profound regret to the Japanese Government.

JD-1: 7143
25843 Navy Trans. 12-6-41 (S)

(Secret)

From: Tokyo
To: Washington
December 6, 1941
Purple
#902 (Part 6 of 14)

4. From the beginning of the present negotiation the Japanese Government has always maintained an attitude of fairness and moderation, and did its best to reach a settlement, for which it made all possible concessions often in spite of great difficulties.

As for the China question which constituted an important subject of the negotiation, the Japanese Government showed a most conciliatory attitude.

As for the principle of Non-Discrimination in International Commerce, advocated by the American Government, the Japanese Government expressed its desire to see the said principle applied throughout the world, and declared that along with the actual practice of this principle in the world, the Japanese Government would endeavor to apply the same in the Pacific area, including China, and made it clear that Japan had no intention of excluding from China economic activities of third powers pursued on an equitable basis.

Furthermore, as regards the question of withdrawing troops from French Indo-China, the Japanese government even volunteered, as mentioned above, to carry out an immediate evacuation of troops from Southern French Indo-China as a measure of easing the situation.

JD-1: 7143
25843 Navy Trans. 12-6-41 (S)

From: Tokyo
To: Washington
December 6, 1941
Purple
#902 (Part 7 of 14)

It is presumed that the spirit of conciliation exhibited to the utmost degree by the Japanese Government in all these matters is fully appreciated by the American government.

On the other hand, the American government, always holding fast to theories in disregard of realities, and refusing to yield an inch on its impractical principles, caused undue delays in the negotiation. It is difficult to understand this attitude of the American government and the Japanese government desires to call the attention of the American government especially to the following points:

1. The American government advocates in the name of world peace those principles favorable to it and urges upon the Japanese government the acceptance thereof. The peace of the world may be brought about only by discovering a mutually acceptable formula through recognition of the reality of the situation and mutual appreciation of one another's position. An attitude such as ignores realities and imposes one's selfish views upon others will scarcely serve the purpose of facilitating the consummation of negotiations.
25843

(Secret)

From: Tokyo
To: Washington
December 6, 1941
Purple
#902 (Part 8 of 14)

Of the various principles put forward by the American government as a basis of the Japanese-American agreement, there are some which the Japanese government is ready to accept in principle, but in view of the world's actual conditions, it seems only a Utopian ideal, on the part of the American government, to attempt to force their immediate adoption.

Again, the proposal to conclude a multilateral non-aggression pact between Japan, the United States, Great Britain, China, the Soviet Union, the Netherlands, and Thailand, which is patterned after the old concept of collective security, is far removed from the realities of East Asia.

The American proposal contains a stipulation which states: "Both governments will agree that no agreement, which either has concluded with any third powers, shall be interpreted by it in such a way as to conflict with the fundamental purpose of this agreement, the establishment and preservation of peace throughout the Pacific area." It is presumed that the above provision has been proposed with a view to restrain Japan from fulfilling its obligations under the Tripartite Pact when the United States participates in the war in Europe, and, as such, it cannot be accepted by the Japanese Government.
JD-1: 7143
25843 Navy Trans. 12-6-41 (S)

From: Tokyo
To: Washington
December 6, 1941
Purple
#902 (Part 9 of 14)

The American Government, obsessed with its own views and opinions, may be said to be scheming for the extension of the war. While it seeks, on the one hand, to secure its rear by stabilizing the Pacific area, it is engaged, on the other hand, in aiding Great Britain and preparing to attack, in the name of self-defense, Germany and Italy two powers that are striving to establish a new order in Europe. Such a policy is totally at variance with the many principles upon which the American Government proposes to found the stability of the Pacific area through peaceful means.

3. Where as the American Government, under the principles it rigidly upholds, objects to settling international issues through

military pressure, it is exercising in conjunction with Great Britain and other nations pressure by economic power. Recourse to such pressure as a means of dealing with international relations should be condemned as it is at times more inhuman than military pressure.
JD-1: 7143
25843   Navy Trans. 12-6-41 (S)

From: Tokyo
To: Washington
        December 6, 1941
        Purple
        #902 (Part 10 of 14)

4. It is impossible not to reach the conclusion that the American Government desires to maintain and strengthen, in collusion with Great Britain and other powers, its dominant position it has hitherto occupied not only in China but in other areas of East Asia. It is a fact of history that one countr— (45 letters garbled or missing)—been compelled to observe the status quo under the Anglo-American policy of imperialistic exploitation and to sacrifice the —es to the prosperity of the two nations. The Japanese Government cannot tolerate the perpetuation of such a situation since it directly runs counter to Japan's fundamental policy to enable all nations to enjoy each its proper place in the world.
JD-1: 7143
25843   Navy Trans. 12-6-41 (S)

From: Tokyo
To: Washington
        December 6, 1941
        Purple
        #902 (Part 11 of 14)

The stipulation proposed by the American Government relative to French Indo-China is good exemplification of the above-mentioned American policy. That the six countries,— Japan, the United States, Great Britain, The Netherlands,

China and Thailand,—excepting France, should undertake among themselves to respect the territorial integrity and sovereignty of French Indo-China and quality of treatment in trade and commerce would be tantamount to placing that territory under the joint guarantee of the governments of those six countries. Apart from the fact that such a proposal totally ignores the position of France, it is unacceptable to the Japanese government in that such an arrangement cannot but be considered as an extension to French Indo-China of a system to the n— (50 letters missed)—sible for the present predicament of East Asia.

JD-1: 7143
25843   Navy Trans. 12-6-41 (S)

From: Tokyo
To: Washington
      December 6, 1941
      Purple
      #902 (Part 12 of 14)

5. All the items demanded of Japan by the American government regarding China as wholesale evacuation of troops or unconditional application of the principle of Non-Discrimination in International Commerce ignore the actual conditions of China, and are calculated to destroy Japan's position as the stabilizing factor of East Asia. The attitude of the American government in demanding Japan not to support militarily, politically or economically any regime other than the regime at Chungking, disregarding thereby the existence of the Nanking government, shatters the very basis of the present negotiation. This demand of the American government falling, as it does, in line with its above-mentioned refusal to cease from aiding the Chungking regime, demonstrates clearly the intention of the American government to obstruct the restoration of normal relations between Japan and China and the return of peace to East Asia.

JD-1: 7143
25843   Navy Trans. 12-6-41 (S)

From: Tokyo
To: Washington
December 6, 1941
Purple
#902 (Part 13 of 14)

5. In brief, the American proposal contains certain acceptable items such as those concerning commerce, including the conclusion of a trade agreement, mutual removal of the freezing restrictions, and stabilization of the Yen and Dollar exchange, or the abolition of extra-territorial rights in China. On the other hand, however, the proposal in question ignores Japan's sacrifices in the four years of the China Affair, menaces the empire's existence itself and disparages its honour and prestige. Therefore, viewed in its entirety, the Japanese government regrets that it cannot accept the proposal as a basis of negotiation.

6. The Japanese government, in its desire for an early conclusion of the negotiation, proposed that simultaneously with the conclusion of the Japanese-American negotiation, agreements be signed with Great Britain and other interested countries. The proposal was accepted by the American government. However, since the American government had made the proposal of November 26th as a result of frequent consultations with Great Britain, Australia, The Netherlands and Chungking, *ANDND** presumably by catering to the wishes of the Chungking regime on the questions of *CHTUALYLOKMMTT**** be concluded that all these countries are at one with the United States in ignoring Japan's position.

JD-1: 7143
25843   Navy Trans. 12-6-41 (S)

---

* Probably "and as."
** Probably "China, can but."

From: Tokyo
To: Washington
December 7, 1941
(Purple—Eng)
#902 (Part 14 of 14)

(NOTE.—In the forwarding instructions to the radio station handling this part, appeared the plain English phrase *"VERY IMPORTANT."*)

7. Obviously it is the intention of the American Government to conspire with Great Britain and other countries to obstruct Japan's efforts toward the establishment of peace through the creation of a New Order in East Asia, and especially to preserve Anglo-American rights and interests by keeping Japan and China at war. This intention has been revealed clearly during the course of the present negotiations. Thus, the earnest hope of the Japanese Government to adjust Japanese-American relations and to preserve and promote the peace of the Pacific through cooperation with the American Government has finally been lost.

The Japanese Government regrets to have to notify hereby the American Government that in view of the attitude of the American Government it cannot but consider that it is impossible to reach an agreement through further negotiations.
25843
JD-1: 7143 (M) Navy Trans. 7 Dec. 1941 (S-TT)

(Secret)

From: Tokyo
To: Washington
December 6, 1941
Purple
#904

Re my #902.
There is really no need to tell you this, but in the preparation of the aide memoire be absolutely sure not to use a typist or any other person.

Be most extremely cautious in preserving secrecy.
Army 25844
JD: 7144 Trans. 12-6-41 (S)

(Secret)

From: Tokyo
To: Washington
December 7, 1941
Purple (Urgent—Very Important)
#907 To be handled in government code

Re my #902.

Will the Ambassador please submit to the United States Government (if possible to the Secretary of State) our reply to the United States at 1:00 p.m. on the 7th, your time.
Army 25850 Trans. 12-7-41 (S)

PART THREE

The Events in Tokyo

The Events in Tokyo

Why the Japanese decided to go to war with the United States may be seen from Japanese sources. The following excerpts consist of the agenda for the Imperial Conference of July 2, 1941, when the broad outlines for Japan's policy were fixed, and the agenda for the Imperial Conference of September 6, 1941, when the first tentative deadline for peace or war was established. Japan's minimum and maximum demands have been included in an annex document.

Pearl Harbor Attack, XX, 4018-4019, 4022-4023, Exhibit 173, Appendix III and V.

AN OUTLINE OF THE POLICY OF THE IMPERIAL GOVERNMENT IN VIEW OF PRESENT DEVELOPMENTS

(Decision reached at the Conference held in the Imperial Presence on July 2)

I. POLICY

1. The Imperial Government is determined to follow a policy which will result in the establishment of the Greater East Asia Co-Prosperity Sphere and world peace, no matter what international developments take place.

2. The Imperial Government will continue its effort to effect a settlement of the China Incident and seek to establish a solid basis for the security and preservation of the nation. This will involve an advance into the Southern Regions and, depending on future developments, a settlement of the Soviet Question as well.

3. The Imperial Government will carry out the above program no matter what obstacles may be encountered.

II. Summary

1. Steps will be taken to bring pressure on the Chiang Regime from the Southern approaches in order to bring about its surrender. Whenever demanded by future developments the rights of a belligerent will be resorted to against Chungking and hostile concessions taken over.

2. In order to guarantee national security and preservation, the Imperial Government will continue all necessary diplomatic negotiations with reference to the southern regions and also carry out various other plans as may be necessary. In case the diplomatic negotiations break down, preparations for a war with England and America will also be carried forward. First of all, the plans which have been laid with reference to French Indo-China and Thai will be prosecuted, with a view to consolidating our position in the southern territories.

In carrying out the plans outlined in the foregoing article, we will not be deterred by the possibility of being involved in a war with England and America.

3. Our attitude with reference to the German-Soviet War will be based on the spirit of the Tri-Partite Pact. However, we will not enter the conflict for some time but will steadily proceed with military preparations against the Soviet and decide our final attitude independently. At the same time, we will continue carefully correlated activities in the diplomatic field.

In case the German-Soviet War should develop to our advantage, we will make use of our military strength, settle the Soviet question and guarantee the safety of our northern borders.

(Pencilled Note: On this occasion the Army and Foreign Minister Matsuoka took a strong attitude toward the Soviet Union, and the Army began concentrating its armed forces in Manchoukuo. This resolution was drawn up to off-set the policies of the Army and the Foreign Minister.)

4. In carrying out the preceding article all plans, especially the use of armed forces, will be carried out in such a way as to place no serious obstacle in the path of our basic military preparations for a war with England and America.

5. In case all diplomatic means fail to prevent the entrance of America into the European War, we will proceed in harmony with our obligations under the Tri-Partite Pact. However, with reference to the time and method of employing our armed forces we will take independent action.

6. We will immediately turn our attention to placing the nation on a war basis and will take special measures to strengthen the defenses of the nation.

7. Concrete plans covering this program will be drawn up separately.

PLANS FOR THE PROSECUTION OF THE POLICY
OF THE IMPERIAL GOVERNMENT
(Agenda for a Council in the Imperial Presence)
September 6, 1941

In view of the increasingly critical situation, especially the aggressive plans being carried out by America, England, Holland and other countries, the situation in Soviet Russia and the Empire's latent potentialities, the Japanese Government will proceed as follows in carrying out its plans for the southern territories as laid in "An Outline of the Policy of the Imperial Government in View of Present Developments."

1. Determined not to be deterred by the possibility of being involved in a war with America (and England and Holland) in order to secure our national existence, we will proceed with war preparations so that they be completed approximately toward the end of October.

2. At the same time, we will endeavor by every possible diplomatic means to have our demands agreed to by America and England. Japan's minimum demands in these negotiations with America (and England), together with the Empire's maximum concessions are embodied in the attached document.

3. If by the early part of October there is no reasonable hope of having our demands agreed to in the diplomatic negotiations mentioned above, we will immediately make up our minds to get ready for war against America (and England and Holland).

Policies with reference to countries other than those in the southern territories will be carried out in harmony with the plans already laid. Special effort will be made to prevent America and Soviet Russia from forming a united front against Japan.

ANNEX DOCUMENT

A LIST OF JAPAN'S MINIMUM DEMANDS AND HER MAXIMUM CONCESSIONS IN HER NEGOTIATIONS WITH AMERICA AND ENGLAND

I. *Japan's Minimum Demands in her Negotiations with America (and England)*

1. America and England shall not intervene in or obstruct a settlement by Japan of the China Incident.

(a) They will not interfere with Japan's plan to settle the China Incident in harmony with the Sino-Japanese Basic Agreement and the Japan-China-Manchoukuo Tri-Partite Declaration.

(b) America and England will close the Burma Route and offer the Chiang Regime neither military, political nor economic assistance.

Note: The above do not run counter to Japan's previous declarations in the "N" plan for the settlement of the China Incident. In particular, the plan embodied in the new Sino-Japanese Agreement for the stationing of Japanese troops in the specified areas will be rigidly adhered to. However, the withdrawal of troops other than those mentioned above may be guaranteed in principle upon the settlement of the China Incident.

Commercial operations in China on the part of America and England may also be guaranteed, in so far as they are purely commercial.

2. America and England will take no action in the Far East which offers a threat to the defense of the Empire.

(a) America and England will not establish military bases in Thai, the Netherlands East Indies, China or Far Eastern Soviet Russia.

(b) Their Far Eastern military forces will not be increased over their present strength.

Note: Any demands for the liquidation of Japan's special relations with French Indo-China based on the Japanese-French Agreement will not be considered.

3. America and England will cooperate with Japan in her attempt to obtain needed raw materials.

(a) America and England will restore trade relations with Japan and furnish her with the raw materials she needs from the British and American territories in the Southwest Pacific.

(b) America and England will assist Japan to establish close economic relations with Thai and the Netherlands East Indies.

II. *Maximum Concessions by Japan.*

It is first understood that our minimum demands as listed under I above will be agreed to.

1. Japan will not use French Indo-China as a base for operations against any neighboring countries with the exception of China.

Note: In case any questions are asked concerning Japan's attitude towards Soviet Russia, the answer is to be that as long as Soviet Russia faithfully carries out the Neutrality Pact and does not violate the spirit of the agreement by, for instance, threatening Japan or Manchuria, Japan will not take any military action.

2. Japan is prepared to withdraw her troops from French Indo-China as soon as a just peace is established in the Far East.

3. Japan is prepared to guarantee the neutrality of the Philippine Islands.

The fall of the Third Konoye Cabinet augured a turn for the worse in Japanese-American relations. The following excerpts from the memoirs of Prince Fumimaro Konoye and the diary of Marquis Koichi Kido, the Lord Keeper of the Privy Seal, illustrate some of the events which led to the formation of the Tojo Cabinet.

International Military Tribunal for the Far East (hereafter cited as IMTFE), Prosecution Document 499, pp. 10,251 ff., 10,283, 10,291.

Prince Fumimaro Konoye's Own Account Of Facts Pertaining To The Resignation Of The 3d Konoye Cabinet

Document 499, Prosecution, IMTFE, pp. 10,251 ff.

The 3d Konoye Cabinet started off with the great mission of readjusting the Japanese-American relations. For this reason, the retirement of Foreign Minister Matsuoka was brought about and as only that was done, it can be said that all efforts were solely exerted toward the accomplishment of this great mission ever since the formation of the Cabinet. However, America's attitude was by no means definite. There were various opinions as to why her attitude was not definite, but the opinion of the War Minister was that since America's basic policy is to advance into Asia, the reason for America's indefinite attitude is fundamental and consequently she lacks sincerity even in her negotiation. However, we continued our negotiation with the view that a temporary compromise and conciliation may be possible in regard to the current situation, even if our basic traditional policies may have been different.

Recently the negotiation reached a state of temporary deadlock due to the occupation of French Indo-China by our troops, but as it became known that we wouldn't go any further, the situation eased somewhat and the negotiation was again resumed. Hence, a message was sent to President Roosevelt on August 28 proposing a conference. Nevertheless, since President Roosevelt, in reply to this stated that he was willing to hold a conference, but would like to have a general agreement reached in regard to the important matters, at least, as a premise, an Imperial Conference was held on September 6 to determine the basis of the counter-measure for this.

As a result of the Imperial Conference it was decided to direct all our efforts toward the diplomatic negotiation to the end, but to resolutely assume a war policy in the event no means for the conclusion of the negotiation is reached by early October.

Since there was a time limit of by early October, the negotiation was carried on hurriedly and as it didn't progress as expected, September passed and October came with the negotiation still not going smoothly. At about that time, the supreme command group became boisterous and stated that they will wait until October 15, but won't extend it beyond that. Therefore, I requested the assembly of the War Minister, the Foreign Minister, the Navy Minister and the President of the Planning Board at Ogigaiso for a final conference on October 12.

However, on the day before the conference, Chief Oka of the Naval Affairs Bureau came and in talking with him, he stated that with the exception of the Naval General Staff, the brains of the Navy don't want a Japanese-American war, but since the Navy, herself, can not say "she can't do it" in view of her approval of the decision of the Imperial Headquarters, the Navy Minister will propose to leave it in the hands of the Prime Minister at tomorrow's conference; so we would like you to decide on continuing the diplomatic negotiation.

Under such circumstances, this important conference was held at 2 p.m. on October 12 at Ogigaiso. . . .

War Minister Tojo, expressing the Army's point of view, stated:

"There is absolutely no hope for a successful conclusion of the diplomatic negotiation."

However, Navy Minister Oikawa stated:

"Let us leave the decision as to whether there is any hope for a successful conclusion of the diplomatic negotiation in the hands of the Prime Minister and the Foreign Minister . . . .

If there is any hope for a successful conclusion of the diplomatic negotiation, we want the negotiation to be continued. . . ."

Against this opinion of the Navy Minister, the War Minister replied:

". . . . I believe that there is no hope for a successful conclusion of the diplomatic negotiation, but if the Foreign Minister is fully confident of success, it may be given further consideration. Does the Foreign Minister have a confidence of success?"

Since Foreign Minister Toyoda's views were asked, the Foreign Minister stated:

"Since there is the second party, I can't say that I am confident of success, but, generally speaking, the important points in the negotiation with America are:

(1) The Tripartite Alliance
(2) The economic problem in China
(3) The question of keeping our troops/T.N. in China.

These three items are the obstacles. Of these, some sort of agreement can be reached in regard to item 1 and 2, but the third item pertaining to the question of keeping our troops /T.N. in China is the most difficult one. Since America is emphatically demanding for the complete withdrawal of troops, I believe a compromise may be reached if we agree to a complete withdrawal of troops as a principle and station troops according to the time and place as specifically designated by an agreement or something between Japan and China, but I believe even this will be considerably difficult."

When this opinion was expressed, the War Minister, objecting emphatically, stated:

"We can't yield on the question of withdrawal of troops. . . ."

Hence, the Prime Minister stated:

"If the War Minister insists, as he does, it is not a question of whether there is any hope for a successful conclusion of the diplomatic negotiation. There definitely is no hope. . . ."

Excerpts From The Diary Of Marquis Kido, 16 October 1941

IMTFE, 10,283.

At 4:00 P. M. Prince Konoye telephoned to say that the Cabinet was going to resign en bloc! I was astounded by the suddenness of this announcement. I visited the Emperor at 4 p.m. to report upon the general resignation of the Konoye Cabinet. At 5 p.m. Prince Konoye tendered the Cabinet Ministers' resignations to the Throne. I was received in audience by the Emperor from 5:30 p.m. to answer his questions regarding the succeeding Cabinet.

Excerpts From The Diary Of Marquis Kido, 17 October 1941

IMTFE, 10,291.

At 11 a.m. Chief Secretary Matsudaira visited me to make arrangements for a senior statesmen's conference. It was held from 1:10 p.m. to 3:45 p.m. in the west ante-chamber of the Palace. . . . I explained the situation of the general resignation. Except for the recommendation of Ugaki by Baron Wakatsuki and the suggestion of a Cabinet under a member of the Imperial Family by General Hayashi, none had a definite opinion.

I asserted that the most important things were the revision of the decision of the last Council in the Imperial presence September 6 and the unity of opinion between the Army and Navy. I suggested a Tojo Cabinet as a solution of these problems. . . .

The final decision for war with the United States was taken in Tokyo after the expiration of the deadline for negotiations on November 29, 1941. The following excerpts from the diary of Marquis Kido and the interrogation of Premier Hideki Tojo highlight the decisions of the conferences between November 29 and December 2, 1941.

International Military Tribunal for the Far East, Exhibit P 1956, pp. 10,452-10,454; Document 2510-A; Document 1209-A; Exhibit 1210, p. 10,523.

EXCERPT FROM ENTRY IN MARQUIS KIDO'S DIARY NOVEMBER 29, 1941

IMTFE, Exhibit P 1966, pp. 10,452-10,454.

From 2 p.m. to 3 p.m. the Emperor asked the Senior Statesmen's opinions concerning the present political situation. The Emperor remarked on the difficult times which we were going through.

Baron Wakatsuki said we were equal to a prolonged war with the U. S. A. in spiritual power, but regarding material power we must make a careful study.

Admiral Okada said that he had grave doubts as to our supply capacity in regard to war materials, and thought the Government's statement about this matter up to date was quite incomplete.

Baron Hiranuma agreed with Mr. Wakatsuki as regards the spiritual strength of the Japanese nation, and urged further measures to awaken patriotic sentiment.

Prince Konoye stated that it was quite regrettable that our negotiations were going to be a failure in spite of our strenuous efforts since last April. But he was of the opinion that there would be no need to resort to a hasty war just because of the rupture of the negotiations as we might be able to reach a wise solution in some way or other, while continuing our struggle against difficulties.

Admiral Yonai said he did not base his opinion on definite

data but it was his desire that we should be careful not to lose what little we possess by trying to avoid becoming poorer by inches.

Mr. Hirota said that although our policy had been to prevent Anglo-American interference in the China Incident, things had reached their present situation. We should be able to seize an opportunity to solve the pending problems between the two countries even after the commencement of hostilities, if we were sincere enough in our diplomatic efforts.

General Hayashi stated that as he had no data for his opinion, he could do nothing but believe the declarations of the Imperial Headquarters and the Government.

General Abe said that according to the Government's statement the negotiations had come to a deadlock in spite of strenuous efforts on our part. He was sure that the Government had studied the world political situation from various angles with laborious minuteness, for which we were thankful. But it would be quite necessary to pay much more attention to the Chinese people than to the war with the U. S. A., otherwise we would lose the fruits of victory in the Chinese Incident.

Mr. Wakatsuki said that the war should be fought to the last, even if there was no chance to win, if it was a defensive one for the cause of our national existence and self-defense, but we should avoid the war if we intended to realize our ideals such as the Asiatic Co-prosperity Sphere or the stabilizing of power in Asia, because such a war would be very dangerous.

Extract From Interrogation Of General Hideki Tojo, March 12, 1946

Document 2510-A, IMFTE.

Q. Yesterday you explained that the policy, after the 6 September 1941 Imperial Conference, was, on the one hand, to negotiate for peace, and on the other, to prepare for war. Did you continue that policy?
A. Yes. I undertook the work as Premier.

. . . .

Q. When and why was a meeting of ex-premiers held prior to the last Imperial Conference of 1 December 1941?
A. You mean the Senior Statesmen?
Q. Yes.
A. That was convened by the Emperor.
Q. When?
A. It was either on the 1st or the 31st.
Q. What was the purpose of calling that meeting?
A. The Emperor was very anxious about the question of war with America and he convened them in order to hear each man's opinion.

. . . .

Q. Did you make any statements at that meeting?
A. Of course I was there too, as the Premier at that time. Yes, I did. The Emperor was there and heard each man's opinion in turn. I was there and from time to time spoke, giving the Government's point of view.
Q. What did you state as the government's point of view?
A. I explained various things, but I don't remember the details now. I explained the inevitableness of war.

. . . .

Excerpt From The Tojo Interrogation Of February 8, 1946

Doc. 1209 A, IMTFE.
Q. Who attended the Imperial Conference on December 1 or 2nd, 1941?
A. I was there as Premier; the President of the Privy Council was there, and all or nearly all of the other Cabinet Ministers, as I recall. The two Chiefs of Staff were there. I am not sure whether the Assistant Chiefs of Staff were there or not, but the Cabinet would know. Those were the responsible people that were there. . . .

. . . .

Excerpt From The Diary Of Marquis Koichi Kido, Lord Keeper Of The Privy Seal, December 1, 1941

Doc. 1632-W-88, IMTFE.

.... At 2 P. M. the Council in the presence of the Emperor was held and at last the war between Japan and the U. S. A. was decided upon. At 4:30 P. M. the Premier visited me to consult about the Imperial Proclamation of War.

WHAT HAPPENED AT PEARL HARBOR?

The actual plan for an attack on Pearl Harbor was drawn up by Admiral Gombai Yamamoto, as illustrated by the following excerpts from the interrogation of Admiral Nagano, Chief of the Naval General Staff, and Navy Minister Shigetaro Shimada.

International Military Tribunal for the Far East, Document 2495-A, pp. 7-9; Document 2496-A, Document 2498-B.

Extract From Interrogation Of Osami Nagano, 21 March 1946, p. 7, 8, 9.

Doc. 2495-A, IMFTE.

Q. Admiral, who was the originator of the plan to attack Pearl Harbor?

A. After being studied by the Combined Fleets the plan was brought forth in the spring of 1941 by Admiral Yamamoto. It was a great secret in the Combined Fleets whereby Admiral Yamamoto and only one or two other officers knew of it.

Q. When was the plan as prepared by Admiral Yamamoto first called to your attention, Admiral?

A. I first found out about this plan officially in October 1941. I heard prior to that that such a plan was being studied.

Q. Admiral, when did you become Chief of the Naval General Staff?

A. In April 1941.

Q. And is it not a fact that this plan of Admiral Yamamoto's was called to your attention at that time?

A. No, it was not. I believe it was at that time that Yamamoto first thought of the plan.

Q. Now, Admiral, you stated that the first time the plan had been called to your attention officially was in October 1941. When was the plan called to your attention unofficially?

A. About July I heard that they were training or practicing such a plan.

Q. And is it not a fact, Admiral, and again I ask you not to answer me too literally but to answer my questions from your knowledge even though you were not personally present and from your knowledge as Naval Chief of Staff as to what was going on in connection with Naval activities in the light of the fact that you were Chief of Staff and as such had general knowledge of Naval activities, is it not a fact that the Japanese Navy started practicing to place into execution the Yamamoto plan to attack Pearl Harbor in the spring of 1941?
A. The plan came into being in the spring but it was not practiced until summer.
Q. And what do you mean by summer?
A. I am not sure but I believe it was about the beginning of July. The Combined Fleets went into Kagoshima and there they practiced coming in low over the mountains and dive bombing.
Q. And is it not a fact also, Admiral, that in addition to those maneuvers, that the fleet also practiced with a specially designed torpedo for use in shallow water such as was known to be the situation in Pearl Harbor?
A. The torpedo was completed during those manuevers. The Combined Fleets spent a lot of time trying out this torpedo and experimenting with it.

Excerpt From Interrogations Of Osami Nagano, 26 March 1946

Doc. 2496-A, IMFTE.
Q. About when, Admiral, did you place your approval upon the plan to attack Pearl Harbor?
A. Either in the end of October or the beginning of November. There was considerable argument between the Fleets and the Naval Operational Bureau. The Fleets were in favor of attacking Pearl Harbor, whereas the Naval Affairs Bureau considered it too much of a speculation and preferred the more conservative method of waiting for the

American Fleet in the South Pacific Islands. Admiral Yamamoto was very adamant in his belief in his plan to attack Pearl Harbor and he threatened to resign along with his staff if that plan were not carried out.
Q. Prior to this time the plan had been perfected by preliminary maneuvers at sea and also on paper at the Naval Headquarters, had it not, Admiral?
A. Yes, the Fleet studied it very greatly.
Q. And when, Admiral, was it that you decided the conflict between the Navy Affairs Bureau and Admiral Yamamoto in favor of the attack on Pearl Harbor?
A. I originally agreed with the Naval Operational Department but as Yamamoto was too avid in about the end of October or early part of November, as I previously stated, I agreed with the plan to attack Pearl Harbor. The Naval Affairs Bureau were in favor of using the plan that they had held for many years of waiting for the American Navy in the South Pacific Islands.
Q. Nevertheless, Admiral, as I understand it, notwithstanding the desire of the Naval Affairs Bureau to adhere to the plan which had been in effect for many years, you came to the conclusion that the plan to attack Pearl Harbor was best and settled the conflict by giving your approval to the Pearl Harbor Plan, is that not correct, Admiral?
A. I was for the plan of the Naval Affairs Department as that seemed to be the more logical but not to have the Commander of the Fleets resign, as he would have, if his plan did not go through, I thought the best thing to do was to approve.
Q. And you did approve, is that correct, the plan for the Pearl Harbor attack?
A. Yes.
Q. As I understand the situation, Admiral, your approval of the same was the decisive factor in carrying through the attack on Pearl Harbor, is that not right?
A. Yes.
Q. And as I understand it, Admiral, I assume that in the

light of that fact, you are willing to assume responsibility for the same. Is that correct, Admiral?
A. Naturally.
Q. Admiral, about when was the fleet first ordered to take position in order to carry through the Pearl Harbor attack?
A. The Fleets were assembled at Chiahima in the middle of November. On November 26 or 27 they started out for Pearl Harbor. . . .
Q. Admiral, as a matter of fact, there was a liaison conference held on or about November 28 or 29, 1941, was there not . . . to complete the determination of war against the United States? is that not correct?
A. I am not sure of the date but I believe you are correct on that. However, until the very last we were hoping that peace could be established and were prepared to abandon the plan until the very last, for the attack on Pearl Harbor. . . .

Excerpts From Interrogation Of Shigetaro Shimada On 23 January 1946

Doc. 2498-B, IMFTE.
Q. Yamamoto proposed his Pearl Harbor attack plan to the General Staff early in 1941, did he not?
A. I heard that he offered it in January of 1941.
Q. At that time he was Commander-in-Chief of the combined fleet, was he not?
A. Yes.
Q. Admiral Nagano authorized him to proceed with a study of the plan in March of 1941, did he not?
A. In that point I don't know the date, but I think it was later.
Q. But it was early in 1941, was it not?
A. I think it was perhaps in May or June.
Q. May or June when his plan was adopted for study?
A. At first the ordinary plan did not have any plans for the attack on Pearl Harbor, but it was made formal in May or

June. The studying and training of a squadron by Yamamoto was begun in May or June of 1941, I think. . ."

. . . .

Q. Now, on November 10, 1941, didn't Vice-Admiral Nagumo issue aboard his flagship, aircraft carrier *Akagi* striking force operation order No. 1, which ordered all forces to complete battle operations by November 20, 1941?
A. I think that is so.
Q. Tankan (Hitokappu) Bay of Etorofu Island in the Kuriles was designated in the striking force order No. 1 as the rendezvous for the task force, was it not?
A. Yes.
Q. Between November 21 and November 27, the task force rendezvoused at Tankan Bay, didn't it?
A. Yes.
Q. The task force left Tankan Bay on November 27, 1941, and sailed East until December 4th or 5th, didn't it?
A. Yes.
Q. Then it altered its course to the Southeast toward Hawaii?
A. Yes.
Q. Upon reaching a point approximately 250 miles from Hawaii the first wave of planes was launched, wasn't it?
A. Yes.
Q. A fleet of from 20 to 30 Japanese submarines from the Sixth Fleet was patrolling outside Pearl Harbor before the strike, wasn't it?
A. Yes.
Q. And a fleet of some 5 or 6 midget submarines attempted to gain entrance to the Harbor, didn't it?
A. Yes. . . ."

THE EVENTS IN TOKYO

The success of the raid on Pearl Harbor was a matter of great pride to the Japanese. The following document is an excerpt from Marquis Kido's diary for December 8, 1941.

International Military Tribunal for the Far East, Document 1632-W-90.

Excerpt From Entry In Marquis Kido's Diary, December 8, 1941

At 12:40 a.m. Foreign Minister Togo telephoned me to consult about the treatment of the personal telegram from President Roosevelt to the Emperor, which had been brought by Ambassador Grew. I advised him to consult the Premier as regards its diplomatic effect and procedure. I said that as for a visit to the Throne, there would be no need of hesitation to make one, for the Emperor would not mind granting an audience even at midnight.

I was informed that Foreign Minister Togo had proceeded to the palace, so I went to the office at 2:40 to see him. When I was going up the Akasaka slope, I saw the rising sun above a building there. I thought it was symbolic of the destiny of this country now that we had entered the war against the U. S. A. and England, the two greatest powers in the world. I closed my eyes and prayed for the success of our Navy planes making an attack upon Pearl Harbor at that time.

At 7:30 a.m. I met the Premier, the Chief of the Army General Staff, and the Chief of the Navy General Staff. I heard from them great news relative to the success of the surprise attack upon Hawaii and felt that the Gods had come to our aid. I saw the Emperor at 11:40 a.m. and talked with him until 12 noon. I was very much impressed by the self-possessed attitude of the Emperor on this day. The imperial Proclamation of War was issued.

PART FOUR

The Events in Berlin

The Events in Berlin

One of the stumbling blocks to an accord between the United States and Japan was the existence of the Tripartite Pact. The following document consists of the most pertinent parts of this treaty, which was signed at Berlin on September 27, 1940.

Nazi Conspiracy and Aggression, V, 355-357.

Excerpts From Tripartite Pact Between Germany, Italy And Japan, September 27, 1940

The Governments of Germany, Italy, and Japan consider it as a condition precedent of a lasting peace, that each nation of the world be given its own proper place. They have therefore decided to stand together and to cooperate with one another in their efforts in Greater East Asia and in the regions of Europe, wherein it is their prime purpose to establish and maintain a new order of things calculated to promote the prosperity and welfare of the peoples there. Furthermore, it is the desire of the three Governments to extend this cooperation to such nations in other parts of the world as are inclined to give their endeavors a direction similar to their own, in order that their aspirations toward world peace as the ultimate goal may thus be realized. Accordingly, the Governments of Germany, Italy, and Japan have agreed as follows:

Article 1

Japan recognizes and respects the leadership of Germany and Italy in the establishment of a new order in Europe.

Article 2

Germany and Italy recognize and respect the leadership of Japan in the establishment of a new order in Greater East Asia.

Article 3

Germany, Italy, and Japan agree to cooperate in their efforts on the aforesaid basis. They further undertake to assist one another with all political, economic, and military means, if one of the three Contracting Parties is attacked by a Power at present not involved in the European war or in the Chinese-Japanese conflict.

. . . .

Article 5

Germany, Italy, and Japan affirm that the aforesaid terms do not in any way affect the political status which exists at present between each of the three Contracting Parties and Soviet Russia.

. . . .

Although Hitler was preoccupied with his European enemies, he had plans for war with the United States at a later date, as shown by the following excerpt from a memorandum of Major (General Staff) Freiherr von Falkenstein, dated October 29, 1940.

Nazi Conspiracy and Aggression, III, 288-289.

SECRET

FUEHRER'S H. Q.
29/10/40

Major (General Staff) Freiherr von Falkenstein
[Addressed to an unspecified General] "Chefsache"

. . . .

5. The Fuehrer is at present occupied with the question of the occupation of the Atlantic Islands with a view to the prosecution of war against America at a later date. Deliberations on this subject are being embarked upon here. Essential conditions are at the present:—

    a. No other operational commitment,
    b. Portuguese neutrality,
    c. Support of France and Spain. . . .

In spite of their ultimate plans for war with the United States, the Germans were anxious to keep America neutral as long as possible. However, in November, 1941, on the eve of the Pearl Harbor attack, they abandoned this policy, as shown by the following excerpts from the "magic" intercepts of two messages between Hiroshi Oshima, the Japanese Ambassador in Berlin, and his Government.

Pearl Harbor Attack, XII, 200, 204.

(Secret)

From: Berlin
To: Tokyo
        29 November 1941
        (Purple)
        #1393 (In 3 parts, complete)

By his request, I was supposed to have called on Foreign Minister Ribbentrop during the evening of yesterday, the 28th. Suddenly, however, he requested that the time be postponed and it was not until 10:30 at night that I finally saw him.

. . . .

1. Ribbentrop opened our meeting by again inquiring whether I had received any reports regarding the Japanese-U. S. negotiations. I replied that I had received no official word.

Ribbentrop: "It is essential that Japan effect the New Order in East Asia without losing this opportunity. There never has been and probably never will be a time when closer cooperation under the Tripartite Pact is so important. If Japan hesitates at this time, and Germany goes ahead and establishes her European New Order, all the military might of Britain and the United States will be concentrated against Japan.

"As Fuehrer Hitler said today, there are fundamental differences in the very right to exist between Germany and Japan, and the United States. We have received advice to the effect that there is practically no hope of the Japanese-U. S. negotiations being concluded sucessfully, because of the fact that the United States is putting up a stiff front.

"If this is indeed the fact of the case, and if Japan reaches a decision to fight Britain and the United States, I am confident that that will not only be to the interest of Germany and Japan jointly, but would bring about favorable results for Japan herself."

I: "I can make no definite statement as I am not aware of any concrete intentions of Japan. Is Your Excellency indicating that a state of actual war is to be established between Germany and the United States?"

Ribbentrop: "Roosevelt's a fanatic, so it is impossible to tell what he would do."

Concerning this point, in view of the fact that Ribbentrop has said in the past that the United States would undoubtedly try to avoid meeting German troops, and from the tone of Hitler's recent speech as well as that of Ribbentrop's, I feel that German attitude toward the United States is being considerably stiffened. There are indications at present that Germany would not refuse to fight the United States if necessary. . . .

(Secret)

From: Tokyo
To: Berlin
November 30, 1941
Purple (CA)
#985 (Part 1 of 3)

. . . .

1. The conversations begun between Tokyo and Washington last April during the administration of the former cabinet, in spite of the sincere efforts of the Imperial Government, now stand ruptured, broken. . . . In the face of this, our Empire faces a grave situation and must act with determination. Will

Your Honor, therefore, immediately interview Chancellor *HITLER* and Foreign Minister *RIBBENTROP* and confidentially communicate to them a summary of the developments. Say to them that lately England and the United States have taken a provocative attitude, both of them. Say that they are planning to move military forces into various places in East Asia and that we will inevitably have to counter by also moving troops. Say very secretly to them that there is extreme danger that war may suddenly break out between the Anglo-Saxon nations and Japan through some clash of arms and add that the time of the breaking out of this war may come quicker than anyone dreams.

The Foreign Ministers of Germany and Italy have left slightly differing accounts of the background of the Pearl Harbor attack. The following documents consist of excerpts from the testimony of Joachim von Ribbentrop at Nuremberg in August and September, 1945, and excerpts from the Diary of Count Galeazzo Ciano for December 3, 4, 5, and 8, 1941.

Nazi Conspiracy and Aggression, Supplement B, 1199, 1201; *ibid.*, V, 691-692.

Excerpts From Testimony Of Joachim Von Ribbentrop, Taken At Nuremberg, Germany, 31 August 1945, 1420-1535 . . .

Nazi Conspiracy and Aggression, Supplement B, 1199.

Q. But you are sure that there were no discussions or any decision reached, either one way or the other, with respect to even the possibility of war between Japan and the United States?

A. No, this was never, to my mind, discussed at all. Of course, this tense feeling was there, which might possibly be said that once it might have been discussed or said, "What will this lead to?" or something. I don't know. I don't remember that very well, but surely the possibility of the war of Pearl Harbor was never discussed in a way as if it was going to happen. On the contrary, if I remember well, we had rather the opposite feeling that things were coming to adjustment.

Q. And you were also sure that there was no encouragement of Japan, looking towards the creation of an incident that might bring about such a war?

A. No, absolutely not. I can say most definitely, no. You know, I tell you, even if something had been—which definitely had been in the Japanese mind,—the Japanese are very close-mouthed. They don't say what they think. My experience with the Japanese taught me that they are very close-mouthed. We never knew exactly where we stood, never. They never said really what was going on.

I remember I told the Fuehrer, that according to the stipulation of the Three Powers Pact since Japan had attacked, we would not have to declare war on the United States of America, formally. So then the Fuehrer decided—he thought this matter over quite a while, and then he gave me a very clear decision in that respect. This is more or less what he said: "If we don't stand on the side of Japan, the Pact is politically dead. But that is not the main reason. The chief reason is the United States is already shooting against our ships. They have been a forceful factor in this war, and they have, through their actions, already created a situation, which is practically, let's say, a situation of war." . . .

Excerpts From Testimony Of Joachim Von Ribbentrop, Taken At Nuremberg, Germany, 10 September 1945, 1130-1215 . . .

Nazi Conspiracy and Aggression, Supplement B, 1201.

Q. Then, summarizing, Hitler was opposed to Japan making any arrangements with the United States?
A. Yes. One can say that.
Q. That was before Pearl Harbor?
A. To my mind, I think a long time before Pearl Harbor. I don't recall it exactly, but one can see that in the press.
Q. Would you say that it was in the spring of '41?
A. I don't really know about dates. It is very difficult for me. I only know my recollection by this: that Pearl Harbor was a complete surprise to us all. We didn't expect anything like that and so these negotiations, of that kind, to my mind, must have been very much earlier. That is the way I recollect it, but I couldn't really tell you exactly when, but I do remember that we had not given to Japan the counsel ever to attack the United States. I don't remember that at all. With the position of the United States short of war, and the shaky attitude of certain Japanese circles, it might perhaps have been understandable, but I don't remember that we ever gave a counsel like that; but perhaps I may explain, chronologically, the way it went. First,

our first dealings with Japan were against Russia. . . . Then came the Three Power Pact which was closed, as I think I said before, in order to keep the United States neutral. Then during the war, since the declaration of Great Britain with war on Germany, the Japanese had discussed at various occasions the idea of attacking England through the south on Singapore. I remember myself discussing with the Japanese in Berlin, I think also in Tokyo, the interest we took in such an attack, on the neutrality of the United States. I remember pointing that out at various occasions.

Q. Well, logically, it was much to your advantage that the United States did not enter the war against Germany.

A. It has always been in my mind, and I remember quite well that I have talked with the Japanese in Berlin, in the sense that it would be in the interest of us all, to keep the United States neutral, which was the main object of the Pact when closed. I don't know whether on the military sector there had been anything. I don't know; I was not informed, but I don't suppose so.

Excerpts From The Diary Of Count Galeazzo Ciano

Nazi Conspiracy and Aggression, V, 691-692.

"December 3.
Wednesday

"Sensational move by Japan. The Ambassador asks for an audience with the Duce and reads him a long statement on the progress of the negotiations with America, concluding with the assertion that they have reached a dead end. Then, invoking the appropriate clause in the Tripartite Pact, he asks that Italy declare war on America immediately after the outbreak of hostilities and proposes the signature of an agreement not to conclude a separate peace. The interpreter translating this request was trembling like a leaf. The Duce gave fullest assurances, reserving the right to confer with Berlin before giving a reply. The Duce was pleased with the communication and said: "We are now on the brink of the inter-continental war which

I predicted as early as September 1939." What does this new event mean? In any case, it means that Roosevelt has succeeded in his maneuver. Since he could not enter the war immediately and directly, he has entered it indirectly by letting himself be attacked by Japan.

"December 4.
Thursday
"Berlin's reaction to the Japanese move is extremely cautious. Perhaps they will accept because they cannot get out of it, but the idea of provoking America's intervention pleases the Germans less and less. Mussolini, on the other hand, is pleased about it.***"

"December 5.
Friday
"A night interrupted by Ribbentrop's restlessness. After delaying two days, now he cannot wait a minute to answer the Japanese and at three in the morning he sent Mackensen to my house to submit a plan for a triple agreement relative to Japanese intervention and the pledge not to make a separate peace. He wanted me to awaken the Duce, but I did not do so, and the latter was very glad I hadn't***"

"December 8.
Monday
"A night telephone call from Ribbentrop; he is overjoyed about the Japanese attack on America. He is so happy about it that I am happy with him, though I am not too sure about the final advantages of what has happened. . . ."

When the Japanese finally struck, the Germans were taken completely by surprise, as shown in the following excerpt from the Nuremberg testimony of Dr. Paul Otto Schmidt, the German Foreign Office Interpreter.

Trial of the Major War Criminals Before the International Military Tribunal, X, 201.

Examination Of Dr. Paul Otto Schmidt At Nuremberg, 28 March 1946, Before The International Military Tribunal By Counsel For Defendant Joachim Von Ribbentrop

Dr. Horn: Witness, were you in a position to observe how Ribbentrop reacted to the news of Japan's attack on Pearl Harbor?

Schmidt: I had no direct opportunity, but in the Foreign Office it was generally known that the news of Pearl Harbor took the Foreign Minister, as indeed the whole Foreign Office, completely by surprise. This impression was confirmed by what a member of the Press Department told me. The Press Department had a listening station for radio news and the official on duty had instructions to inform the Foreign Minister personally of important news at once. When the first news of Pearl Harbor was received by the listening station of the Press Department, the official on duty considered it of sufficient importance to report it to his chief, that is to say, the head of the Press Department, who in turn was to pass it on to the Foreign Minister. He was however—so I was told—rather harshly rebuffed by the Foreign Minister who said it must be an invention of the press or a canard, and he did not wish our Press Department to disturb him with such stories. After that, a second and third message about Pearl Harbor was received, I think a Reuters report had also been received by the listening station; and the head of the Press Department then again plucked up courage and, in spite of the order not to disturb the Foreign Minister, he once more gave him this news.

PART FIVE

The American-Japanese Conversations

The American-Japanese Conversations

Between April and December 1941, a series of diplomatic conversations took place between the United States and Japan for the purpose of seeking a possible adjustment of the differences between the two powers. The following documents consist of selections from the diplomatic papers concerning these negotiations from August to December, 1941.

Foreign Relations of the United States: Diplomatic Papers, 1941, Volume IV, The Far East, pp. 425-438, 468-469, 483, 492, 633-634, 683-684, 707, 720-721; *Papers Relating to the Foreign Relations of the United States, Japan: 1931-1941*, II 554-559, 576-579; 588-589, 697-698, 701-704, 710-714, 743-744, 755-756, 764-770.

Memorandum By The Secretary Of State

Foreign Relations, Japan, II, 554-559.

[WASHINGTON,] August 17, 1941.

The Ambassador of Japan called to see the President at the latter's request. Following some few exchanges of preliminary remarks, the President then became serious and proceeded to refer to the strained relations between our two countries. He referred to the Ambassador's visit to me and the latter's request for a reopening of the conversations between our two Governments. The President commented briefly on the policies and principles that this Government has been standing for in its relations with Japan, and he made some contrast to Japan's opposite course of conquest by force, et cetera. He concluded by saying that our attitude of opposition to Japan's course has been made well known, and that the next move is now up to Japan. The President inquired of the Ambassador if he had anything in mind to say in connection with the situation. Thereupon the Ambassador drew out of his pocket an instruction which he said was from his Government, in which the Japanese Government set forth some generalities and asserted very earnestly that it desired to see peaceful relations preserved between our two countries; that Prince Konoye feels so seriously and so earnestly about preserving such relations that he would be disposed to meet the President midway, geographically speaking, between our two countries, and sit down together and talk the matter out in a peaceful spirit.

The President thereupon said that this Government should really bring the matters between the two Governments literally up to date and that he would, therefore, offer certain observations about the position of this Government; he added that he regretted the necessity of so doing but that he had no other recourse. The President said he had dictated what he was about to say and that he would read it to the Ambassador and then hand him the written instrument containing the oral conversation. This the President proceeded to do as follows:

(Here follows text of the oral statement printed *infra*.)

The President, after some little delay in the conversation so as to set apart the first statement which he read to the Ambassador, then proceeded to turn to the Ambassador's request to the Secretary of State and to himself for a resumption of the conversations. The President made further references to Japan's opposing course of conquest by force and bitter denunciation of this country by the Japanese Government-controlled press and then coming to the request for a reopening of the conversations he repeated our former statements to the Japanese Government that, of course, we could not think of reopening the conversations if the Japanese Government is to continue its present movement of force and conquest supported by its bitter press campaign against this country.

Thereupon the President proceeded to read to the Ambassador the following statement, which is self-explanatory:

(Here follows text of the statement printed on page 280.)

The Ambassador received each paper in writing and said he

would communicate both to his Government. He reiterated from time to time that his Government was very desirous of preserving peaceful relations between the two countries and he took no issue with the President relative to the reasons set forth by this Government for discontinuing conversations with Japan.

C(ORDELL) H(ULL)

Oral Statement Handed By President Roosevelt To The Japanese Ambassador (Nomura) On August 17, 1941

During the past months the Governments of the United States and of Japan, through the Secretary of State and the Japanese Ambassador in Washington, have engaged in protracted conversations directed toward exploring the possibility of reaching a sound basis for negotiations between the two countries relative to the maintenance of peace with order and justice in the Pacific. The principles and policies which were under discussion in these conversations precluded pursuit by either Government of objectives of expansion by force or by threat of force.

On July 24 last the President of the United States informed the Japanese Government through the Japanese Ambassador in Washington that he was willing to suggest to the Governments of Great Britain, the Netherlands and of China that they make a binding and solemn declaration that they had no aggressive intentions with regard to Indo-China and that they would agree that the markets and raw materials of Indo-China should be available to all Powers on equal terms. The President stated further that he would be willing to suggest to the Powers mentioned that they undertake this declaration, in which the United States would be willing to join, upon the understanding that the Government of Japan would be disposed to make a similar declaration and would be further disposed to withdraw its military forces from Indo-China.

Notwithstanding these efforts, the Government of Japan has continued its military activities and its disposals of armed forces at various points in the Far East and has occupied Indo-China with its military, air and naval forces.

. . . .

Such being the case, this Government now finds it necessary to say to the Government of Japan that if the Japanese Government takes any further steps in pursuance of a policy or program of military domination by force or threat of force of neighboring countries, the Government of the United States will be compelled to take immediately any and all steps which it may deem necessary toward safeguarding the legitimate rights and interests of the United States and American nationals and toward insuring the safety and security of the United States.

Statement Handed By President Roosevelt To The Japanese Ambassador (Nomura) On August 17, 1941

Reference is made to the question which the Japanese Ambassador raised on August 8 during a conversation with the Secretary of State whether it might not be possible for the responsible head of the Japanese Government and the Government of the United States to meet with a view to discussing means whereby an adjustment in relations between the United States and Japan might be brought about. The thought of Prince Konoye and of the Japanese Government in offering this suggestion is appreciated.

. . . .

In case the Japanese Government feels that Japan desires and is in position to suspend its expansionist activities, to readjust its position, and to embark upon a peaceful program for the Pacific along the lines of the program and principles to which the United States is committed, the Government of the United States would be prepared to consider resumption of the informal exploratory discussions which were interrupted in July and would be glad to endeavor to arrange a suitable time and place to exchange views. The Government of the United

States, however, feels that, in view of the circumstances attending the interruption of the informal conversations between the two Governments, it would be helpful to both Governments, before undertaking a resumption of such conversations or proceeding with plans for a meeting, if the Japanese Government would be so good as to furnish a clearer statement than has yet been furnished as to its present attitude and plans, just as this Government has repeatedly outlined to the Japanese Government its attitude and plans.

Memorandum Of Conversation

Foreign Relations, Japan, II, 576-579.

[WASHINGTON,] August 28, 1941

The Japanese Ambassador called by appointment made at his request at the Secretary's apartment. He expressed his appreciation for the Secretary's having arranged to have the Ambassador see the President that morning. The Ambassador said that he felt much encouraged from his interview with the President to hope for a successful outcome of our common effort to bring about an improvement in the relations between the two countries, and he added that he has telegraphed a full account of that interview to his Government.

The Ambassador said that it was his personal opinion that the suggestion of the President that the meeting between the President and the Japanese Prime Minister be held at Juneau would be agreeable to his Government and that the Prime Minister would probably proceed thither by a Japanese warship, making the journey in about ten days.

. . . .

The Secretary then pointed out to the Ambassador the desirability of there being reached in advance of the proposed meeting an agreement in principle on the principal questions which were involved in a settlement of Pacific questions between the two nations. He dwelt upon the serious consequences from the point of view of both Governments which would ensue if the meeting failed to result in an agreement as a consequence of issues arising which could not be resolved, and he expressed the view that the meeting should therefore have as its purpose the ratification of essential points already agreed to in principle. . . .

The Ambassador reviewed the points in regard to which difficulties had been encountered in the conversations, namely: (1) Japan's relations to the Axis, (2) the question of the retention of Japanese troops in North China and Inner Mongolia, and (3) the question of the application of the principle of non-discrimination in international commercial relations. He noted that only in regard to the question of the retention of Japanese troops in North China, concerning which he had no information that his Government had modified its attitude, did he anticipate real difficulty. He observed that with regard to Japan's relations with the Axis there should be no difficulties, as the Japanese people regarded their adherence only nominal and as he could not conceive of his people being prepared to go to war with the United States for the sake of Germany. He said he thought our attitude in regard to self-protection was entirely reasonable. The only difficulty that he saw was that to ask that Japan give a blank check for action that the United States might take against Germany in the name of self-defense was equivalent to asking for a nullification of the Tripartite Pact.

The Secretary commented that the Japanese Government had entered into the Tripartite Pact at a most critical moment in our efforts to extend aid to England, and Japan's action therefore was given particular emphasis in this country. In addition, Mr. Matsuoka kept reasserting gratuitously Japan's alignment with the Axis. The Secretary said he felt that unless something was done to counteract the effect upon the American people, it might prove a source of serious embarrassment to the President upon his return from the proposed meeting. The Secretary went on to refer to the actual situation in our relations with Germany, to the fact that although no shooting is taking place we are maintaining patrols all the way to Iceland.

The Japanese Ambassador said that with regard to the China question it was the idea of the Japanese Government that we exercise our good offices in bringing the Chinese and Japanese together leaving China and Japan to reach a direct settlement among themselves whereas the United States Government desired to discuss with Japan the basic terms on which peace was to be concluded.

. . . .

The Secretary said that we were involved in this matter through Japan's requesting this Government to exercise its good offices. In order to exercise such good offices it was necessary for us to have the confidence and friendship of the Chinese Government before and after exercising those good offices. We could not, he said, propose that the Chinese negotiate with Japan until we knew what the basic terms were which Japan intended to propose and it can be imagined what a difficult situation would be created if, after a meeting between Prince Konoye and the President, an explosion should take place in China as a result of dissatisfaction with the results of that meeting. The Secretary explained further that we could not now afford to have the Chinese think that we were ignoring their interests in going ahead with any arrangements and that it was our idea to help the Japanese achieve the purpose of establishing friendship with China on a solid basis. In this way the Secretary said we could work together, Japan and the United States, in order to make the most of the potentialities of the 500,000,000 people of China as a trading nation.

The Ambassador commented that of course the China question was a very important matter but in view of the widespread press comments to the effect that the situation had now come to a show-down between Japan and the United States were there not other questions pending between the United States and Japan even apart from the China question which could be disposed of at the meeting with a view to tiding over a critical situation.

The Secretary replied that it was quite true that there were these other questions but that the China question was one of the pivotal questions underlying relations between the United States and Japan and if this question remained unsettled to the satisfaction of all there would remain the roots of future instability and trouble. The Ambassador said that he recognized the soundness of what the Secretary said especially in view of the French Indo-China situation. Mr. Ballantine said he assumed that what the Ambassador had reference to was the Japanese assurance that they would withdraw their troops from French Indo-China as soon as the China affair was settled.

The Ambassador then recapitulated briefly what the Secretary had said, namely, that the Secretary considers that there should be an agreement in principle on the outstanding questions of importance prior to the holding of the meeting, that the meeting would serve the purpose of ratifying agreement in principle already reached, that the Secretary considered that the Chinese question was one of the pivotal subjects calling for settlement, and that this Government in exercising its good offices between China and Japan would have to consider the basic terms on which Japan proposed to negotiate. The Secretary said this represented his views. The Ambassador said that he recognized that what the Secretary said was quite reasonable. The Ambassador had misgivings as to how far the Japanese Government could go on account of the internal political difficulties in Japan. He said, however, that Prince Konoye was a man of great courage and was prepared to assume great risks in bringing to a successful conclusion an effort to improve relations.

J(OSEPH) W. B(ALLANTINE)

Memorandum By The Secretary Of State

Foreign Relations, Japan, II 588-589.

[WASHINGTON,] September 3, 1941

At the request of the President, the Japanese Ambassador called at the White House this afternoon. The President proceeded at once to read the written oral statement . . . which had been prepared in reply to the communication recently sent to the President by the Japanese Prime Minister. He emphasized certain points as he read. He particularly emphasized the fact that he appreciated the difficulties of Prince Konoye in connection with the Japanese internal situation, but he added that he has dificulties here which he hoped that Prince Konoye and his Government would appreciate. The President referred to his recent conversations with Prime Minister Churchill, especially that portion relating to plebiscites at the end of the war as the best means of settling many differences and as the soundest policy of dealing with conditions existing between different races. He cited several instances existing at the end of the World War, which were effectively dealt with by plebiscites.

The President then proceeded to read his letter to Prime Minister Konoye . . . . The Ambassador inquired if the President was still favorable to a conference and the President replied that he was, but that it was very important to settle a number of these questions beforehand, if the success of the conference was to be safeguarded to the extent warranted by the holding of such a meeting. It was also emphasized that if and when we had secured sufficient assurances from the Japanese Government that it stands earnestly for all of the principles which this Government has been proclaiming as applicable to the Pacific area, it would be necessary for us to discuss the matter fully with the British, the Chinese and the Dutch, since there is no other way to effect a suitable peaceful settlement for the Pacific area; that any settlement must be on a basis that will restore confidence and friendliness among the nations concerned; in no other way can a suitable economic structure be rebuilt for that area. The Ambassador seemed to appreciate this viewpoint. Both the President and I repeatedly emphasized the necessity for his Government to clarify its position on the question of abandoning a policy of force and conquest and on three fundamental questions concerning which difficulties had been encountered in our discussion of the Japanese proposal of May twelfth and the discussion of which we had not pursued after the Japanese went into Indo-China. The Ambassador said that Prince Konoye, while preferring to go to Hawaii, would be disposed to go to any place in the Pacific where there was suitable anchorage.

The Ambassador then proceeded to say that he had a despatch from Tokyo referring to the fact that certain elements of opposition to the proposals of the Prime Minister existed and were active in their opposition. He said that the Government, however, is determined to overcome such opposition. He stated that a meeting between the President and the Prime Minister would enable Japan to overcome these disagreements at home and that the opposition would gradually get in line with the Government. He said that Konoye thinks that he and the President can discuss the three questions which were left untouched when the Japanese went into Indo-China in July, mainly the question relating to the complete evacuation of Japanese troops from China, the question of non-discrimination in commerce, et cetera, et cetera, and the Tripartite Pact.

It was made clear to the Ambassador that several days should be consumed by his Government both in clarifying and stating strongly its position on the principles already referred to and their application so far as China is concerned, and also that their Government should by word and act in every way possible devote some time at once to the education and organization of public opinion in support of the proposals for a peaceful settlement, as already set forth.

C(ORDELL H(ULL)

Memorandum By The Adviser On Political Relations (Hornbeck)*

Foreign Relations, 1941, Far East, pp. 425-428.

[WASHINGTON,] September 5, 1941

The chief danger attendant upon the holding of a meeting between the President and the Japanese Prime Minister is that if such a meeting is held there must emanate from it an agreement. The only kind of an agreement that could possibly be arrived at would be an agreement in most general terms. Such an agreement would not (in the light of what we know of this

*Unsigned "Comment on the question of holding (at this time) a conference."

country's attitude and policy and of what we are now given regarding Japan's attitude and policy) represent any real meeting of the minds of the two persons who could become parties to it, and still less would it represent a meeting of the minds of the people of the two countries thus committed by it. In entering into such an agreement neither of the parties to it would intend or expect that his country would, by the consummation of that agreement, be diverted from its present principles, objectives, policies or even procedures. Each of the parties would be motivated in large part by political *fears* and *hopes;* each would be playing for time and hoping for miracles to come; each would be expecting that a make-shift and make-delay agreement would be advantageous for his side; each would be expecting to tell his own people far less than the whole truth about the meeting and about the agreement.

For the Japanese Premier, most of this would be "all to the good." Not so, however, for the American President. The world is not expecting of Japan today any battle for peace, any support of high principles, any aid for countries resisting aggression: Japan is one of the three allied aggressor powers and Japan intends to remain in the Tripartite Alliance for a good while to come. The United States has proclaimed itself the "arsenal of democracy" in support of principles and in resistance to aggressor powers; the world expects of the United States that it will not compromise with any aggressor power and that, on the contrary, it will assist the countries which are being aggressed against by giving them aid (and comfort) and by withholding aid (and comfort) from aggressor powers.

The United States has done no injury to Japan or to the world. Japan has done injury to both the United States and to the world.

The holding by the President of the United States now of a rendezvous with the Premier of Japan would be, so far as the United States is concerned, a gesture born of lack of confidence in the present position (actual military capacity) of the United States. It would be utterly unlike the meeting between the President and the British Prime Minister. It would more nearly resemble meetings which were held between Mr. Chamberlain and Mr. Hitler. Whatever might be said in some quarters of the "courage," the "vision" and the "nobility" of attempts to make and to maintain peace, this gesture would be construed and interpreted by, to and for the Japanese—and the Germans—as an indication of weakness and uncertainty on the part of the United States. And, it would give a terrific jolt to the Chinese and the Dutch and the Russians and even the British.

And then—the agreement—. It would not put a stop to Japanese aggression. It would not bring to an end Japan's effort to conquer China: it would on the contrary tend to facilitate that effort. It would not give the United States any *time* that we would not have in the absence of it. It would not afford us security. It might, if we relied on it as a factor in our defense, lead us faster and more surely toward war—not war with Germany alone but war with Germany *and* Japan, a war from which on our side the Chinese and the Russians might be missing.

For, if the United States makes an agreement with Japan, there would be no reason for us to assume with any confidence that the Chinese would continue to resist Japan or that the Soviet Union would not make an agreement with Japan. Then, were there such developments, the world line-up would be the United States and Great Britain (two only) against the Tripartite Alliance (Japan included) . . . .

The Chinese question is the central question now, and it will be that for a good while to come, in the problem of the Far East. That question cannot be disposed of without China's having a "say-so." And it cannot be disposed of between Japan and China without a military victory by Japan over China or a dissolution (which cannot be other than gradual) of Japan's military effort in and against China.

Whatever is necessary as a factual condition precedent for peace in western Europe is necessary, in broad terms of similarity, as a factual condition precedent for peace in eastern Asia.

To wean Japan away at this time—on paper or in appearance —from the Axis would be an achievement spectacular in aspect but of no substantial political or military value. For, Japan is not helping Germany except in a negative way (which she is doing only because the United States overestimates Japan's capacity to injure us) and Japan will not be helping Germany in any positive way unless and until the United States goes to war with Germany (at which time, if and when, it is problematical what Japan would do).

From the point of view of United States interests: Conclusion of an agreement with Japan is not an urgent desideratum. We are not in great danger vis-a-vis Japan and Japan is not capable of doing us any great injury. Japan, involved and weakened as she is by the "Chinese Incident," does not possess military capacity sufficient to warrant an attack by her upon the United States with any reasonable expectation on her part or ours of her defeating us in war. Were Japan to attack us, we could with a wisely strategic use of less than one-half of our Navy maintain a sound defensive position while we prepared for an ultimate offensive.

The degree of "tension" between the United States and Japan is exaggerated. The facts of the situation that now exists are working real hardship to Japan (as a nation at war) but are not working any real hardship to the United States. This condition of "tension" can continue for an indefinite period without our suffering much. Were Japan to make war on us, she could interfere for a while with our procuring of tin and rubber. But, there is a low minimum of likelihood that Japan will make war on us for (a) there are easier wars that she might make nearer home and (b) she is already at war with China and making out none too well there, and (c) she is waiting for clear signs—which are not likely to come in the near future— that the Germans are winning against either the Soviet Union or Great Britain. (If, however, Japan should get an agreement with us, the chance of her attacking the Soviet Union would be substantially increased.) There is little for us to gain but much for Japan to gain should a conclusion now of an agreement between the two countries be consummated. We are not "in a hole" and we need no helping out. Japan is "in a hole," she needs helping out, and she is trying to get us to be her helper. (But at the same time she is neither willing nor able to give up her position in the Axis Alliance.) She is half whipped in her war with China—and she hopes that, with the "lift" that conclusion of an agreement between her Premier and the President of the United States would give her, she will either be able to knock out China or be able to avoid being knocked out by China.

The Ambassador In Japan (Grew) To President Roosevelt

Foreign Relations, 1941, Far East, pp. 468-469.

TOKYO, September 22, 1941

DEAR FRANK: I have not bothered you with personal letters some time for the good reason that letters are now subject to long delays due to the infrequent sailings of ships carrying our diplomatic pouches, and because the developments in American-Japanese relations are moving so comparatively rapidly that my comments would generally be too much out of date to be helpful when they reached you. But I have tried and am constantly trying in my telegrams to the Secretary of State to paint an accurate picture of the moving scene from day to day. I hope that you see them regularly.

As you know from my telegrams, I am in close touch with Prince Konoye who in the face of bitter antagonism from extremist and pro-Axis elements in the country is courageously working for an improvement in Japan's relations with the United States. He bears the heavy responsibility for having allowed our relations to come to such a pass and he no doubt now sees the handwriting on the wall and realizes that Japan has nothing to hope for from the Tripartite Pact and must shift her orientation of policy if she is to avoid disaster; but whatever the incentive that has led to his present efforts, I am convinced that he now means business and will go as far as possible, without incurring open rebellion in Japan, to reach a reasonable understanding with us. In spite of all the evidence of Japan's bad faith in times past in failing to live up to her commitments, I believe that there is a better chance of the present Government implementing whatever commitments it may now undertake than has been the case in recent years. It seems to me highly unlikely that this chance will come again or that any Japanese statesman other than Prince Konoye could succeed in controlling the military extremists in carrying through a policy which they, in their ignorance of international affairs and economic laws, resent and oppose. The alternative to reaching a settlement now would be the greatly increased probability of war,—*Facilis descensus Averno est*—and while we would undoubtedly win in the end, I question whether it is in our own interest to see an impoverished Japan reduced to the position of a third-rate Power. I therefore must earnestly hope that we can come to terms, even if we must take on trust, at least to some degree, the continued good faith and ability of the present Government fully to implement those terms.

I venture to enclose a copy of a letter which I recently wrote to a Japanese friend who had expressed the hope that the United States would ultimately come to sympathize and to cooperate with Japan in pursuing her "legitimate interests and aspiration." The letter was sent by my friend, on his own initiative, to Prince Konoye.

My admiration of the masterly way in which you have led and are leading our country in the present turmoil in world affairs steadily increases.

Faithfully yours, JOSEPH C. GREW

The Secretary Of State To President Roosevelt

Foreign Relations, 1941, Far East, p. 483.

When the Jap Prime Minister requested a meeting with you he indicated a fairly basic program in generalities, but left open such questions as getting troops out of China, Tripartite pact, non-discrimination in trade on Pacific.

We indicated desire for meeting, but suggested first an agreement in principle on the vital questions left open, so as to insure the success of the conference.

Soon thereafter, the Japs *narrowed* their position on these basic questions, and now continue to urge the meeting at Juneau.

My suggestion is to recite their more liberal attitude when they first sought the meeting with you, with their much narrowed position *now,* and earnestly ask if they cannot go back to their original liberal attitude so we can start discussions *again* on agreement in principle *before* the meeting, and reemphasizing your desire for a meeting—

President Roosevelt To The Secretary Of State

Ibid.

HYDE PARK, N. Y., September 28, 1941.

I wholly agree with your pencilled note—to recite the more liberal attitude of the Japanese when they first sought the meeting, point out their much narrowed position now, earnestly ask if they cannot go back to their original attitude, start discussions again on agreement in principle, and reemphasize my hope for a meeting.

F (RANKLIN) D. R (OOSEVELT)

The Ambassador In Japan (Grew) To The Secretary Of State

Foreign Relations, 1941, Far East, 492.

TOKYO, October 1, 1941—9 p.m.
(Received 9:36 p.m.)

1561. For the Secretary and Under Secretary only. 1. My Polish colleague learns from his intimate contacts in the Black Dragon Society that the proposal of the Prime Minister to meet the President on American soil is now generally known in political circles in Tokyo and that the proposal is generally applauded, even in military circles, on the ground that the economic situation in Japan renders a settlement with the United States absolutely essential. It is said that delegations from important political groups have called on Prince Konoye to assure him that the country as a whole will support him in his endeavors to reach an agreement. These circles are under the impression that the Japanese Government has already agreed to meet the position of the United States but they further aver that, if the conference takes place, the Prime Minister will be obliged to accept the American conditions because it would be unthinkable for him to return to Japan having failed in his mission.

2. The circles mentioned above attach importance to the fact that Prince Konoye purposely absented himself from Tokyo on the anniversary of the conclusion of the Tripartite Alliance, that the celebration was reduced to a minimum and that German elements in Japan are now under close surveillance by the police.

3. The information in paragraph 1 above tends to support the repeated assurances conveyed to me by the Foreign Minister that all dificulties can and will be ironed out at the proposed conference between the responsible heads of the two Governments.

GREW

Memorandum By The Ambassador In Japan (Grew)

Foreign Relations, Japan, II, 697-698.

[TOKYO,] October 25, 1941

The informant* called on me at his own request this evening. He told me that just prior to the fall of the Konoye Cabinet a conference of the leading members of the Privy Council and of the Japanese armed forces had been summoned by the Emperor, who inquired if they were prepared to pursue a policy which would guarantee that there would be no war with the United States. The representatives of the Army and

---

*A reliable Japanese informant.

Navy who attended this conference did not reply to the Emperor's question, whereupon the latter, with a reference to the progressive policy pursued by the Emperor Meiji, his grandfather, in an unprecedented action ordered the armed forces to obey his wishes. The Emperor's definite stand necessitated the selection of a Prime Minister who would be in a position effectively to control the Army, the ensuing resignation of Prince Konoye, and the appointment of General Tojo who, while remaining in the Army active list, is committed to a policy of attempting to conclude successfully the current Japanese-American conversations.

The informant emphasized to me that the recent anti-American tone of the Japanese press and the extreme views expressed by pro-Axis and certain other elements gave no real indication of the desire of Japanese of all classes and in particular of the present political leaders that in some way or other an adjustment of relations with the United States must be brought about. He added in this connection that Mr. Togo, the new Foreign Minister, had accepted his appointment with the specific aim of endeavoring to pursue the current conversations to a successful end and it had been understood that should he fail in this he would resign his post.

The belief is current among Japanese leaders that the principal difficulty in the way of an understanding with the United States is the question of the removal of Japanese armed forces from China and Indo-China, but these same leaders are confident that, provided that Japan is not placed in an impossible position by the insistence on the part of the United States that all Japanese troops in these areas be withdrawn at once, such a removal can and will be successfully effected.

The informant, who is in contact with the highest circles, went on to say that for the first time in ten years the situation at present and the existing political set-up in Japan offer a possibility of a reorientation of Japanese policy and action.

J(OSEPH) C. G(REW)

THE AMBASSADOR IN JAPAN (GREW) TO THE
SECRETARY OF STATE
(Substance)

Foreign Relations, Japan, II, 701-704.

TOKYO, November 3, 1941—3 p.m.
(Received 4:19 p.m.)

1736. The Ambassador reports for Secretary Hull and Under Secretary Welles as follows:

(1) He cites a leading article from the Tokyo *Nichi Nichi* of November 1 . . . adding that a banner headline declaring "Empire Approaches Its Greatest Crisis" introduced a despatch from New York with a summary of a statement the Japanese Embassy reportedly gave to the *New York Times* regarding the need of ending the United States-Japanese economic war. Both the article and the *Nichi Nichi* editorial . . . are believed to be close reflections of Japanese sentiments at present.

(2) The Ambassador refers to his various telegraphic reports during several months past analyzing the factors affecting policy in Japan and says he has nothing to add thereto nor any substantial revision to make thereof. In his opinion, a conclusive estimate may be had of Japan's position through the application to the existing situation and the immediate future of the following points:

(a) It is not possible for Japan to dissociate either Japan or the conflict with China from the war in Europe and its fluctuations.

(b) In Japan political thought ranges from medieval to liberal ideas and public opinion is thus a variable quantity. The impact of events and conditions beyond Japan may determine at any given time which school of thought shall predominate. (In the democracies, on the other hand, owing to a homogeneous body of principles which influence and direct foreign policy and because methods instead of principles are more likely to cause differences of opinion, public opinion is formed differently.) For example, in Japan the pro-Axis elements gained power following last year's German victories in Western Europe; then Japanese doubt of ultimate German victory was created by Germany's failure to invade the British Isles, this factor helping to reinforce the moderate elements; and finally Germany's attack on the Soviet Union upset the expectation of continued Russo-German peace and made the Japanese realize that those who took Japan into the Tripartite Alliance had misled Japan.

(c) An attempt to correct the error of 1940 may be found in the efforts to adjust Japanese relations with the United States and thereby to lead the way to conclusion of peace with China, made by Prince Konoye and promised by the Tojo Cabinet. If this attempt fails, and if success continues to favor German arms, a final, closer Axis alignment may be expected.

(d) The Embassy in Japan has never been convinced by the theory that Japan's collapse as a militaristic power would shortly result from the depletion and the eventual exhaustion of Japan's financial and economic resources, as propounded by many leading American economists. Such forecasts were unconsciously based upon the assumption that a dominant consideration would be Japan's retention of the capitalistic system. The outcome they predicted has not transpired, although it is true that the greater part of Japan's commerce has been lost, Japanese industrial production has been drastically curtailed, and Japan's national resources have been depleted. Instead, there has been a drastic prosecution of the process to integrate Japan's national economy, lacking which there might well have occurred the predicted collapse of Japan. What has happened to date therefore does not support the view that continuation of trade embargoes and imposition of a blockade (proposed by some) can best avert war in the Far East.

(3) The Ambassador mentions his telegram No. 827, September 12, 1940 (which reported the "golden opportunity" seen by Japanese army circles for expansion as a consequence of German triumphs in Europe). He sent this telegram under circumstances and at a time when it appeared unwise and futile for the United States to adopt conciliatory measures.

The strong policy recommended in the telegram was subsequently adopted by the United States. This policy, together with the impact of world political events upon Japan brought the Japanese Government to the point of seeking conciliation with the United States. If these efforts fail, the Ambassador foresees a probable swing of the pendulum in Japan once more back to the former Japanese position or even farther. This would lead to what he has described as an all-out, do-or-die attempt, actually risking national hara-kiri, to make Japan impervious to economic embargoes abroad rather than to yield to foreign pressure. It is realized by observers who feel Japanese national temper and psychology from day to day that, beyond peradventure, this contingency not only is possible but is probable.

(4) If the fiber and temper of the Japanese people are kept in mind, the view that war probably would be averted, though there might be some risk of war, by progressively imposing drastic economic measures is an uncertain and dangerous hypothesis upon which to base considered United States policy and measures. War would not be averted by such a course, if it is taken, in the opinion of the Embassy. However, each view is only an opinion, and, accordingly, to postulate the correctness of either one and to erect a definite policy thereon would, in the belief of the Embassy, be contrary to American national interests. It would mean putting the cart before the horse. The primary point to be decided apparently involves the question whether war with Japan is justified by American national objectives, policies, and needs in the case of failure of the first line of national defense, namely, diplomacy, since it would be possible only on the basis of such a decision for the Roosevelt administration to follow a course which would be divested as much as possible of elements of uncertainty, speculation, and opinion. The Ambassador does not doubt that such a decision, irrevocable as it might well prove to be, already has been debated fully and adopted, because the sands are running fast.

(5) The Ambassador emphasized that, in the above discussion of this grave, momentous subject, he is out of touch

with the intentions and thoughts of the Administration thereon, and he does not at all mean to imply that Washington is pursuing an undeliberated policy. Nor does he intend to advocate for a single moment any "appeasement" of Japan by the United States or recession in the slightest degree by the United States Government from the fundamental principles laid down as a basis for the conduct and adjustment of international relations, American relations with Japan included. There should be no compromise with principles, though methods may be flexible. The Ambassador's purpose is only to ensure against the United States becoming involved in war with Japan because of any possible misconception of Japan's capacity to rush headlong into a suicidal struggle with the United States. While national sanity dictates against such action, Japanese sanity cannot be measured by American standards of logic. The Ambassador sees no need for much anxiety respecting the bellicose tone and substance at present of the Japanese press (which in the past several years has attacked the United States intensely in recurrent waves), but he points out the shortsightedness of underestimating Japan's obvious preparations to implement an alternative program in the event the peace program fails. He adds that similarly it would be shortsighted for American policy to be based upon the belief that Japanese preparations are no more than saber rattling, merely intended to give moral support to the high pressure diplomacy of Japan. Action by Japan which might render unavoidable an armed conflict with the United States may come with dangerous and dramatic suddenness.

GREW

Memorandum By The Ambassador In Japan (Grew)

Foreign Relations, Japan, II, 710-714.

[TOKYO,] November 10, 1941

The Foreign Minister recalled the conversation which he had had with me on October 30, when he said that he was firmly of the opinion that the maintenance of friendly relations between the United States and Japan was a practicable proposition. He went on to say that he had given constant thought to this matter and that he had determined to put forward every effort to re-establish relations between the two countries on a friendly basis and to maintain peace in the Pacific. It was the purpose of the present Cabinet to continue with the project of establishing a "Great East Asia" as a contribution toward world peace. Mr. Togo said that ever since he has assumed office he had been intensively studying the documents relating to the conversations which have thus far taken place. Fresh proposals had been formulated and had been sent to Admiral Nomura, who had been instructed to enter into negotiations with the President and the Secretary of State. I interrupted the Foreign Minister to say that our Government had been careful to emphasize that it was engaged in "preliminary and exploratory conversations" with the Japanese Government. Mr. Togo replied that he was well aware of that fact, but that he wondered whether the time had not come to enter into formal and official negotiations. However, he said that he did not wish to press the point.

Mr. Togo went on to say that only recently Mr. Kurusu had been dispatched to Washington to assist Admiral Nomura in conducting the conversations. . . .

What he most keenly felt, the Foreign Minister continued, from reviewing the documents recording conversations which have thus far taken place was that the knowledge and appreciation of the United States with regard to the realities of the situation in the Far East are unfortunately inadequate. Although Mr. Hull had admitted that Japan is a stabilizing force in the Far East, the position taken by the United States throughout the conversations had not been in harmony with that fact. Unless the American Government should take full cognizance of the fact that Japan has been engaged in hostilities with China for four and a half years, then the admission of Japan's being a stabilizing force in the Far East would have in actuality no meaning. Mr. Togo said that Mr. Hull, in a conversation with Mr. Wakasugi on October 16, recalled that he recalled that he had told former Ambassador Saito that he recognized Japan as a stabilizing force and would be prepared to express such recognition in an official manner. The Minister went on to say that the population of this country is steadily and rapidly increasing; it was now about one hundred million; and it was necessary to assure raw materials necessary for their existence. It was his opinion that unless the American Government realizes this fact as among the realities of the situation, successful conclusion to the conversations would be difficult. During the conversations carried on for a period of more than six months, the Japanese Government had repeatedly made proposals calculated to approach the American point of view, but the American Government for its part had taken no step toward meeting the Japanese position and had yielded nothing —it had perhaps taken a more advanced position. Those being the facts, "we in Japan are led to wonder what is the degree of sincerity of the American Government in continuing the conversations." He said that national sentiment will not tolerate further protracted delay in arriving at some conclusion. Referring to the fact that the Diet is shortly to meet, he emphasized that the position is daily becoming more pressing. He expressed the hope that the American Government would take a statesmanlike position and view the problems to be resolved from the broadest possible viewpoint—that it would try to settle these problems "with one sweep." It was his opinion that otherwise the prospects of overcoming the present difficulties would be small.

. . . .

The Foreign Minister remarked that he was quite prepared to admit that the Embassy is endeavoring to report accurately on the situation in the Far East, but that, in view of the position which is being taken by the American Government, he wondered whether the American Government has in fact a correct appreciation of the realities. To illustrate his point, he wished to cite the question of the stationing of Soviet troops in Outer Mongolia, which was universally recognized to be a part of China. So far as he knew no one had objected to the presence of Soviet troops in Outer Mongolia. With regard to my comment on the phrase "stabilizing force in East Asia," the Foreign Minister said that there should be a satisfactory interpretation of that phrase from a common-sense point of view. With regard to my observations on the question of assuring to Japan sources of raw materials the Foreign Minister said that this was a question which had been debated over a period of years at Geneva and eleswhere. He did not wish to go into the fundamentals of the question, but he thought that he could advert briefly to the importance of commercial and economic relations between the United States and Japan. The freezing by the United States of Japanese assets had stopped supplies of many important raw materials to Japan. Economic pressure of this character is capable of menacing national existence to a greater degree than the direct use of force. He hoped that the American Government would take into consideration circumstances of this character and realize the possibility that the Japanese people, if exposed to continued economic pressure might eventually feel obliged resolutely to resort to measures of self-defense.

The Minister went on to say that Japan had been engaged in extensive hostilities for a period of more than four years, and that if Japan were called upon to sacrifice the fruits of such protracted hostilities she must inevitably collapse. If the American Government realized this fact a speedy conclusion to the conversations will be easy.

I pointed out the apparent inconsistency between the Minister's emphasis on the insistence of Japan that she retain the fruits of hostilities and Japan's acceptance of the principle of refraining from aggression and the use of force.

The Foreign Minister replied that Japan is not conducting a war of aggression and that therefore no question arises of her retaining the fruits of aggression. It is his impression that the American Government is now resorting, under the plea of self-defense, to measures over and beyond those that are generally recognized by international law. He expressed the opinion that it might not be out of place for Japan to ask the United States not to put too liberal a construction on the principle of self-defense. In any event, it was his opinion that theoretical discussions would not promote the conversations, which he thought should be pursued along realistic lines.

The conversation then turned to another matter which is covered by a separate memorandum.

J(OSEPH) C. G(REW)

The Ambassador In Japan (Grew) To The Secretary Of State
(Substance)

Foreign Relations, Japan, II, 743-744.

TOKYO, November 17, 1941—8 p.m.
(Received November 17—2:09 p.m.)

1814. The Ambassador, referring to his previous telegram No. 1736 of November 3, 3 p.m., final sentence, emphasizes the need to guard against sudden Japanese naval or military actions in such areas as are not now involved in the Chinese theater of operations. He is taking into account, therefore, the probability of the Japanese exploiting every possible tactical advantage, such as surprise and initiative. He advises his Government accordingly of the importance of not placing the major responsibility in giving prior warning upon the Embassy staff, the naval and military attaches included, since in Japan there is extremely effective control over both primary and secondary information. The Embassy would not expect to obtain any information in advance either from personal Japanese contacts or through the press; the observation of military movements is not possible by the few Americans remaining in the country, concentrated mostly in three cities (Tokyo, Yokohama, Kobe); and with American and other foreign shipping absent from adjacent waters the Japanese are assured of the ability to send without foreign observation their troop transports in various directions. Japanese troop concentrations were reported recently by American consuls in Manchuria and Formosa, while troop dispositions since last July's general mobilization have, according to all other indications available, been made with a view to enabling the carrying out of new operations on the shortest possible notice either in the Pacific southwest or in Siberia or in both.

The Ambassador expresses the Embassy's full realization that the present most important duty perhaps is to detect any premonitory signs of naval or military operations likely in areas mentioned above and states that every precaution is being taken to guard against surprise. He adds that the Embassy's field of naval or military observation is restricted almost literally to what could be seen with the naked eye, and this is negligible. Therefore, the United States Government is advised, from an abundance of caution to discount as much as possible the likelihood of the Embassy's ability to give substantial warning.

GREW

Draft Proposal Handed By The Japanese Ambassador (Nomura) To The Secretary Of Of State On November 20, 1941

Foreign Relations, Japan, II, 755-756.

1. Both the Governments of Japan and the United States undertake not to make any armed advancement into any of the regions in South-eastern Asia and the Southern Pacific area excepting the part of French Indo-China where the Japanese troops are stationed at present.

2. The Japanese Government undertakes to withdraw its troops now stationed in French Indo-China upon either the restoration of peace between Japan and China or the establishment of an equitable peace in the Pacific area.

In the meantime the Government of Japan declares that it is prepared to remove its troops now stationed in the southern part of French Indo-China to the northern part of said territory upon the conclusion of the present arrangement which shall later be embodied in the final agreement.

3. The Government of Japan and the United States shall cooperate with a view to securing the acquisition of those goods and commodities which the two countries need in Netherlands East Indies.

4. The Governments of Japan and the United States mutually undertake to restore their commercial relations to those prevailing prior to the freezing of the assets.

The Government of the United States shall supply Japan a required quantity of oil.

5. The Government of the United States undertakes to refrain from such measures and actions as will be prejudicial to the endeavors for the restoration of general peace between Japan and China.

Memorandum By Mr. Joseph W. Ballantine To The Secretary Of State

Foreign Relations, 1941, Far East, pp. 633-634.

[WASHINGTON,] November 22, 1941

MR. SECRETARY: With reference to the Japanese proposal of November 20 for a *modus vivendi* and our memorandum containing suggestions for possible comment that might be made orally to the Japanese in regard to their proposal . . . there are given below additional suggestions for possible comment.

With reference to item three in regard to cooperation in obtaining from the Netherlands East Indies materials which our two countries need, it is not clear why the Japanese Government desires to limit this proposal to the Netherlands East Indies. It would appear to us that, if the Japanese Government could see its way clear to adopting our proposal in regard to commercial policy, the field for cooperation by the two countries would not be limited to any one area but would extend to the entire world. It would seem to us that the Japanese proposal takes no account of our broad offer which was renewed in very specific terms in the paper which was given to the Japanese

Ambassador on November 15. It would seem to us that such a proposal would be open to possible criticism. That is to say that, whereas Japan was insisting on preferential treatment for itself in certain areas, in other areas it was asking for cooperation of the United States in obtaining for Japan the very kind of economic opportunities which Japan was trying to deny to third countries elsewhere. This Government has consistently advocated broadening the basis of world trade not from any selfish point of view but from the point of view of providing stable peace and elimination of chronic political instability and recurrent economic collapse. Such a program would provide means of raising living standards all over the world, thus promoting the well-being of all peoples.

With reference to the provision that the Government of the United States should supply Japan a required quantity of oil, it may be observed that until very recently the United States was supplying Japan with an ever-increasing amount of petroleum products, even to the extent where there was widespread public criticism in the United States of permitting this to continue. The period since 1937 was marked, on the one hand, by a tremendous increase in imports into Japan from the United States of petroleum products and, on the other hand, according to reports reaching us, by a progressive curtailment in the amounts of oil released in that country for normal peacetime consumption. There is no desire in this country to deny to Japan petroleum products needed for its normal economy, but the increased consumption of American petroleum products in Japan for a military purpose brings to the fore a question which we have called to the attention of the Japanese Ambassador, namely, that the Japanese association with the Axis powers is doing the United States tremendous injury.

With regard to the fifth point in the Japanese proposal, you might emphasize again what you said to the Japanese Ambassador on November 20, namely, that, when the Japanese complain about our helping China, the public in this country wonders what is underneath the Anti-Comintern Pact; that Japanese statesmen ought to understand that we are helping China for the same reason that we are helping Britain; that we are afraid of the military elements throughout the world led by Hitler; and that the methods adopted by the Japanese military leaders in China are not unlike Hitler's methods. You might then ask what the Ambassador thinks would be the public reaction in this country if we were to announce that we had decided to discontinue aid to Great Britain. You might say that in the minds of the American people the purposes underlying our aid to China are the same as the purposes underlying our aid to Great Britain and that the American people believe that there is a partnership between Hitler and Japan aimed at dividing the world between them.

J(OSEPH) W. B(ALLANTINE)

Memorandum Of A Conversation

Foreign Relations, Japan, II, 764-770.

[WASHINGTON,] November 26, 1941.

The Japanese Ambassador and Mr. Kurusu called by appointment at the Department. The Secretary handed each of the Japanese copies of an outline of a proposed basis of an agreement between the United States and Japan and an explanatory oral statement.

After the Japanese had read the documents, Mr. Kurusu asked whether this was our reply to their proposal for a *modus vivendi*. The Secretary replied that we had to treat the proposal as we did, as there was so much turmoil and confusion among the public both in the United States and in Japan. He reminded the Japanese that in the United States we have a political situation to deal with just as does the Japanese Government, and he referred to fire-eating statements which have been recently coming out of Tokyo, which he said had been causing a natural reaction among the public in this country. He said that our proposed agreement would render possible practical measures of financial cooperation, which, however, were not referred to in the outline for fear that this might give rise to misunderstanding. He also referred to the fact that he had earlier in the conversations acquainted the Ambassador of the ambition that had been his of settling the immigration question but that the situation had so far prevented him from realizing that ambition.

Mr. Kurusu offered various depreciatory comments in regard to the proposed agreement. He noted that in our statement of principles there was a reiteration of the Stimson doctrine. He objected to the proposal for multilateral non-aggression pacts and referred to Japan's experience of international organizations, citing the case of the award against Japan by the Hague tribunal in the Perpetual Leases matter. He went on to say that the Washington Conference Treaties had given a wrong idea to China, that China had taken advantage of them to flaunt Japan's rights. He said he did not see how his Government could consider paragraphs (3) and (4) of the proposed agreement and that if the United States should expect that Japan was to take off its hat to Chiang Kai-shek and propose to recognize him Japan could not agree. He said that if this was the idea of the American Government he did not see how any agreement was possible.

The Secretary asked whether this matter could not be worked out.

Mr. Kurusu said that when they reported our answer to their Government it would be likely to throw up its hands. He noted that this was a tentative proposal without commitment, and suggested that it might be better if they did not refer it to their Government before discussing its contents further informally here.

The Secretary suggested that they might wish to study the documents carefully before discussing them further. He repeated that we were trying to do our best to keep the public from becoming uneasy as a result of their being harangued. He explained that in the light of all that has been said in the press, our proposal was as far as we would go at this time in reference to the Japanese proposal; that there was so much confusion among the public that it was necessary to bring about some clarification; that we have reached a stage when the public has lost its perspective and that it was therefore necessary to draw up a document which would present a complete picture of our position by making provision for each essential point involved.

The Secretary then referred to the oil question. He said that public feeling was so acute on that question that he might almost be lynched if he permitted oil to go freely to Japan. He pointed out that if Japan should fill Indo-China with troops our people would not know what lies ahead in the way of a menace to the countries to the south and west. He reminded the Japanese that they did not know what tremendous injury they were doing to us by keeping immobilized so many forces in countries neighboring Indo-China. He explained that we are primarily out for our permanent futures, and the question of Japanese troops in Indo-China affects our direct interests.

Mr. Kurusu reverted to the difficulty of Japan's renouncing its support of Wang Ching-wei. The Secretary pointed out that Chiang Kai-shek had made an outstanding contribution in bringing out national spirit in China and expressed the view that the Nanking regime had not asserted itself in a way that would impress the world. Mr. Kurusu agreed with what the Secretary had said about Chiang, but observed that the question of the standing of the Nanking regime was a matter of opinion. His arguments on this as well as on various other points were specious, and unconvincing.

The Ambassador took the occasion to observe that sometimes statesmen of firm conviction fail to get sympathizers among the public; that only wise men could see far ahead and sometimes suffered martydom; but that life's span was short and one could only do his duty. The Ambassador then asked whether there was no other possibility and whether they could not see the President.

The Secretary replied that he had no doubt that the President would be glad to see them at any time.

Mr. Kurusu said that he felt that our response to their proposal could be interpreted as tantamount to meaning the end, and asked whether we were not interested in a *modus vivendi.*

The Secretary replied that we had explored that. Mr. Kurusu asked whether it was because the other powers would not agree; but the Secretary replied simply that he had done his best in the way of exploration.

The Ambassador when rising to go raised the question of publicity. The Secretary replied that he had it in mind to give the press something of the situation tomorrow, and asked what the Ambassador thought. The Ambassador said that he did not wish to question the Secretary's right to give out what he desired in regard to the American proposal. The Ambassador said he would like to have Mr. Wakasugi call on Mr. Ballantine on Thursday to discuss further details.

J(OSEPH) W. B(ALLANTINE)

Oral Statement Handed By The Secretary Of State To The Japanese Ambassador (Nomura) On November 26, 1941

[WASHINGTON,] November 26, 1941.

The representatives of the Government of the United States and of the Government of Japan have been carrying on during the past several months informal and exploratory conversations for the purpose of arriving at a settlement if possible of questions relating to the entire Pacific area based upon the principles of peace, law and order and fair dealing among nations. These principles include the principles of inviolability of territorial integrity and sovereignty of each and all nations; the principle of non-interference in the internal affairs of other countries; the principle of equality, including equality of commercial opportunity and treatment; and the principle of reliance upon international cooperation and conciliation for the prevention and pacific settlement of controversies and for improvement of international conditions by peaceful methods and processes.

It is believed that in our discussions some progress has been made in reference to the general principles which constitute the basis of a peaceful settlement covering the entire Pacific area; that it would be helpful toward creating an atmosphere favorable to the successful outcome of the conversations if a temporary *modus vivendi* could be agreed upon to be in effect while the conversations looking to a peaceful settlement in the Pacific were continuing. On November 20 the Japanese Ambassador communicated to the Secretary of State proposals in regard to temporary measures to be taken respectively by the Government of Japan and by the Government of the United States, which measures are understood to have been designed to accomplish the purposes above indicated.

The Government of the United States most earnestly desires to contribute to the promotion and maintenance of peace and stability in the Pacific area, and to afford every opportunity for the continuance of discussions with the Japanese Government directed toward working out a broad-gauge program of peace throughout the Pacific area. The proposals which were presented by the Japanese Ambassador on November 20 contain some features which, in the opinion of this Government, conflict with the fundamental principles which form part of the general settlement under consideration and to which each Government has declared that it is committed. The Government of the United States believes that the adoption of such proposals would not be likely to contribute to the ultimate objectives of ensuring peace under law, order and justice in the Pacific area, and it suggests that further effort be made to resolve our divergences of views in regard to the practical application of the fundamental principles already mentioned.

With this object in view the Government of the United States offers for the consideration of the Japanese Government a plan of a broad but simple settlement covering the entire Pacific area as one practical exemplification of a program which this Government envisages as something to be worked out during our further conversations.

The plan therein suggested represents an effort to bridge the gap between our draft of June 21, 1941 and the Japanese draft of September 25 by making a new approach to the essential problems underlying a comprehensive Pacific settlement. This plan contains provisions dealing with the practical application of the fundamental principles which we have agreed in our conversations constitute the only sound basis for worthwhile international relations. We hope that in this way progress toward reaching a meeting of minds between our two Governments may be expedited.

Document Handed By The Secretary Of State To The Japanese Ambassador (Nomura) On November 26, 1941

Strictly Confidential,
Tentative and Without
Commitment.

WASHINGTON, November 26, 1941

Outline Of Proposed Basis For Agreement Between The United States And Japan

SECTION I.

Draft Mutual Declaration of Policy

The Government of the United States and the Government of Japan both being solicitous for the peace of the Pacific affirm that their national policies are directed toward lasting and extensive peace throughout the Pacific area, that they have no territorial designs in that area, that they have no intention of threatening other countries or of using military force aggressively against any neighboring nation, and that, accordingly, in their national policies they will actively support and give practical application to the following fundamental principles upon which their relations with each other and with all other governments are based:

(1) The principle of inviolability of territorial integrity and sovereignty of each and all nations.

(2) The principle of non-interference in the internal affairs of other countries.

(3) The principle of equality, including equality of commercial opportunity and treatment.

(4) The principle of reliance upon international cooperation and conciliation for the prevention and pacific settlements of controversies and for improvement of international conditions by peaceful methods and processes.

The Government of Japan and the Government of the United States have agreed that toward eliminating chronic political instability, preventing recurrent economic collapse, and providing a basis for peace, they will actively support and practically apply the following principles in their economic relations with each other and with other nations and peoples:

(1) The principle of non-discrimination in international commercial relations.

(2) The principle of international economic cooperation and abolition of extreme nationalism as expressed in excessive trade restrictions.

(3) The principle of non-discriminatory access by all nations to raw material supplies.

(4) The principle of full protection of the interests of consuming countries and populations as regards the operation of international commodity agreements.

(5) The principle of establishment of such institutions and arrangements of international finance as may lend aid to the essential enterprises and the continuous development of all countries and may permit payments through processes of trade consonant with the welfare of all countries.

SECTION II.

Steps To Be Taken by the Government of the United States and by the Government of Japan

The Government of the United States and the Government of Japan propose to take steps as follows:

1. The Government of the United States and the Government of Japan will endeavor to conclude a multilateral non-

aggression pact among the British Empire, China, Japan, the Netherlands, the Soviet Union, Thailand and the United States.

2. Both Governments will endeavor to conclude among the American, British, Chinese, Japanese, the Netherland and Thai Governments an agreement whereunder each of the Governments would pledge itself to respect the territorial integrity of French Indo-China and, in the event that there should develop a threat to the territorial integrity of Indo-China, to enter into immediate consultation with a view to taking such measures as may be deemed necessary and advisable to meet the threat in question. Such agreement would provide also that each of the governments party to the agreement would not seek or accept preferential treatment in its trade or economic relations with Indo-China and would use its influence to obtain for each of the signatories equality of treatment in trade and commerce with French Indo-China.

3. The Government of Japan will withdraw all military, naval, air and police forces from China and from Indo-China.

4. The Government of the United States and the Government of Japan will not support—militarily, politically, economically—any government or regime in China other than the National Government of the Republic of China with capital temporarily at Chungking.

5. Both Governments will give up all extraterritorial rights in China, including rights and interests in and with regard to international settlements and concessions, and rights under the Boxer Protocol of 1901.

Both Governments will endeavor to obtain the agreement of the British and other governments to give up extraterritorial rights in China, including rights in international settlements and in concessions and under the Boxer Protocol of 1901.

6. The Government of the United States and the Government of Japan will enter into negotiations for the conclusion between the United States and Japan of a trade agreement, based upon reciprocal most-favored-nation treatment and reduction of trade barriers by both countries, including an undertaking by the United States to bind raw silk on the free list.

7. The Government of the United States and the Government of Japan will, respectively, remove the freezing restrictions on Japanese funds in the United States and on American funds in Japan.

8. Both Governments will agree upon a plan for the stabilization of the dollar-yen rate, with the allocation of funds adequate for the purpose, half to be supplied by Japan and half by the United States.

9. Both Governments will agree that no agreement which either has concluded with any third power or powers shall be interpreted by it in such a way as to conflict with the fundamental purpose of this agreement, the establishment and preservation of peace throughout the Pacific area.

10. Both Governments will use their influence to cause other governments to adhere to and to give practical application to the basic political and economic principles set forth in this agreement.

The Secretary Of State To The Ambassador In Japan (Grew)

Foreign Relations, 1941, Far East, pp. 683-684.

WASHINGTON, November 28, 1941—7 p.m.

796. For the Ambassador and the Counselor only. Following the Japanese proposals of November 20, the Department gave consideration to a number of alternate proposals and counter-suggestions or combinations thereof which suggested themselves to the Department for possible presentation to the Japanese Government. At one time the Department considered the question of presenting to the Japanese Government simultaneously with the proposal which was actually given them on November 26, an alternate plan for a temporary *modus vivendi*. The draft under consideration at that time called for a temporary *modus vivendi* to be in effect for a period of 3 months during which time conversations would continue toward the working out of a comprehensive peaceful settlement covering the entire Pacific

area. At the end of the period of the term of the *modus vivendi* both Governments would confer at the request of either to determine whether the extension of the *modus vivendi* was justified by the prospects of reaching a settlement of the sort sought.

The draft *modus vivendi* which we were considering contained mutual pledges of peaceful intent, a reciprocal undertaking not to make armed advancement in northeastern Asia and the northern Pacific area, southeast Asia and the southern Pacific area, an undertaking by Japan to withdraw its forces from southern French Indo-China, to limit those in northern Indo-China to the number there on July 26, 1941, which number should not be subject to replacement and Japan should not in any case send additional naval, military or air forces to Indo-China. This Government would undertake to modify its freezing orders to the extent to permit exports from the United States to Japan of bunkers and ship supplies, food products and pharmaceuticals with certain qualifications, raw cotton up to $600,000 monthly, a small amount of petroleum within categories now permitted general export on a monthly basis for civilian needs, the proportionate amount to be exported from this country to be determined after consultation with the British and Dutch Governments. The United States would permit imports in general provided that raw silk constitutes at least two-thirds in value of such imports. The proceeds of such imports would be available for the purchase of the designated exports from the United States and for the payment of interest and principal of Japanese obligations within the United States. This Government would undertake to approach the British, Dutch and Australian Governments on the question of their taking similar economic measures.

At a certain point in our consideration of the draft *modus vivendi* the representative in Washington of the British, Dutch, Australian and Chinese Governments were consulted.

After careful consideration of all factors in the situation within the United States and in the general world situation, including the reaction and replies of the Governments mentioned above, it was decided that we should drop the draft *modus vivendi* which we had had under consideration. That draft *modus vivendi* was not handed to the Japanese, and the fact that this Government had considered a *modus vivendi* was not mentioned to them.

The Department has informed you in separate telegrams of the documents handed the Japanese Ambassador on November 26 and of the conversation which took place on that date.

HULL

The Ambassador In Japan (Grew) To The Secretary Of State

Foreign Relations, 1941, Far East, p. 707.

TOKYO, December 1, 1941—8 p.m.
(Received December 1–3:02 p.m.)

1874. For the Secretary and Under Secretary. 1. During the past few days I have talked with several prominent Japanese, most of whom appear to be already familiar with the terms of the Department's recent draft proposal and some of whom have been in direct personal touch with the Foreign Minister. They generally reflect a pessimistic reaction, emphasizing what they purport to regard as the unconciliatory "tone" of the draft and the difficulty of bridging over the Japanese and American positions. They all, however, appear to desire continuance of the Washington conversations.

2. In all recent talks I have emphasized my personal view that the American draft conveys a broad-gauge objective proposal of the highest statesmanship, offering to Japan in effect the very desiderata for which she has ostensibly been fighting and a reasonable and peaceful way of achieving her constantly publicized needs. The Japanese Government is now in a position to mould public opinion to the justified conception that Japan can now achieve without force of arms the chief purposes for which she has hitherto allegedly been fighting. These unofficial views have been indirectly conveyed to the Foreign Minister. I have furthermore expressed astonishment that the

Prime Minister, at this critical moment, should have seen fit to deliver so bellicose an address as his speech yesterday, and I have indicated the serious and deplorable impression which that speech is bound to exert on the American Government and people.

3. Tonight's newspapers report that the Cabinet at its meeting today, while realizing the difficulty of adjusting the respective positions of the two countries, nevertheless determined to continue the Washington conversations.

GREW

The Ambassador In Japan (Grew) To The Secretary Of State

Foreign Relations, 1941, Far East, pp. 720-721.

TOKYO, December 5, 1941—5 p.m.
(Received 7:50 p.m.)

1895. For the Secretary and Under Secretary only. You will no doubt be aware that the American proposal is being represented here to the press and to the public as a mere restatement of "fanciful principles which ignore the realities of the situation," and that no intimation whatever has been given out that the proposal, if implemented, would provide Japan by peaceful and orderly processes with that security—political as well as economic—which she affects to seek by exercise of force. The response of most Japanese to whom we have said the American proposal, far from being a formulation of fanciful principles designed to preserve the old order of things, is a well-balanced, constructive, practical and forward-looking plan for creating order out of the disorders of the past, has been to express strong disappointment that the private individual is not in a position to form any intelligent opinion with regard to a matter of such supreme importance, while some have said that if the American proposal is actually such as we have described it to be, an attitude of intransigence on the part of the Japanese would be viewed with regret by the masses.

It is impossible to forecast precisely what effect publication of our proposal would have. Undoubtedly reaction to certain phases of the proposal, notably complete evacuation of China, would be strong and might be so violent as to eliminate the last possibility of an agreement. However, there would seem to be even greater risks of the elimination of that possibility if the points at issue continue in Japan to be befogged by ignorance and misrepresentation. I feel sure that you will have considered the wisdom of publishing the proposal as soon as possible after consultation with the Japanese Government but even without the latter's assent if that should not be forthcoming, publication to be accompanied by a statement substantially along the lines of the thought expressed in paragraph 2 of my 1874, December 1, 8 p.m.

A prominent Japanese in close touch with Government circles wrote to me in handwriting yesterday *inter alia*:

"The situation is most deplorable. I may understand how you feel and you know how I feel. Allow me to write to you frankly what I have now in my mind. After speaking with friends and studying their frame of mind I come to conclude that they feel without having the knowledge of the true nature of your document of the 26th November as if we received an ultimatum from Washington. Under such unfortunate psychology of your people the only way left us, I think, is that your government will broadmindedly take our proposal as a base of discussion for the *modus vivendi* with a view of arriving at final settlement on the line of your proposal. From sheer desire for happy ending I have to write you."

I believe this letter to be a fair criterion of public opinion here.

GREW

Index

Abe, Nobuyuki, 251
Air attack against Pearl Harbor, disbelief in possibility of, 74-75; Short's testimony about defense against, 77; warning about possibility of, 34
Aircraft, Kimmel's complaints about shortage of, 37 ff.; Short's complaints about shortage of, 77 ff.
Aircraft carriers, 36, 56
Alerts, Short's testimony about, 62-63, 68-69, 74
American-Japanese conversations, 15, 44 ff., 124 ff.; excerpts from, 277-318; Germany and, 266-268, 270; rupture of, 47, 267, 268. *See also* Hull, Nomura, *modus vivendi*, deadline date
Antares, U.S.S., 106
Anti-Comintern Pact, 13-14, 305
Army Pearl Harbor Board, and delay of warning message, 178; Bratton's testimony before, 175; Lockard's testimony before, 85-95; Short and, 60; Tyler's testimony before, 95-101
Arnold, H. H., 66, 128, 142

B-17's, flight to Hawaii of, 74, 84, 98-99
Ballantine, Joseph W., 284, 304-306, 309
Bangkok, 41
Barrage balloons, message about, 73
Battleships, reasons for disposition of, 38
Beardall, John R., 197, 199, 200 ff., 219 ff.
Berlin, events in, 263-373; Japanese messages to, 51
Bratton, Rufus, 75, 156 ff., 167, 173, 175-176
Brewster, Owen, 80
Burgin, Henry T., 69
Burma, 127, 133, 141, 143, 244

Cabinet, U. S., November 7, 1941 meeting of, 124

Canton Island, 67
Casualties, at Pearl Harbor, 26
Chiang Kai-shek, 14, 144, 229, 307
China, 14, 15, 123, 129; Japanese attitude toward, 226-227, 241-243, 244 ff., 248, 282 ff., 294, 295, 299 ff., 303 ff., 305 ff.; opposition to U. S.-Japanese rapprochement of, 284, 286 ff., 307; U. S. proposal concerning, 313 ff.
Christmas Island, 67
Churchill, Sir Winston S., 285, 287
Ciano, Galeazzo, 269, 271-272
Clausen Investigation, 14-part message and, 175-176
Coal strike, November 1941, 125
Codes, Japanese, destruction of, Marshall's testimony about, 168; Short's testimony about, 71
Communism, 14
Condor, U.S.S., 104
Congress, U. S., contemplated special message to, 133-134, 144, 145
Cooper, Jere, questioning of Marshall by, 163-165; questioning of Kramer by, 215-218

Deadline date, of negotiations, 44, 45, 46, 56, 71
"Do-don't message": *See* War warning message
Dutch East Indies, 15, 50, 123; Japanese attitude toward, 227 ff., 243, 244-245, 303-305; question of Japanese attack on, 124, 133, 135, 141 ff.; Short's testimony concerning, 70

Earle, John B., testimony of, 114-117
"East wind rain": *See* Winds code
Elliott, George E., Lockard's testimony about, 90 ff.; testimony of, 79-89
Enterprise, U.S.S., 36
Espionage, Japanese, in Hawaii, 43
Eterofu Island, 258

319

Falkenstein Memorandum, 265
F. B. I., radio communications of, 179
Ferguson, Homer, questioning of Marshall by, 168-173
Follow-up orders, Short's testimony on, 75, 78
Ft. Shafter, 83
Fourteen-part message, 18, 183; arrival of, 194, 195, 203, 205; delay in delivery to Marshall of, 170-173; delivery of, 196-203, 206 ff.; Roosevelt's reaction to, 221-223; testimony concerning: Kimmel's, 53 ff., 57; Kramer's, 194-215; Marshall's, 155 ff.; Miles', 174-175; Safford's, 184-186; Short's, 72; text of, 225-237
Frank, Walter H., questioning of Lockard by, 90-95; questioning of Tyler by, 95-102
Freezing, of Japanese assets, 304, 313, 314, 315

Gearhart, Bertrand W., questioning of Marshall by, 165-168, 180-182
Germany, 13, 14, 20; Japanese relations with, 51, 242, 269, 282 ff., 293, 298; Konoye and, 287 ff.; U. S. relations with, 122, 266-267, 270-272; and Tripartite Pact, 264, 282
Gerow, Leonard T., 61, 78, 128, 134, 142; and war warning, 148, 161, 166
Great Britain, 305, 306, 313; Japan and, 123 ff., 241, 271; Konoye and, 285 ff.; U. S. aid to, 124-125, 133, 143, 146, 174; and winds code, 217
Grew, Joseph C., 43; letter to Roosevelt from, 290-291; memorandum by, 293-294; message from Hull to, 314-316; recommendations of, 295 ff.; reports from, 292-293, 295-298, 298-302, 302-303, 316-317, 317-318; war warning from, 303-203
Grunert, George, 95, 96
Guam, 166

Halsey, William F., 38, 57
Hamilton Field, 74
Hawaii, Department of, 61 ff.; time zone of, 55, 163, 211-212, 214-215

Hayashi, Senjuro, 251
Hewitt, H. Kent, questioning of Outerbridge by, 103-109
Hewitt Inquiry, testimony of Earle before, 114-117; testimony of Outerbridge before, 103-109; testimony of Safford before, 188-189
Hiranuma, Kiichiro, 250
Hirohito, Emperor, and fall of Konoye, 249, 293-294; Pearl Harbor and, 259; Roosevelt's message to, 51, 133, 144, 223; and Senior Statesmen Conference, 250-251, 252
Hirota, Koki, 251
Hitler, Adolf, assumption of power by, 13; expansion policies of, 123; and Japan, 15, 268; and Pearl Harbor, 270; and the U. S., 123, 265, 266 ff.; and U. S.-Japanese negotiations, 270
Hitokappu Bay, 258
Hopkins, Harry L., 18, 221-223
Hornbeck, Stanley K., 286-290
Hull, Cordell, delivery of one o'clock message to, 211, 213, 214; and 14-part message, 54, 55, 167-168, 208-209; and "magic," 172; memoranda by, 277-279, 284-286; message to Grew from, 314-316; November 26 interview with Japanese of, 306-314; proposal of *modus vivendi* and, 303-306; quoted, 71; Stimson on, 124 ff., 139. *See also* American-Japanese conversations, Ultimatum, Hull's alleged

Imperial Conferences: *See* Japan, Government of
Indo-China, 15, 18, 123, 49-50, 219, 315; Japan and, 133, 134, 141, 143, 144, 211, 223, 227 ff., 242, 244-245, 246, 294, 303 ff.; Roosevelt and, 280-281, 285; U. S. proposals concerning, 313 ff.
Information, Kimmel's charges of withholding of, 41-59; Short's charges of withholding of, 67 ff., 76; Short's receipt of, 63-68
Information Center, Ft. Shafter, 81 ff., 92-94, 95-96, 101

INDEX

Intercepts, Japanese: *See* Information, "magic"
Isolationists, 15; and Pearl Harbor, 20, 146
Italy, Japanese demands for declaration of war and, 271-272; and Tripartite Pact, 264

Japan, 13, 14; army, attitude of, 293-294; economic demands of, 304, 305; economic difficulties of, 293-295, 296 ff., 301; Kimmel's interpretation of plans of, 49; Miles' interpretation of intentions of, 174; *modus vivendi* proposals by, 303-304; navy, attitude of, 247; probability of surprise attack by, 298-303; proposals of, 125, 228, 229; proposals to, 306-314; threat of, 122 ff., 137 ff., 139 ff.; Tripartite Pact and, 263-264; war decision of, 250 ff., 252-253
Japan, Government of, conferences of, July 2, 1941, 241-243; November 29, 1941, 250-251; December 1, 1941, 252-253; council of, September 6, 1941, 243-245, 247, 251; maximum concessions of, 245; minimum demands of, 244-245. *See also* American-Japanese negotiations

Kagoshima, 225
Kaminski, Harold, 103; testimony of, 110-113
Keefe, Harold B., 195; questioning of Marshall by, 175-180
Kido, Koichi, 246; and fall of Konoye Cabinet, 249; excerpts from diary of, 249, 250, 253, 259; and Proclamation of War, 253; suggests Tojo as Prime Minister, 249
Kimmel, Husband E., 77; battle reports of, 25-32; career of, 32-33; Marshall on warnings to, 181; Safford's interest in defense of, 188-189; and Short, 74-75; testimony of, 32-58
Knox, Frank, 55, 126; and 14-part message, 167-168, 196 ff., 200-201; Kramer's visit to, 200-201; and one o'clock message, 213, 214; and State Department conference, Dec. 7, 1941, 204, 208; Stimson on activities of, 133, 134, 135, 139, 142, 143, 144, 145
Konoye, Fumimaro, and conference of November 29, 250; and China, 296; difficulties of, 290-291; fall of cabinet of, 124, 249, 293-294; memoirs of, 246-248; opposition to, 285; proposed meeting with Roosevelt of, 16, 227-228, 246-247, 279 ff., 281 ff., 283-284, 285-286, 286-290, 292-293
Kra, Isthmus of, 18, 36, 133, 143, 146, 211
Kramer, Alwin D., Safford on, 186 ff., 190; Schulz on, 220-222; testimony of, 193-219
Kurusu, Saburo, 299; November 26 interview with Hull of, 306-314; Stimson on, 125; Tokyo's instructions to, 46 ff., 68
Kurile Islands, 19, 258

Lockard, Joseph L., 79; Elliott's testimony about, 81; testimony of, 89-95
Lucas, Scott, 218-219

MacArthur, Douglas, 125, 131, 132, 151; alerting of, 142, 175; reports from, concerning winds code, 191-192
"Magic" intercepts, breaking of code of, 16; testimony concerning: Marshall's, 151 ff., 171-172; Miles', 175; Short's, 76-77; Stimson's 145; text of, 225-237
Malaya, 50, 123, 124, 135, 139 ff., 211
Mandated Islands, secret flight over, 128, 142-143
Marshall, George C., 17, 18; activities of, December 6, 1941, 159-160; horseback ride of, 19, 21, 156; instructions to Short from, 61; Miles' testimony on actions of, 175; and Philippines, 125; Short's testimony about, 61, 63 ff., 76-78; Stimson's testimony about, 126 ff., 139 ff.; testimony of, 147-182; and war message, 67

Martin, F. L., 64, 69
Matsuoka, Yosuke, 242, 246, 282
McCoy, Frank R., 112
McCollum, Arthur N., and 14-part message, 185 ff., 197, 199, 207; and one o'clock message, 211, 212, 214
Midway Island, 37, 56
Miles, Sherman, 75, 147; and "magic," 152, 173; and Stimson, 134; testimony of, 173-175; and Wilkinson, 201
Mitchell, William D., questioning of Marshall by, 147-163
Modus vivendi proposals, 17, 318; Ballantine's memorandum on, 304-306; Hull and, 314-316; reply to, 306 ff.; Stimson on, 126, 139; text of Japanese, 303-304
Monaghan, U.S.S., 113
Mussolini, Benito, and declaration of war, 271-272

Nagano, Osami, testimony of, 254-257
National Theater, 224
Naval Court of Inquiry, and winds code, 52
Navy Department, U. S., Kimmel's testimony on actions of, 39, 43, 50-58
Netherlands, 313; and proposed Konoye-Roosevelt meeting, 285-288; and *modus vivendi*, 315. See also Dutch East Indies
Newton, J. H., 38
Nichi Nichi, 295
Nimitz, Chester, 37
Nomura, Kichisaburo, 299; conversations with Hull of: August 28, 1941, 281-284; September 3, 1941, 284-286; November 26, 1941, 306-314; conversation with Roosevelt, 277-281; *modus vivendi* proposal of, 303-304; Stimson on, 125. See also American-Japanese conversations

Ogigaiso conference, 247-248
Oikawa, Keshira, 247
Oil, and Japanese-American relations, 139, 304, 305, 309

Okada, Keisuke, 250
One o'clock message, December 7, 1941, Kramer's testimony on, 208-215; Marshall's testimony on, 157-159; text of, 237
Opana, radar station at, 80, 82; and Japanese planes, 97-99; operating hours of, 81-82, 90; operators' departure from, 85-86
Oshima, Hiroshi, 266-267
Outer Mongolia, 300-301
Outerbridge, William W., testimony of, 103-109

Pacific Fleet, U. S., attack on, 19; casualties of, 26; cooperation of army with, 74-75; destruction of, 13, 20; disposition of ships of, 38; Kimmel and, 33, 58
Pearl Harbor, attack on, 13, 16, 25, 30, 254-255; events at, 26-117; failure to appreciate danger to, 18, 50, 60, 68, 73, 132, 135, 136, 146, 162, 218-219, 224; Ribbentrop and, 269 ff.; ships in harbor of, *see* Ships-in-harbor message
Pearl Harbor Day, Kido's activities on, 259; Kramer's activities on, 209-215; Marshall's activities on, 156 ff.; Stimson's activities on, 134-135
Philippines, 180, 182; danger to, 18, 34, 50, 60, 132, 136, 162; Japanese concessions concerning, 245; Japanese threat to, 123, 124, 141, 143; supplies for, 134
Phillips, Walter C., 69, 159
Pilot message, Marshall's testimony on, 167 ff.; text of, 53, 225
Pye, William S., 39

Radar, arrival of equipment for, 90; Elliott's testimony concerning, 79-89; Lockard's testimony about, 89-95; Stimson on, 125, 131; Tyler's testimony about, 95-103; use of, at Pearl Harbor, 19, 79
Reconnaissance, Kimmel's measures for, 36 ff.
Ribbentrop, Joachim von, interview with Oshima of, 266-267; Japan-

INDEX

ese warnings to, 268; and Pearl Harbor, 269, 272-273; testimony of, 269-271
Richardson, Seth W., questions by, to Elliott, 79-89; Kramer, 193-215; Safford, 183-192; Schulz, 219-223
Roberts Commission, Kaminski's testimony before, 110-114; and radar intercept, 84; Short and, 59; and winds code, 188
Roosevelt, Franklin D., 14, 15, 16, 55, 308; advice of military to, 123; and cabinet, 124; and 14-part message, 18, 167, 197, 199-200, 221-225; Grew's letter to, 290-291; Mussolini's opinion of, 272; and Nomura, 277-286; note from Hull to, 291-292; prediction of surprise attack by, 126, 129; Ribbentrop's opinion of, 267; Stimson on, 126 ff., 139 ff.
Rostov, 134
Russell, Henry D., 99, 100
Russia, 313; Germany's attack on, 122; Germany's interest in Japanese attack on, 271; and Japan, 16, 122-123, 242, 243, 288 ff., 296, 300-301; and Tripartite Pact, 264

Sabotage, Marshall's testimony on Short's actions against, 149-151; Short's measures against, 60-63, 67, 70, 76; Stimson's testimony on Short's actions against, 137
Sabotage alert, reply to, 66; testimony on: Marshall's, 149-151, 165, 166; Short's 65 ff.; Stimson's, 137 ff.; text of, 65-66, 130
Safford, Laurence F., Kramer's reply to testimony of, 217 ff.; testimony of, 183-191
Sampan, capture of, 40, 108
Schmidt, Paul O., testimony of, 273
Schulz, Lester R., testimony of, 219-225
Scrambler phone, 19; Short's testimony on, 67, 75; Marshall's testimony on, 159, 178 ff. *See also* One o'clock message
Senior Statesmen Conference, 250-251, 252

Shanghai, Japanese expedition from, 127, 141
Shimada, Shigetaro, 254; testimony of, 257-258
"Ships-in-the-harbor" message, testimony about: Kimmel's, 42 ff., 50, 56; Marshall's, 153, 180-182; Short's 71; text of, 42
Short, Walter C., 17; expectations of, 75; Kimmel on, 34; Marshall on, 147-151, 165-166, 168, 180, 181; Stimson on, 128 ff.; 136-138; testimony of, 59-77
Siam, Gulf of, 134, 135
Singapore, 70, 123, 133, 143; expected attack against, 163; German interest in attack on, 271
Smith, Walter Bedell, 171, 172, 173, 175
Sonnett, John F., questioning of Earle by, 114-117
Soong, T. V., 144
Spaatz, Carl A., 61
Standley, William H., questioning of Kaminski by, 110-114
Stark, Harold R., 126, 139, 143, 204, 205, 224; and 14-part message, 157, 197, 198, 207-208, 210; and November, 1941, crisis, 128; and one o'clock message and war warning message, 159, 160, 177, 207-208
Stimson, Henry L., 55; and 14-part message, 167-168, 208; notes of, 138-146; statement by, 121-138
Submarines, contacts of U. S. forces with, 20, 30; midget, 108-109, 258; reports about, 40; testimony about: Earle's, 114-115; Kaminski's 112-114; Outerbridge's, 103 ff.

Tankan Bay, 19, 258
Thailand, 36, 313; danger to, 50, 127, 132-133, 139 ff.; Japanese policy toward, 41, 214, 232 ff., 242, 244-245
Time differential, between Washington and Hawaii, 55; Kramer on, 211-212, 214-215; Marshall on, 163
Togo, Shigenori, 259, 294, 316; Grew's interview with, 298-302
Tojo, Hideki, 16, 250, 259, 317; ap-

pointment as Prime Minister of, 249, 294; Konoye on, 247-248; Stimson on, 124; testimony of, 251-252; and U. S.-Japanese relations, 296
Tokyo, events in, 241-259
Toyoda, Teijiro, 248
Tripartite Pact, 226, 232, 248, 287 ff., 296; anniversary of, 293; excerpts from text of, 263-264; and Pearl Harbor, 270
Truce, proposal of: See *modus vivendi*
Turner, Richmond K., 53, 197, 198, 204
Tyler, Kermit, 79; reply of, concerning spotted planes, 84; testimony of, 95-103

Ultimatum, Hull's alleged, documents pertaining to, 306-314; Japanese reaction to, 316, 317, 318; Short's testimony concerning, 70, 72; Stimson on, 127-128. 140. See also U. S. note, November 26, 1941
Ultimatum, Japanese, to U. S., testimony concerning: Kimmel's, 54, 55, 57; Short's, 75
Ultimatum, proposal of, 140
United States, diplomatic crisis with Japan of, 13; German policy toward, 206-207; Japanese plans for war with, 242, 243; Konoye's opinions about actions of, 246 ff.; negotiations of, with Japan: See American-Japanese negotiations; note of, to Japan, November 26, 1941, 47, 51, 53, 56, 70, 72, 126, 140, 184, 194, 225, 229 ff., 309-314, 316
Upson, John, 86, 87

Wakasugi, Kaname, 299, 309
Wakatsuki, Rejeiro, 249, 250, 251
Wake Island, delivery of planes to, 36-37, 56, 57; Halsey at, 30; possible attack on, 164
Wang Ching-wei, 308

War, contingencies for American involvement in, 124, 133, 146, 174
War Cabinet, 133, 142
War Department, U. S., Short's testimony concerning actions of, 60, 69 ff., 74 ff., 78; Stimson's defense of, 135-138
War Warning Message, November 27, 1941; testimony concerning: Kimmel's, 17 ff., 39 ff.; Marshall's, 147-149, 164-165, 165-167; Miles', 175; Short's, 63 ff., 69, 74, 78; Stimson's, 124, 128-132, 137-138; text of, 63-64
War Warning Message, December 7, 1941, testimony concerning: Marshall's 158-159, 160-163, 177-180; Short's, 67, 73, 75; text of, 67, 160-161
Ward, U.S.S., report of action of, 30; testimony concerning: Earle's 115-117; Kaminski's, 112-114; Kimmel's, 40; Outerbridge's, 103-109
Wardman Park Hotel, 200
Warm Springs, Ga. 134
Washington, events in, 121-237
Welles, Sumner, 49, 134, 144, 294
Western Union, 159, 179
White House, delivery of 14-part message to, 198-199, 200; delivery of one o'clock message to, 213
Wilkinson, T. S., 77, 204, 205; and 14-part message, 197, 199, 200 ff., 207; Kramer's visit to, 201-202
"Winds" code, 17, 183; testimony concerning: Kimmel's 52, 57; Kramer's, 215-219; Marshall's 153-155; Safford's, 186-192; Short's, 71; texts of, 153-154
"Winds Implementing" message, testimony concerning: Japanese, 191-192, 217; Kramer's 215-219; Marshall's 153-155; Safford's, 188 ff.

Yamamoto, Gombai, 254-255, 256, 257, 258
Yonai, Mitsumasa, 250-251